SCHOOL DEVELOPMENT SERIES

General Editors: David Hopkins and David Reynolds

MONITORING EDUCATION

MONITORING EDUCATION
Indicators, Quality and Effectiveness

Carol Taylor Fitz-Gibbon

CASSELL

Dedicated to Taylor Fitz-Gibbon and Robin Zack Fitz-Gibbon Jeppesen and everyone's grandchildren: may they receive a better world.

Cassell
Wellington House   370 Lexington Avenue
125 Strand   New York
London WC2R 0BB   NY10017 - 6550

First published 1996
Reprinted 1998

British Library Cataloguing-in-Publication Data
A catalogue record for this book is available from the British Library

ISBN 0-304-33070-1 (hardback)
ISBN 0-304-32983-5 (paperback)

Typeset by Action Typesetting, Gloucester
Printed and bound in Great Britain by
Redwood Books, Trowbridge, Wiltshire

Contents

Series Editors' Foreword

In the last few years, Carol Fitz-Gibbon has established herself as one of the most original thinkers within the field of school effectiveness. We are therefore delighted that she has taken the opportunity that a book provides to generate this integrated, comprehensive and trenchant statement about performance indicators, educational policies and much else besides.

Fitz-Gibbon argues that if we conceive of education as a highly complex system, then simple attempts to describe 'good schools' or 'effective practices' are misjudged. Instead we require sensitive systems of performance indicators that are used to feedback information to the producers of education at a local level, who can advance their own development as they interpret the date in their 'live' contexts.

Importantly, she rejects attempts to evaluate institutions from the 'outside' of the educational system as practised in the OFSTED model, and rejects associated 'fear-based' systems. Instead she celebrates self-evaluating educational systems and outlines in useful detail the ALIS and YELLIS systems which currently involve over a thousand schools and colleges in data collection and data feedback systems of the highest quality and utmost importance.

As simplistic politically driven concerns about 'performance evaluation', 'effectiveness', 'efficiency' and 'appraisal' become ever more pervasive, this book serves as a timely reminder of the complexity of the educational world we live in. As a statement of the philosophy and practice of a well constructed system of educational evaluation and management that prefers the still small voice of rationality to the emotional debates of others, this book is of the utmost importance and relevance to all in education in the 1990s.

David Hopkins
David Reynolds

September 1995

Preface

WHY WRITE A BOOK?

Thomas Kuhn in his investigation of the nature of science ('*The Structure of Scientific Revolutions*') pointed out that researchers in mature disciplines communicate through research articles, there being no time before fast-paced discoveries to write books. Indeed much of the scientific interchange which followed the claims of 'cold fusion' was even more immediate, on the worldwide, almost instantaneous, electronic networks (Close, 1992).

Clearly, a book is not the place to publish current results of research. Logically, the only reason for writing at length seems to be to say more than can be said in shorter forms of communication. The reason for this book, then, is length and that is due to an attempt to consider educational monitoring in breadth – to touch many bases – and to put forward a coherent philosophy as well as to present the experience gained from developing a monitoring system of the first generation.

The reader may or may not find the philosophical parts helpful, but for me they seem to offer a framework for understanding an increasingly complex world. The literature on the evolution of complex systems seems to provide some clues to life, some guides as to how to tackle social problems. Perhaps we need some philosophy to fill the vaccum left by the limited successes of idealistic socialism and in response to the observable success of markets in some fields.

Can the search for a humane society best be tackled by adherence to doing science as well and as honestly as possible? What are the consequences which follow from a recognition that the future is fundamentally unpredictable?

A NOTE ABOUT CITATIONS AND CRITICISMS

At various points in this book what I have to say seems to me so obvious and reasonable as to be hardly worth saying. Unfortunately, some positions seem less obvious to others and criticism creeps in. Criticism is generally taken badly and I am not keen on losing friends. But, as Popper has argued, criticism is essential to science. So criticism there must be, but *who* is criticized is not important – it is the ideas that matter. So I felt much relieved when I decided not to name anyone I was criticizing. Each person criticized is, by the way, someone who could be designated either 'a notable professor' or a major politician – criticisms are directed at the powerful.

The decision not to name anyone criticized introduces an element of natural justice. Universities are being assessed on research, and one measure under consideration is the citation count – a count of how many times a piece of work is referenced by others. This serves as an indicator of the impact of the research on the research community. One objection often raised to the use of the citation count is that work which is in error will be referenced frequently because it needs criticizing – and this will be confounded with positive citations, thus corrupting the performance indicator. Now if we all follow the practice of not naming those whose work is criticized, the names will not be cited in the references and so will not benefit the persons concerned and not invalidate the citation counts.

Acknowledgements

I wish to thank all those who in various ways made this book possible and also those hundreds of people who have become involved in the monitoring of education through projects such as ALIS, the A-Level Information System. I particularly want to thank Peter Tymms, whose exceptional skills have helped immeasurably to make hectic years joyful and productive.

People in the Office:

Currently
Sandra Lovell, John Ardley, Kalvinder Dhillon, Hazel Glass, Brenda Ward, Michael Wilson.

Formerly
Ros Armstrong, Val Clifford.

The Data Management and Research Teams:

Currently
Kathy Clegg, Neil Defty*, Christopher Egdell**, Chris Noton, Paul Skinner, Nicola Stephenson*, Paul Trower, Luke Vincent, Martin Wright.

Formerly
David Clark, Peter Clarke, Vaughn Jackson, Mike Lacy, Simon Leung, Ross Macrae*, Darren Wilkinson.

* members of the after-work video team
** Director of *The Curse of the OFSTED Man* video.

People who have played an important role in developing or sustaining the monitoring projects:

David Anderson, Vivian Anthony, Chris Benneworth, Richard Bishopp, Chris Boothroyd, Aldric Brown, Peter Clark, Mr. E. Coomber, Tom Crompton, Peter Daly, Malcolm Dawson, Stella Dixon, Bryan Dockrell, Michael Duffy, John Dunford, Patrick Eavis, Tony Edwards, Roger Edwardson, David Elsom, Ed Elvish, Margaret Eve, Bob Fisk, Reed Gamble, John Gammon, John Garmston, Trevor Gilson, Peter Goff, Harvey Goldstein, Lisa Griffiths, Ken Gulliver, Margaret Hobrough, Bill Hodgson, Gordon Hogg, Akbar Ibrahim, Peter Jones, James Kennedy, Moira Kilkenny, Lord Lucas, Colin MacLean, Wendy Mason, Peter Matthews, Colin McCabe, Imelda

McDaid, Archie McGlynn, Andrew McPherson, Nick Meagher, John Morgan, Keith Murdoch, Sue Muse, Keith Nancekievil, Stuart Nichols, Desmond Nuttall, Brian Oglethorpe, David Oliver, Richard Parker, Wally Pearson, Don Povey, Maureen Purvis, David Reynolds, Stephen Sharp, Harvey Stalker, Lin Stebbings, Neil Straker, Meryl Thompson, Chris Tipple, Ram Wallace, Brian Wilcox, Ian Wilson, Kenneth Wright.

People who read a draft of this book, however all errors of omission and commission are mine alone:

Jean Taylor Hammerton, Charles Ian Howarth, Alastair McGregor, Peter Tymms.

PART ONE

Introduction

Chapter 1

Introduction

This book is about education but it is also about how we think about and try to solve social problems.

Education is the compulsory treatment, the complex social system in which everyone is required to participate. You can avoid the law all your life, hardly ever go to a doctor and never bother with psychologists, but you have only to reach the age of 5, or thereabouts, to merit compulsory treatment by educators. Education is the social science with clout: the non-voluntary intervention. Once you reach 'school age', educators lay claim to thousands of hours of your time. Education, the universal right, is an offer which is rarely refused.

This unparalleled call on the time and efforts of the nation's youth places education in a position of great responsibility. Educators have more opportunities than other professionals to have enormous influence on the next generation. Research and development in education should be a major national investment – but not, perhaps, as currently practised.

How we choose to think about, investigate, design and monitor education will be closely similar to our approaches to other social problems. Furthermore, if we could get education right, then not only would we have learned better techniques for dealing with other problems but the number of such problems might well be steadily reduced.

DEVELOPING QUALITY IN EDUCATION

We are all in favour of quality. 'To have life and to have it more abundantly' is how someone expressed the idea of quality of life, some time ago. We would like people in all walks of life and in all countries to have life and to have a constantly improving quality of life. The question is how to get there.

Nobody is against 'quality', so of course everyone is in favour of assuring quality – but how do we know whether or not we are achieving 'quality'? Do we set targets? If so, how? What is quality anyway? Is quality the same thing for you as for the next person? We are told that quality is 'suitability for purpose'. What if systems are not simply either suitable or unsuitable but are suitable to varying degrees? How much quality is feasible within constraints of time and money? How do we know to what degree we are assuring quality? What kinds of systems deliver quality? We are not talking here of quality widgets, but of quality of life, or the educational outputs that lead on to quality of life.

Another definition of quality is 'doing what you said you would do'. But what if what you said you would do was very meagre – or impossibly ambitious? How do we choose to say the right things and then assure ourselves and others that we are applying 'suitable' procedures and doing things in ways reasonably consistent with what we reasonably promised, all things considered?

To assure quality in any defensible way we shall have to measure, not just our own institutions but also similar ones. We can then get some idea of what is feasible. Are others doing better or worse, achieving more or less with similar resources? To find out we shall need to monitor. We shall need to keep an eye on outcomes. By so doing we may get some idea about whether we are achieving attainable quality.

How, then, do we get quality into education? The hypothesis developed in this book is that our best strategy lies in improving the information in the system, particularly by defining and measuring the many outcomes that we care about and feeding back the measurements *to the units of responsibility*.

To live effectively is to live with adequate information

(Norbert Wiener, originator of cybernetics)

An effective educational system needs good information. This notion sounds so innocuous and unexceptional as to be hardly worth stating. But years of work will be needed to get the information systems working at every level – nursery, primary, secondary and tertiary – in such a way that they have maximum positive impact and avoid the negative impact which can arise from poorly conceived systems which threaten rather than inform, distract rather than energize, and demoralize rather than promote professionalism. Old habits die slowly but if recent work on the nature of 'complex systems' is correct we almost certainly need to adopt new mental models for managing education. Approaches to management predicated on the presumption of unrealistic levels of wisdom must give way to approaches more in line with a complex and unpredictable reality. Knowing where we want to get to demands values, but finding out how to get there requires science and design: giving a complex system sufficient information to get there in multiple *self*-organizing units, each of which may take a different route. The units need to know if they are getting closer and we may never understand exactly how we get there: fudging and nudging our way forward, guided by good information on outcomes. Notions of prescription and control must be replaced with a sense of science, of information and investigation.

INPUT – PROCESS – OUTPUT – OUTCOME

There is a tendency for people working in an area such as education to develop the habit of using a certain vocabulary – jargon – without explanation. Jargon is necessary as a simple shorthand, but it can be very easily explained. A very simple organizing idea is that of intake–process–output (or sometimes the longer-term 'effects' are called 'outcomes'). Students enter a phase of education, such as nursery school, they are looked after and taught (these being the 'processes' of schooling – what goes on in school), and at the end of the year they are different. They are different not only because of the schooling, but partly because they have grown up, and partly because they have been learning from experiences at home, with friends and generally in their life outside school. Some of the differences in the students might be due to the processes experienced at school – learning letters, for example. Do children learn letters better at some schools than others? If so, are those students also happier at school, or more miserable? Do the students who have learned letters better continue to make greater progress, or has the learning put them off school so that they will drop out as soon as possible? These are the kinds of questions that we need to consider by measuring *many* outcomes of schooling – learning outcomes, attitudes, behaviour. In order to try to sort out which of the outcomes are simply characteristic of the student and which are related to the processes of schooling, we need to measure a fair number of things that vary, i.e. 'variables'. We need, in fact, to develop tentative models of how the system works – the inputs, the processes and the outputs or outcomes. Trying to keep track of a system can be called monitoring.

PERFORMANCE INDICATORS, COMPLIANCE INDICATORS AND MONITORING

Before going any further, a couple of definitions should be attempted, despite Popper's eminently logical advice against defining words with more words.

A 'performance indicator' can be defined as an item of information collected at regular intervals to track the performance of a system (Fitz-Gibbon, 1990). A major distinction should be made between performance indicators and compliance indicators (Richard, 1988). Compliance indicators are checks as to whether some *required* features have been implemented. For example, if a school must comply with certain safety procedures or must deliver a certain number of hours per week in certain subjects, then checks on these facts would constitute compliance indicators, usually simply yes or no statements. Performance indicators, on the other hand, need to be designed to reflect our understanding of how a system works.

Monitoring means 'keeping track of the performance of a system, largely by the use of performance indicators focused on outcomes'. However, by monitoring I shall generally mean not only the regular collection of performance indicators, but also their being reported back to the units responsible, i.e. *monitoring with feedback*.

An example of a set of performance indicators constituting a monitoring system is ALIS – the A-level Information System. Input measures are the students' achievement at age 16 along with other characteristics such as gender and home background. Processes are features of the school or college, including teaching and learning processes. Outputs are not just the grades achieved at age 18 but also students' aspirations and levels of satisfaction with their courses. The ready reception of the ALIS project, which provides extensive 'accountability' data, including what has recently come to be called 'value added', contrasts with the reception encountered by government-imposed testing systems in England, Scotland and Wales: boycotts, leaks and general resistance. The contrast is marked and it is hoped that this book will provide many clues as to the possible explanations and the ways forward.

The monitoring-with-feedback systems which we are now developing for all phases of schooling seem, with hindsight it must be admitted, to fit very aptly

- with ideas developed in management by W. Edwards Deming;

- with ideas about the nature of information and problem-solving put forward by philosopher/scientists such as Karl Popper and H. A. Simon;

- with currently developing understanding of 'unpredictable', complex

5

systems, the quiet revolution in science which is described by Davies (1987) and Waldrop (1992) among others.

The growth of measurement-based systems, such as ALIS, raises important questions about other approaches to seeking quality in education – such as some kinds of inspection and some kinds of management – which are quite possibly not just useless but actually damaging; practices which not only take resources out of education but also mislead and hinder efforts to promote quality, thus providing negative value for money.

THE UK EXAMINATION SYSTEM: A VITAL MEASURE OF OUTPUT

In the UK, more than in most other countries, we are very close to having highly effective monitoring systems and performance indicators in secondary education. This is because the UK has well-established procedures for independent, external examinations taken by large proportions of students. With the addition of courses developed by informed people working on vocational qualifications, there could soon be fair and external measures to form a framework for monitoring and feedback across the ability range.

In the USA there is increasing recognition of how much such systems are needed. The search is on for 'curriculum-embedded, authentic, high stakes testing', i.e. what the UK has always called 'exams': 'curriculum embedded' because the assessments are designed to test what has been taught; 'authentic' because sudents actually work out problems, respond to data, and write essays rather than simply ticking boxes; and 'high stakes' because students care about these examinations – they have consequences. In the UK we have become so used to the existence of examinations and the highly professional, well-organized examination boards which run them, that we are in danger of forgetting what an essential and essentially fair system of assessment they represent. This is a controversial issue and since assessment will be at the heart of many monitoring systems some chapters are devoted to this important topic.

In short, in considering quality in education we shall have to consider the nature of assessment. Thanks to the unsung heroes of educational assessment – the examination boards – assessment in the *academic* realm is something that the UK already has well worked out, although some improvements are needed, as always. One urgent need is to extend to vocational areas the development of equally fair and effective systems.

MONITORING IN THE NEXT DECADE

If the education profession does not participate in the creation of performance indicators, quality assurance systems and monitoring, then others will impose such systems. To help us, there exists a body of carefully built-up knowledge called social science. Systems designed with a knowledge of social science should be more likely to work than systems designed without the benefit of accumulated knowledge. Furthermore, there are exciting changes in science, as scientists increasingly turn their attention to the study of *complex systems*. Whether these new mental models will provide useful guides remains to be seen, but they must be considered, for education is, above all, a *complex system*. If the developing sciences of complexity are correct, we should probably expect education to be most effective when it consists of hierarchies of self-organizing units which thrive on the edge of chaos.

AUDIENCES

This book is about the ways in which complex systems in general, and schools and colleges in particular, can become most effective. The solution put forward is a framework which provides feedback on the many outcomes that are valued. For whom, then, is this book intended? For all those who are, in any fashion, making the educational system work:

- staff in schools and colleges and their professional associations;
- those in government, public service and governing bodies who take some responsibility for education;
- students of social science;
- the 'chattering class' in general, particularly people involved in making complex systems work.

It is hoped that this book can point some ways forward and thus contribute to the ongoing process of designing systems that work.

I have been concerned to indicate in this one book the knowledge base needed to distinguish good data from poor. An accountancy firm is currently offering to re-package data already available to schools and analyse 'value added' on the assumption that all A-levels are equally difficult. The assumption is false and some teachers may be quite wrongly criticized if no one can challenge the report of the accountancy firm. Set this along with the controversies over the publication of 'league tables' and it seems clear that the leaders of education – teachers, managers and their professional associations – need to be well informed as never before.

I particularly hope that politicians with a scientific rather than ideological cast of mind will find the book informative. I cannot share the cynical view that no politician will admit ignorance and seek to be guided by evidence. Indeed, economic indicators are providing experience in politics of the value of monitoring complicated systems. The book does not fit into either a right-wing or a left-wing stereotype. It is about science.

Because the book introduces arguments and portrays current conflicts in education, it could serve as an introductory reading for studies in education. Cognitive conflict promotes learning.

A good course in research methods contains information on *measurement*, *design* and *statistics*, and this book includes these topics because they form the relevant knowledge base needed for monitoring. Those already knowledgeable in these fields may wish to skip Chapter 3 on design and some of Parts 4 and 5, but on the other hand they may find some fresh perspectives there.

US readers will find frequent reference to education in the USA and an Appendix providing a brief comparison of US and UK structures and approaches to assessment.

NUMBERS

Not everybody shares the enthusiasm for numerical indicators which permeates this book. There are, for example, those who call anyone proposing to use numbers a logical positivist. From what little I know of the Vienna Circle, I do not think any practising scientist espoused logical positivism. Popper is the philosopher who has spoken most cogently to scientists (Magee, 1975), and it is his philosophy which is referred to here. Suffice it to say, for the moment, that there are indeed reasons to be wary of numbers. Measurement gives messages and has an impact on that which is measured and on the whole system. Anticipating that impact is vital in the design of monitoring systems. The dangers provide no reason to avoid the power and usefulness of numbers. There are, indeed, 'lies, damned lies and statistics', but if you are going to lie it is a lot easier to lie without statistics than with statistics. Furthermore, once you try to measure a few obvious things, you discover that, if you have no statistics, the person whom you most fool may be yourself.

STRUCTURE OF THE BOOK

With the exception of the Introduction, each Part has an introductory page describing the chapters in it.

Part 1 Introduction

Part 1 consists of this introductory chapter and three others. Chapter 2 is a short but important chapter on four kinds of data. This provides a quick guide to what appears to cause constant confusion. It represents a simple set of ideas which should be taught to everyone, in school. So important is one kind of data – experimental data – that Chapter 3 is devoted to it even though, in the present book, it is something of an option. Chapter 4 is there in case anybody doubts that education faces grave problems: there are some vignettes to bring the issues alive.

Part 2 Philosophical considerations

This Part celebrates the delight of finding so much convergence of ideas among a number of leading thinkers, each coming from very different experiences and backgrounds. It is a speculative look at the ideas of a number of scientists/philosophers. Perhaps it provides a valuable framework for thinking about systems in general and how to make them work.

Part 3 ALIS: An up-and-running indicator system

It seemed important, before going further into the design of monitoring systems, to give a concrete example. The A-level Information System has been providing 'value added' measures to schools and colleges for over a decade. In conjunction with the Secondary Heads' Association 16+ Value Added Project, this information was going into more than 800 schools in 1994. Developments of other monitoring-with-feedback systems (YELLIS and PIPS, both benefiting from the support from the National Association of Head Teachers) are referred to briefly at the end of the Part.

Part 4 Measurements for monitoring systems

At the heart of a monitoring system must lie a statistical information system – we measure that which we care about enough to bother measuring. The quality of the measures we use for assessing achievement, attitudes and vocational courses matters greatly and chapters in this Part deal with those topics. In particular, measures of achievement lie at the heart of educational monitoring and represent an area of considerable debate, much of it puzzling to those not involved. There are the issues of the impact of assessment on teaching, the reporting of results, the use of continuous assessment versus end-of-course tests, and the methods which can be applied for assessment in 'vocational' areas.

Part 5 Basic statistical procedures for monitoring

A few simple concepts from statistics will go a long way in performance monitoring – they will at least start us on a journey which is nowhere near finished. Statistical concepts are quite accessible when set in a familiar situation, and everyone concerned with education is now becoming familiar with such terms as 'regression' and 'residuals'. There are chapters on 'value added' and 'relative ratings' to provide some basis for these necessary concepts. Because there is a particular problem in monitoring if only highly aggregated data are available, such as school averages rather than data on individual students, one chapter is devoted to a problem known as the 'ecological fallacy'.

Part 6 The design of performance indicator systems

This Part looks to the present and the future but could easily be skipped unless you are yourself designing indicator systems. It starts with a general rationale which can be applied in tackling the design of any set of performance indicators. Some criteria for performance indicators are discussed and the final chapter looks to the future – as far as performance monitoring is concerned, these are early days.

Part 7 The impact of monitoring on other systems

When performance monitoring systems are in place they are likely to have profound effects on the way in which a number of other educational systems work. Chapter 20 considers the impact on management – what styles work? Chapter 21 considers one of the management strategies often linked with performance indicator systems – performance-related pay. The role of local education authorities is considered in Chapter 22, and Chapter 23 actually questions the validity of inspectors' judgements. (In over 100 years of inspection, those conducting inspections have provided no evidence of the reliability, let alone the validity, of their judgements) Chapters 24 and 25 complete this consideration of the impact which information systems may have.

Part 8 Conclusions

A brief chapter concludes the body of the book. References, Appendices and an Index complete the book.

Monitoring systems are here to stay, if only because of computers. Consequently, a major task for the next few decades will be to get these systems to work in ways that are beneficial for society as a whole, for staff and students in educational institutions and for the advancement of knowledge. As will become apparent, people are hurt when there is a lack of information or when a system is given misinformation, so one might misquote Wiener: 'To live humanely is to live with adequate information.'

Chapter 2

Four Kinds of Data

The four kinds of data briefly described here will be referred to frequently through-out the book. Too often attempts are made to draw inferences which cannot be jus-tified on the basis of the available data. Too often only simple data are available and the more informative data have not been collected. This situation contributes to many practical and human problems and much stress in the functioning of all our social systems. Examples of problems in the educational system are given in Chap-ter 3 after this brief introduction to four kinds of data.

Some readers may see this chapter on methodology as an unnecessary diver-sion, especially the argumentative part about experiments, but it seems necessary. This is so because there appears to be little general knowledge about how to resolve social issues, how to collect convincing data, how to establish, if not 'proof', at least something a good deal more secure than assertions dressed up with a few numbers. The concept of testing policies by experiments is not supported not only by politicians (who are largely inadequately educated[1]) but even by social scien-tists, who seem singularly fainthearted about experiments, being content with elab-orate theories without adequate evidence. However, these concepts need elabora-tion. Let us proceed.

FOUR KINDS OF INFORMATION

Numbers are less likely to be misused or misinterpreted if clear distinctions are made between four kinds of data:

- raw data;
- comparisons;
- fair comparisons, i.e. 'residuals' based on statistical models;
- really fair comparisons – based on experimental data or what is known in medicine as 'clinical trials' or 'randomized controlled trials' (RCTs).

The point to be made here is that numerical information is not necessarily inter-pretable. The extent to which you can learn from it depends upon the nature of the data and especially the framework in which they were collected – what is some-times called the 'design' of the investigation. Simple raw information (data) often leads us to realize that we need yet more information before we can make sense of it, in particular before it can be used as a basis for informing actions.

Raw data

Raw data are simply measurements such as '70 per cent of students said yes', or '10 students were absent last week'. They are simple to understand, but often almost impossible to interpret. For example, suppose a secondary school collected data on students' attitudes in each year group and found that, overall, 70 per cent said they generally enjoyed lessons. Is this an acceptable figure? Is it acceptable that almost a third did not report enjoying lessons? We know exactly what has been measured and yet we are still left with considerable doubts as to how to interpret the data.

Comparative data

In an attempt to interpret raw data we turn to making comparisons. We might break the school's data down and find that the 13–14-year-olds were the most negative towards school. Should their teachers be accused of turning students off school? Is there cause for concern? Is the pattern simply typical of the 13–14-year-old age group, perhaps related to their in-between status – not new to the school but not yet in classes clearly focused on up-coming examinations? In other words, we can compare the attitudes of each year group but perhaps these comparisons are not fair; they may be missing some important patterns which need to be taken into account. We could wait and see what next year's data look like. But if a trend develops – say a downward trend over the years – is this to be attributed to changing teenage attitudes in general or just to our own school in particular? Are there changes in the intake: different abilities, different home backgrounds? Do these matter?

How can we find comparisons which help us to interpret the data? We need some way of knowing what sort of data are reasonable, only to be expected, and what are getting 'out of line'. We need to know when to rejoice, when to be satisfied and when to worry. The same problem arises in the interpretation of examination results. Are they good or only what was to be expected from those students?

Fair comparisons or 'residuals'

In order to know what kind of data might reasonably be expected we need to use *models* which suggest what factors have to be taken into account. How do we know what these factors are? The models can be guessed at (or, to put it more pompously, 'derived from theory') but they need to be tested against the data. Thus we might think that attitudes are affected by age, home background, sex and ability – we would then need to check out the extent to which this is so. We can look for these relationships in one school's data, but that will not tell us if that school is different from other schools. If we find differences between the attitudes of different ability groups, it could be because of something that is done or not done in the school, or it could be a generally found pattern. *The idea of 'self-evaluation', using only one school's data, is one likely to lead to disappointment and confusion.* What is needed is a large set of data from many schools so that we will be able to make fair comparisons: comparing like with like. If, for example, we found that high- and low-ability students generally had different attitudes, and that these attitudes also varied with age, we could begin to make fair comparisons. We could compare like with like by comparing the attitudes of 13–14-year-old boys with those of boys of the same ability in several other schools. If we found that only 30 per cent of the 13–14-year-old boys of high ability at one school were positive about school, we might be worried. But if we found out that at other schools the figure was only 25 per cent, our initial dismay might be tempered with the realization that the school was not out of line, and in fact had results slightly better than might have been predicted.

In statistical terminology, a 'residual' is defined as the difference between the result obtained and the result predicted from measurements of factors known to be correlated with the outcomes.

Residual = Actual result – Predicted result

where the predicted result is 'predicted' from a model which takes account of factors known to be associated with the outcome. Residuals have come to be called 'value added'.

The computation of residuals is basically the calculation of what is left over after taking account of the effects of important factors which influence the results. Residuals provide fair comparisons, fair performance indicators – although *fairer* comparisons might be a more accurate designation, since not everything will have been taken into account.

The factors which have to be taken into account are those which correlate, or co-vary, with the measured outcomes, and which are therefore called *covariates*. There will be other things influencing the outcomes which have not been measured and are not, therefore, taken into account. The effects of some of these unmeasured 'variables' will be present in the residuals, and the effects of the errors of measurement will also be present in the residuals. Thus only a part of the residual can be seen as possibly indicating the 'effect' of the school, or of parts of the school, on students.

The need to take inputs into account can be illustrated with an example from outside education. If you were studying the death rates in towns you would need to take account of the number of old people in the town. It would not be 'fair' or sensible to compare towns that had a predominance of young families with retirement towns.

Residuals might be called *fair comparative* data, *adjusted data* or *contextualized data*. It has recently become fashionable in the UK to speak of residuals in terms of 'value added', and the concept is further discussed in chapter 14.

Really fair comparisons: Experimental data

When we simply measure the way the world is, as in monitoring or in conducting surveys, we find out that many measurements are related. In general, all good things are positively correlated, i.e. they tend to be found together. Thus high achievement, a wealthy home, good health, a low accident rate and favourable attitudes to school are positively correlated, meaning they are often found together in the same people. This basically is a finding that the world is far from even-handed or fair. These kinds of survey findings can help us to make comparisons which are more fair, but they have limitations. There is always the suspicion that important factors have been left out.

The main problem arises in interpreting the results of actions we might take to make improvements. Suppose nursery school education is provided in a district and we wonder if it is worthwhile – does it improve students' subsequent achievements? If we collected data on those who did or did not go to nursery school and found that those who did were subsequently more positive to school and achieving more highly, could we then conclude that the nursery provision *caused* these differences?

The very fact that parents placed their children in nursery school might have meant they were different from parents who did not choose nursery schools. Maybe the 'nursery school parents' were more likely to have money, to have jobs, to be two parents rather than one, to be older parents or even parents more concerned with their children's adjustment to school. There may have been *pre-existing differences* which had not been taken into account and which might account for the children of these parents being different later in their schooling.

The point is that if groups are self-selecting they may be different in many ways which we have not even thought about. We cannot think of everything, so what can we do to make the comparisons fairer? The solution to this problem is now widely recognized, following the work of Sir Ronald Fisher in the first half of the twentieth century, interestingly recounted by his daughter (Box, 1978). In medicine it is known as a clinical trial. If we want to know what effect nursery education has, we have to run carefully designed experiments: clinical trials. Two 'equivalent' groups are created by, say, coin tossing, and one group receives nursery education while the other does not. Any differences on any factor will have been randomly assigned between the two groups. The larger the groups are, the smaller the likely differences between them on *any factors* – those which we have thought about and also those which we have not thought about. Randomization compensates for ignorance. If the only difference between two groups was whether or not they had nursery education, then any subsequent differences in outcomes could be reasonably attributed to nursery education.

SUMMARY

Four kinds of data have been described and categorized on the basis of how informative they are: simple raw data, comparative data, fair comparisons represented by residuals calculated from empirically established relationships, and the gold standard: experimental data or really fair comparisons – the data derived from procedures known in medicine as clinical trials or randomized controlled trials.

The next chapter gives a solution to the ethical question so often related to experiments – are they fair? The reader more interested in monitoring systems and performance indicators might wish to skip that chapter. It uses the example of nursery education.

NOTES

1 George Porter, President of the Royal Society and Nobel Laureate, remarked that he would rather deal with politicians without educational qualifications than with people who had read Politics, Philosophy and Economics at Oxford, 'which makes them anti-scientific'.

Chapter 3

Experiments: Finding Out the Effects of Actions

By an 'experiment' is meant what the elementary science in the National Curriculum calls, quite rightly, 'a fair test'. If you want to find out the effect of an action, you try to set up a fair test. In medicine, such experiments are called clinical trials. Not only are they recognized as the essential gold standard of evidence, but they are often required before new drugs can be released onto the market.

The term 'experiment' is used as in Campbell and Stanley (1966) to mean a controlled experiment, i.e. an intervention with participants randomly assigned to 'treatment' groups. It is assumed that *field* experiments, not *laboratory* experiments, will be most appropriate for educational research. (Field experiments are conducted in natural settings such as ordinary classrooms, as opposed to laboratories.) Education *is itself* an intervention, one to which everyone is subjected and which is designed to have certain effects. It is surprising, therefore, that educational research in the UK does not use the experimental method to any large extent. The reasons may derive in part from the dominance of sociology in British educational research traditions. Another reason may be that social science in general has been poorly served by statistics and statisticians, who are fond of large data sets. One such wrote, for example:

> The literature on research designs has been concerned largely with
> randomised experiments where different combinations of 'treatments'
> can be assigned at random to experimental units, where these might be
> fertilisers and field plots in agriculture, or drugs and patients in
> medicine. In education and the social sciences such possibilities are rare
> although where they do occur, for example in psychology, then the
> traditional procedures will apply.

This was hardly an encouragement to experimentation. Experiments were relegated, by this influential statistician, to the role of small-scale efforts in psychology, and their power to inform was not extolled but almost denigrated. It is not surprising that politicians in the UK seem unaware of the difference between correlational studies (what we have here called 'fair comparisons') and experimental tests ('really fair comparisons' or fair tests). They are not being given good advice, it seems.

Experiments should not be thought of as artificial, laboratory exercises from which it will be difficult to generalize. 'Field' experiments can be conducted in exactly the settings which are of concern. Indeed, experiments to inform policy decisions can be and have been undertaken. An excellent summary of a number of controlled research studies is provided by Lazar (1977), who chaired a consortium examining the effects of nursery education. All the projects reported represented

15

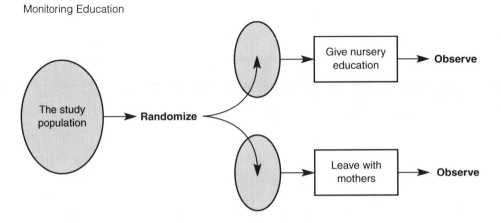

Figure 3.1 *An experimental design for investigating the effects of nursery education*

randomly controlled field trials to test the hypothesis that the provision of nursery education to severely deprived pre-schoolers would yield important benefits later in the child's life. The hypothesis was supported. This excellent research into the effects of pre-school education was done in the US. The design of the experiment is shown in Figure 3.1. The points to note are as follows:

- The study population needs to be carefully described – whence came the random samples? The results cannot safely be generalized to dissimilar populations.

- The method of randomization might be simple or stratified – stratified randomization can take account of various important factors. For example, the randomization procedure might ensure equal numbers of boys and girls in each group.

- If the 'treatment' of interest is the nursery education, then the no-nursery group is often called the 'control group'. However, it is important to know what was happening to the control group – it should really be regarded as an alternative treatment.

- Once the experiment has been conducted, the observations of the outcomes can continue for years. The Ypsilanti, Michigan Highscope project followed up pupils from such experiments annually through the years when they were 3 to 11 years old, then at 14, 15, 19 and 27 years of age (Lazar and Darlington, 1982).

ETHICAL CONSIDERATIONS BEHIND EXPERIMENTS

Randomized controlled trials, i.e. procedures with 'experimental' and 'control' groups, may provide good scientific evidence, people argue, but they are not ethical. For example, would it be ethical to provide nursery education only to a few? The implication behind such a question is that we already know that nursery education is good and that it is therefore unethical to give it randomly to some and not to others. If we *did* know that nursery education was always beneficial, then that argument would be correct. But are we sure? Perhaps nursery education is harmful, at least for some children, and some research has suggested that the learning experiences of pre-school children at home with the middle-class mothers are richer than those of pre-schoolers in nursery schools (Tizard and Hughes, 1984).

Nursery education is already haphazardly available to some and not to others, i.e. there is uneven provision. Is uneven provision ethical if haphazard, but unethical if designed systematically to enable us to learn the effects?

Some very good research has demonstrated that pre-school education leads to many benefits – *for some study populations*. The problem is that the results might not be applicable throughout the UK. The study population consisted of children from the severely stressed and deprived US inner cities. When the benefits of nursery education are extolled (as they currently are), we are rarely informed that of the pupils who were provided with nursery education in, for example, the exemplary Ypsilanti, Michigan pre-school project,

- nearly one fifth were in remedial programmes at the age of 14;
- 57 per cent of the nursery-educated had a delinquency record;
- by age 19, nearly one in four of the nursery-educated had been charged with a serious crime.

These figures were all substantial improvements over those *not* given pre-school education, for whom the figures were 39 per cent in remedial programmes, 75 per cent delinquency at age 14, and 38 per cent charged with a serious crime by age 19. However, the figures show that those experiments may not be immediately applicable to all pupils in the UK, where we are still generally somewhat behind the US in crime rates and reading problems.

The experiments were vital to policy-making in the US, especially since they were replicated by many different teams working in different cities so that generalizability was built into the series of clinical trials and considerable confidence could be placed on the findings. Another factor of vital importance in these experiments was the possibility of evaluating not only effects (benefits) but also costs, thus permitting the strongest possible evidence to be presented for policy decisions: analyses of costs and benefits.

However, the problem of generalizing from the intensely deprived study populations in the US to the whole of the UK seems to have been forgotten in the glow of hearing of $6 return on every $1 spent. For some reason there is now a national consensus in the UK, reflected in the recommendations of the National Commission on Education (1993), that nursery education for all should be the goal. UK industry may have been influenced by its own desire to (a) retain female workers and (b) have their children cared for at public expense rather than having to provide workplace facilities.

> Backed by Howard Davies, Director general of the Confederation of British Industries, the new forum Employers for Childcare, called on the Government to increase funding, set a national framework for services, and lay down national standards. . . . The Employers for Childcare document 'Good Childcare, Good Business', . . . lines up the BBC, British Airways, British Gas, British Telecom, Co-operative Bank, Grand Metropolitan, Kingfisher, Midland Bank, Rover Group, Shell UK and the

TSB group with the pre-school lobby . . .

(Rowan, 1993, pp. 6–7)

However, motives do not matter – what matters is outcomes, including costs. The outcomes must be broadly measured, encompassing effects not only on children but also on the labour force, on parents, on tax returns, on benefit payments etc.

There are obviously many issues to be disentangled:

- The generalizability of findings on rather different study populations.
- The nature of the pre-school programmes: the successful ones were 'cognitively oriented'. Unlike many 'playschools', they had activities explicitly aiming to increase children's mental competencies, including making choices and planning.
- The training of staff.
- The staff/pupil ratios (the successful ones recommend 1 to 10 or better).
- The inclusion of parents.
- The provider: LEAs have been prevented from spending or even surviving in some cases; business would rather the state provided; and if provision depends on parents the most at-risk pupils might not get nursery education.
- The social outcomes – are they good for the not-at-risk child?
- The costs, including savings due to the fact that working mothers can stay off public assistance.

Rowan's 1993 presidential address to the education section of the British Association for the Advancement of Science rightly called for more research with proper control groups. But she also noted the problem of the time-scale: 'Longitudinal research into the benefits of nursery education should be commissioned but meanwhile (we can't wait for 10 or 20 years) there is surely enough evidence to make investment in under-fives a priority' (Rowan, 1993, p. 22). This returns us to the topic of monitoring. We need fair comparisons (residuals) but we also need experimental evidence. Although the experimental evidence will be slow, it is the surest way to obtain sound evidence. The summer 1989 issue of the (US) *Journal of Educational Statistics* (Wainer, 1989) was devoted to methodology, and the consensus was:

> There is *no substitute* for properly designed experiments. No fancy
> statistical analysis can work magic on a badly confounded set of data.
> The best message to convey is that many interesting and important
> questions must remain doubtful until experimenters obtain the funding,
> control and authority to carry out the proper research. (Emphasis
> added)

Most educational policies could benefit from being put to a fair test. If policies were routinely piloted in the framework of an experimental design, we might gradually begin to understand the costs and benefits of decisions which affect millions.

Should the UK repeat the US experiments in nursery education? An early small study did, commendably, provide some experimental evidence based on different types of nursery provision in what were then the stable mining communities of the West Riding of Yorkshire (Smith and James, 1975). In trying to draw conclusions they found considerable local complexity.

> Detailed exposition of the results rapidly leads to explanations of the position in a particular school, or the attitudes of a particular teacher. (Smith and James, 1975, p. 237)

> Far from the policy question being answered, it has been made infinitely more complex; new forms of pre-school intervention have been developed, different approaches shown to have different but equally valid results, and effectiveness to be as much a product of *local conditions* as of any experimental programme. (Smith and James, 1975, p. 238) (Emphasis added)

This finding of complexity in the details is a theme of this book, as will become apparent in Part 2, but the broad simplicities, the bounded nature of the complexity, may still be available to guide policy. Taguchi, the famous Japanese engineer, will set up hundreds of experiments to test out the effects and interactions of dozens or more variables before starting up a production line. Social scientists seem to expect a few dozen experiments to yield definitive conclusions even though they are dealing with far more complex 'production lines'.

There should be experiments *and* monitoring to study the effects of pre-school interventions. Indeed, some of the effects found in the West Riding experiments were as strong as any generally seen (e.g. effect sizes as large as 0.6). Moreover, as Smith and James argued, there remains a feeling that the pre-school years hold great promise because they provide a 'chance to intervene before any cycle of failure has built up, where there is a high degree of parental interest and enthusiasm' (Smith and James, 1975, p. 238).

This suggests that *deprived* pre-schoolers at least need to be given nursery education on the basis of the experimental findings already available. Perhaps – but will every child benefit? We might start with provisions for the most deprived and then expand the provision gradually, monitoring the impact. The policy issue becomes one of *'for what proportion* of the population should nursery school be provided?'* This kind of question is best answered by a series of experiments premised on the following:

- Those most in need should receive the service.

- The cut-off point for 'most in need' is not precise and is assessed only with difficulty.

- There is certainly a borderline group about whom there would be debate because the level of need cannot be precisely assessed. The borderline group can even be defined by the errors of measurement.

- The only ethical way to assign children who are in the borderline

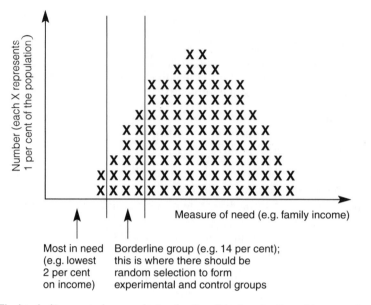

Fig. 3.2 *The borderline control group design for the ethical evaluation of interventions which are thought to benefit the most needy.*

group is randomly, and this random assignment provides the basis for establishing a 'borderline control group' (Fitz-Gibbon and Morris, 1987, pp. 156–160). The borderline group, then, should be randomly assigned to make a 'treatment' group and a control group (Figure 3.2).

The borderline control group could and should be used to evaluate many policies, such as: the placement of children in special needs classes; the development of classes for mentally gifted students; the provision of vocational courses as an alter-

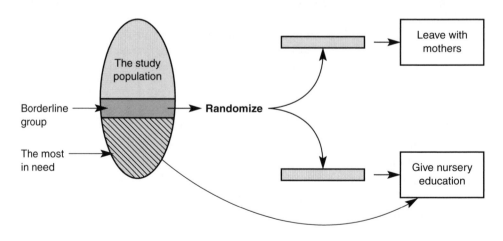

Fig. 3.3 *Borderline control group design.*

native for some, and a determination of the optimal proportion. Even if, in each new initiative, only six students a year were randomly assigned at sites around the country, within a couple of years we would have built up a large experiment.

What are the obstacles? Politicians, in particular, want simple answers, not 'we need more evidence'. Another obstacle is that many people feel they know the answer and do not need to check it. However, setting out to do good is *not* a guarantee that your effects will be beneficial. No matter how good the intentions, things can go badly and surprisingly wrong. Unfortunately, evaluations of interventions have generally focused on immediate outcomes and some have relied on the 'feel good' kind of outcome – general client satisfaction. In a study unusual for its mix of methods and long time-scale, McCord (1978) reported counselling and practical help given over a period of five years to 'at-risk' young males in their teens. Thirty years later they remembered their social workers with affection, and reported the help that had led them away from crime (e.g. 'I was put on the right road', 'I think I would have ended up in a life of crime', 'I probably would be in jail'). However, objective measures, based on records such as the number of arrests, seriousness of crimes and recidivism, showed either no differences or differences in favour of those *not* provided with help. 'Intervention programs risk damaging the individuals they are designed to assist' commented the author.

Had the treatment, the help provided, been harmful? Perhaps the teenagers, poised to observe their own growing up, interpreted the help, sent at state expense without it being requested, as confirmation that someone could see they were helpless, incompetent, and in need of outside assistance. Did a self-labelling effect have negative long-term outcomes on the whole family? Or did interactions with social workers produce later internal conflicts, and raise expectations which were later shattered? We might never know, but this exceptional follow-up highlights two points: (1) long-term outcomes need checking; (2) good intentions do not guarantee good outcomes.

DOES THE LACK OF EXPERIMENTATION IN EDUCATION MATTER?

Lack of experimental data leaves social scientists in ignorance of the effects of actions which might be taken. The result is that very serious problems are described but not effectively treated. Ignorance cannot be seen as comfortable or desirable. Quite apart from the professional pride that might be taken in actually having some firm evidence, as in the case of the impact of pre-school education on at-risk children, there are very serious social problems that we hope can be addressed through schools and with which we are making very little headway because of the lack of an experimental approach. For example, drug education programmes may have increased the use of drugs rather than decreased the use of drugs. The death of Ahmed Ulla in Manchester was blamed, by some, on the anti-racist teaching in the school (Macdonald *et al.*, 1989). I recall a prominent researcher on racism addressing a meeting and advocating a particular style of anti-racist teaching. He was asked what evidence he had that the procedures he was recommending so forcefully – much like those used in Manchester – were actually beneficial in their impact rather than possibly negative in their impact. His reply was that he was not that kind of researcher. If he had no evidence, why did he feel that he was in a position to make recommendations for actions? And why did those funding him not worry about this situation?

Lack of knowledge means that people suffer. For example, bad advice, based on a confusion between residuals and experimental evidence, cost thousands of hard-pressed teachers their free time, needed for refreshment and lesson preparation, in stressful inner-city teaching jobs. On the basis of survey research, two noted US researchers observed that schools which had longer schools days and better attendance had higher achievement measures. They drew the inference that lengthening the school day and the school year would improve achievement in inner-city schools. Even though their interpretations of the data were very quickly and effectively challenged by Karweit (1976), who pointed out that the short school days and high absences were in inner-city schools and the long days were in suburban schools, simple prescriptions to lengthen the school day were nevertheless adopted in a large number of school districts throughout the US. These changes in allocated time did not bring the advances in achievement predicted by the researchers. Moreover, the over-stated research has cost teachers dearly.

Should the Hippocratic Oath be taken by educational researchers? I think so, and by inspectors too, but that is another chapter.

Chapter 4

Do We Really Need Performance Indicators?

A complex system must learn in two ways: from strong inferences derived from the conduct of experiments and from constant checking on its own performance. That is, a complex system needs both experimental data (type 4 data as per Chapter 3) and constant monitoring in the framework of a model (type 3 data). In the future, people may be amazed at the way in which complex systems have been allowed to trundle blindly along with very little in the way of accurate feedback on their performance. Such flying blind was possibly excusable or even inevitable given the difficulty of managing large amounts of information about highly complex organizations. With computers available, the excuse fades. Furthermore, effective organizations should probably work in such small modules that each module has some indication of its own effectiveness. However, useful indicators are rarely readily available; they have to be engineered in, designed into the system.

With the advent of computing power, we can now manage complex organizations more effectively. We can feed back vast amounts of information to the system about the system's performance. This we do by the creation of systems of performance indicators. Public administration can become a fascinating research enterprise in social science.

This is easily said, but less easily done. We will not get performance indicators right the first time. The problems are too great. However, we seem, in some instances, to be getting them wrong in a most predictable, peculiar and unintelligent away.

In this chapter are a few examples of indicators which are corruptible and therefore corrupting and damaging. (Cooley (1983) coined the useful terms 'corrupting' and 'corruptible' – drawing attention to the impact of indicators in a prescient article dealing with 'monitoring and tailoring'.)

EXAMPLES OF CORRUPTIBLE AND/OR CORRUPTING INDICATORS OUTSIDE EDUCATION

Law Courts

Law Courts are required to report the time lapse between an arrest and an appearance in court. However, rather than clog the system with enormous amounts of such measurements, four-week periods are selected as samples. It is the delay times in these samples which are reported. The system is corruptible in that the four-week samples are known in advance. It is, therefore, entirely possible to postpone the arrival of a case in court if it has been too long on the books and could be more conveniently dealt with at a later time outside the four-week reporting period. Not only is the system corruptible, but it is acting, to some extent, against its own purpose, which is, presumably, to reduce the delay time between arrest and appearance in court. On the other hand, it can be argued that a reasonable amount of investigation before something goes to court demands a reasonable delay time. What is reasonable? Only comparative data or quantitative studies of a convincing nature could answer such a question. The system as set up is clearly corruptible.

Telephone repairs

A system of monitoring the work of telephone repair men was instituted which involved simply counting the repairs accomplished per hour. The problem was that the problems needing attention were displayed on a screen and the repair men could choose which problem to work on. The obvious strategy to employ was to solve the quick and simple problems and keep putting off any problem which was difficult to solve. This example illustrates the need to talk with the people whose work is being monitored. They are the experts; they can tell you how the system is working, can work, where it goes wrong, where it does not achieve its aims and what the obstacles and problems are. It is difficult for anybody to supervise another person if the person being supervised always has more information than the person supervising. Surveillance is, therefore, exceedingly difficult and the very best management strategy is to keep people working for the long-term good of the enterprise. The desire to tie performance to pay can lead to some silly systems, as illustrated by this simple indicator of the number of repairs per hour.

The Herald of Free Enterprise

The Herald of Free Enterprise transported cars and people across the English Channel and was one of many such ferries built to a design with well-known flaws: the cars were loaded into a cargo area in the lower part of the ship, a procedure known as 'roll-on–roll-off', and the problem was that this cargo hold had no dividers. It was one large cavity. Should water ever get into this, it could swill to one side and tilt the ship over. Even more alarming, it was well known to those who operated these ships that the cargo doors had often been open instead of sealed when the ships set sail, running the risk that water would enter the cargo hold and capsize the ship. There was no safety design which prevented a ship from leaving if the cargo doors were still open. The captain had asked for an automatic signal to show him the state of the doors on the bridge but had not been provided with one. The danger of an accident was increased by the ship's need to take on water as ballast to bring it down to the level of the Zeebrugge roll-on facility. Further, the captain had been ordered to reduce the crossing time by 20 minutes, and this left him no time to pump out the ballast before departing (Sutherland, 1992, p. 251).

In calm seas, within sight of land, the Herald of Free Enterprise sank with the loss of 180 lives in the most appalling circumstances of a mass drowning.

Those responsible for the design and management of this shipping service should have been considered culpable. They had ignored information and the advice of those who knew the job, and had set up performance indicators which had fatal consequences. The ship's sailing time was monitored very closely, since it was trying to keep to a tight timetable. This was equivalent to a performance indicator of turnaround time. In contrast, the number of times the ship left in an unsafe condition with the cargo doors open was not monitored. Such dangerous events carried no consequences. The pressure, therefore, was on the crew to keep to schedule. There was not, it seems, an equivalent pressure to stay within safe limits.

Water service performance indicators

An example of a potentially corrupting indicator was that imposed on the water industry when it was required to report the number of samples taken per month. A simple count of the number of samples failed to reveal that some samples were quick and easy to collect whilst other very important samples were more difficult and time-consuming to collect. If scientists were held accountable only for the number of samples, not for the type, the strategy would be to collect quick and simple samples, whether or not they were adequate for monitoring the quality of the water. Fortunately, in the case of the water industry, scientists could afford to ignore the performance indicator because, if challenged, they would have had strong scientific evidence about the nature of their enterprise. They could demonstrate very clearly the need for time-consuming samples of some complexity, so they could probably resist the corrupting influence of such a simple-minded indicator. The indicator might have been made non-corrupting if it had been set in the context of many other indicators and if comparative data had been collected and shared among water authorities.

This particular example illustrates, however, the easier situation facing scientific enterprises, in which the data are less debatable than in social science.

Near misses

An example from the air travel industry illustrates this effect of context. Pilots are allowed to report 'near misses', in which their aeroplane is almost in an accident, without giving their name. This allows the monitoring of 'near misses' so that people can examine the system, and track down airports or practices or situations in which near misses are occurring in order to learn how to avoid not only near misses but their inevitable eventual consequence, actual collisions. This system has confidentiality built into it because otherwise pilots might fear that their jobs would be at stake and they might under-report near misses. The near miss is, for example, to some extent a matter of judgement; it is not an objective, clear-cut phenomenon. *Whenever there is an element of judgement, the element of fear in the system has a chance to act more strongly, leading to corrupted data.* Confidentially may then be essential to the collection of adequate information.

The general point here is that the context in which the indicator is collected is all-important. If the indicator is to be related to pay, for example, then its influence is potentially very strong and dangerous. If, on the other hand, the indicator is part of an investigation of how the system is functioning, then it becomes a matter of interest rather than a source of fear, and corrupting effects can be resisted.

EXAMPLES OF INDICATORS IN SCHOOLS

Truancy

Schools must provide figures on their rates of truancy. A high rate of truancy published in newspapers could deter many parents from choosing to send their children to that particular school. Headteachers are therefore redefining truancy; most absences will become excused absences. Since there is no simple way of checking on the report of the school about its truancy rate and no proposals to put any funds into doing so, this indicator is fallible in the extreme because it is subject to being corrupted at source. It illustrates well Deming's observation that 'wherever there is fear, we get the wrong figures'. It should be noted that this is a source of disinformation in the system. It is making the system less fit. It may stop people collecting good data. Schools should be concerned about truancy, but when they are forced to publish the figures in the local press, in a climate of fear, those figures become useless or, worse than useless, misleading.

Percentage pass rates

Another example of a corrupting indicator is the frequently published percentage pass rate collected in government league tables – a source of great distortion in education now that such figures are brought under the glare of publicity. What is the problem with the percentage pass rate, such as the percentage achieving grades A–C in GCSE, or the percentage passing A-level examinations? The problem is that it focuses teachers' attention on the borderline. There is no point in worrying about students who are likely to get a B, even if with effort they might be able to achieve an A. As long as the student is not going to fall below a C, they can be safely ignored. The students to concentrate on are those likely to fall below the border, and every effort should be made to either push them off the course if it is a post-16 non-compulsory course, or to concentrate teaching effort on this borderline group. Indeed, one school abandoned a special needs teacher to create a post aiming at students likely to achieve grade D in GCSE. Extra attention would be paid to them to push them above the critical C/D borderline. This was not a strategy justified in cost–benefit terms or educational terms, i.e. such students' life chances would be more affected than the students who, with similar extra help, might move from a B to an A. The justification was entirely to alter the performance indicator. This is a corrupting effect of such a measurement.

SATs

Another corruptible system was the government's plans for testing at ages 7 and 11 and 14 (testing at age 16 was already in place in the form of examinations called the General Certificate of Secondary Education (GCSE) – a system of blind, externally marked examinations which is almost incorruptible, although leaving the names of candidates and their centre on the papers when they are marked is like working with dirty test tubes. It is not generally recognized as adequate methodology.) The testing at ages 7, 11 and 14 was to be done by teachers in classrooms under non-standardized conditions and peculiar recording conventions. Before SATs appeared, I asked a high official in the body responsible for the tests (Schools Examination and Assessment Council (SEAC) if I had missed some vital component of the system. Was it correct that teachers were to mark tests and the results of those tests were to be published so that we could evaluate how good the teaching was in that school? Did there not seem to be a flaw in this system? He could not reassure me but retreated, as most SEAC officials would under pressure, to 'We have no choice, it's politically driven'. There was, of course, a system of moderation introduced. This, along with the reluctance of teachers to be other than exceed-ingly hard working and honest, probably would have ensured a reasonable set of results if the marking scheme had been reasonable. One illustrative anecdote was provided by a student who, as a maths teacher, was moderating the SAT results for an entire local education authority (LEA). If a pupil had not reached a specific level, the pupil could be awarded a 'W', meaning 'working towards'. The student who was the moderator discovered that out of 32 Ws awarded in his LEA, his own school accounted for 28 of them. Presumably, in most other schools, Ws had been generously awarded a higher grade or ungenerously awarded a lower grade, but had been studiously avoided in some way. His comment was, 'We were the honest fools, we won't be next time.' The SATs, I would argue, were a corruptible system. They might work for a year or two, but once a nearby school produced a fabulous set of results, the temptation to be particularly lenient in judgemental aspects of awarding grades would be strong indeed.

Indicators can be corrupting in two ways: they can tempt people simply to dis-tort the indicator, as in truancy rates, or people might take the indicator seriously, and try to affect it but in so doing adopt behaviour which has an impact which is quite contrary to the desired impact of improved quality, and improved fitness. This would be the case with percentage pass rates.

CAN THE NET EFFECT OF INDICATORS BE GOOD?

It is possible to produce examples of the good effect of indicators and, indeed, it is the impact of indicators on behaviour which is the most important issue. Indicators must surely be designed to improve performance, not distract from it.

An example of the good effects of indicators might be the economic indicators which monitor economic activity. It is an area in which politicians are trying very hard to get good information because they cannot control the indicators beyond a certain amount. Thus the exchange rate, the growth in the economy and rate of inflation are indicators that political parties find it difficult to subvert. In the field of economics, politicians must try to change the reality and let the indicators show. There are limits to how often, for example, the method of calculating unemploy-ment figures can be changed.

VIGNETTES OF SOME CURRENT PROBLEMS IN THE EDUCATION SYSTEM

The UK already has one of the most closely monitored systems in the world, thanks to our system of examinations at 16 and 18 years of age. Large proportions of the students we teach are submitted for examination: the end-product is assessed and in a way which is impressively fair and thorough, a viewpoint elaborated in the chapters on assessment. But whilst we have excellent data available, they have not been used as effectively as they could be. They have not been used to provide teachers with feedback which relates to their effectiveness.

There are different kinds of effectiveness. Classroom control is one, and on this teachers get feedback. Teachers know when they are getting from students the behaviour they are looking for, because the feedback is there before their eyes: immediate and unambiguous. But what of effectiveness in inducing learning? At the end of, say, two years of teaching towards an examination, when the results arrive, teachers wonder: are these excellent or average results? Did other teachers working with similar students get better results? Has every student lived up to his or her potential or have I been more successful with some than with others? They may have some hunches about the answers but further information has proved to be widely welcomed. The further information needed is that which provides fair comparisons by showing what has come to be called the 'value added' per student. (The topic of value added is taken up in Chapter 14.)

There have been some problems in the UK educational system in recent years and these can often be traced to the lack of good information and/or confusion about the interpretations which can be made of the four kinds of data described in Chapter 2. Below are a few examples of these problems. Each example has been created to illustrate a point. None refers to a particular incident, though you might find parallels in reality. It would be likely, however, that there would be all kinds of complications and mitigating circumstances in a real situation, and doing justice would require a book for each example. The examples, then, are included for their heuristic value only.

Example 1. A CEO stated that he has set a target of 10 per cent improvement in examination results for his inner-city schools

---

We might ask, why 10 per cent? Why not 2 per cent or 20 per cent? The CEO did not have any data to justify that target as reasonable – he just set it. Then it was up to teachers to deliver. How did he know whether or not the schools were under-performing? Which particular schools was he referring to? Surely they were not all the same just because they were all 'inner city'? More precisely, which departments in which schools?

This was lazy leadership, not bothering to know the situation in detail, not finding out what was working well and deserved praise rather than exhortation, not identifying and addressing specific problems but just casting general asper-sions: 'you're all at fault'. The setting of the target carried the implicit message to teachers: 'You are not doing what is possible: you need to try harder, and get better results.' How could such a message be delivered in the absence of any convincing analysis that might support the truth of such a statement?

The judgement on an entire body of teachers was highly unlikely to be true. When we look at the data on effectiveness of schooling, we find great variations between departments even within one school. There is effectiveness and ineffec-tiveness, random variation and some consistency. Management should avoid group punishments just as any teacher learns that punishing a class for the misde-meanour of one or two of its members is a grave mistake. Injustice develops right-eous anger.

The system was failing the CEO and leading him to unproductive and possibly destructive actions. The system had probably failed to train him in research meth-ods and had failed to provide him with interpretable information. He may have drowned in data but have been unable to make sense of it. He had examination results galore, but no way to interpret them fairly, and he did not know enough to request or buy in the expertise needed. His management training was almost cer-tainly deficient and the accountants who recommended that local authorities should monitor the schools should have indicated the need for resources to enable such monitoring to be undertaken with justice. Thus, there may be quite a number of systems needing adjustment if CEOs are going to function effectively.

> **Example 2. A school obtaining many high-grade results is told by a local authority inspector that he wonders if the results, good as they look, are as good as they should be, given the type of pupils enrolled.**

Here we see an inspector struggling to be fair by being tough on the high achievers. But that is annoying to the high achievers, given that the inspector has only a hunch. Again, the system has failed the inspector and this failure is having a knock-on effect elsewhere in the system. The inspector has access to large amounts of comparative data but has neither the training nor the resources to come up with fair interpretations. And some of the data may not be interpretable, due to a lack of critical pieces of information.

> **Example 3. A CEO prepared reports on schools in his district. He wrote to one headteacher, requesting his comments on the fact that the school's A-level results were below the average for the district.**

This sounded like a criticism and the headteacher wrote back, saying 'How much below average? And how much below average would be reasonable given the pupils in the school?' A fair, precise question to which the CEO had no answer. The CEO had tried looking at free school meals, but had read that this measure was inadequate, and, anyway, none of the A-level candidates seemed to be in receipt of free school meals, so he was not sure it was relevant.

> **Example 4. An HMI watched three lessons in an A-level Chemistry class. On the basis of this sample drawn from the 180 lessons given to that class that year by that teacher, the HMI complained to the head-teacher that the teacher was dictating notes and seemed organized but not inspired. The headteacher humoured the HMI, not wanting to pro-voke a bad report.**

Neither the HMI nor the headteacher knew how effective the teacher was. It could have been the case that the results in that class were unusually good, in so far as other chemistry teachers that year, working with students who had similar prior achievements, had achieved lower grades. But this kind of information was not available, so both the headteacher and the HMI were operating in the dark, making assumptions, judging on an inadequate basis.

Suppose that fair comparative information had been available and had shown the teacher to be effective. If the data showing this had been made available to the HMI before his visit, how then would the teacher have been described by him in discussion with the headteacher? 'Traditional yes, but very methodical. Good chap.' Or perhaps the HMI would have stood by his dislike of the teaching methods and said: 'Well, this is the problem with A-levels. You get good results by bad teaching. The students will not really understand the work and probably will dislike the subject.' But these statements, an attempt to interpret data, are predicated on some unfounded assumptions. *Do* the students dislike the subject? Is there a particular type of teaching which 'gets good results' at A-level, in all subjects? Does the inspector know this for a fact or does he just have a hunch?

Example 5. Inspectors visit a set of inner-city schools and declare that the major problem is that teachers' expectations are too low.

The inspectors do not tell us how they know this. Teachers are bitter but some meekly wonder if the inspectors are right. Wasn't there some research which proved this? The inspectors also were probably thinking of the research, which they vaguely believed proved that low expectations led to low achievement.

We must assume that the inspectors are trying to do a good job. They are going to have to say something at the end of a visit, and this was the currently safe point to make, given that many professors of education were propounding this view, having not yet discovered the flawed nature of the research into this concept. So inspectors blamed the teachers and no one could prove or disprove the statement. And the net result was that no one was any the wiser as to what could be done. No one knew whether the schools were uniformly effective or ineffective, and whether some teachers were getting brilliant results or not. How were 'expectations' to be changed? No one knew where the magic switch was in a teacher's brain to change their perceptions, so no one could actually put the 'expectations' hypothesis to the test. Giving teachers false information, as was done in the original research on teacher expectations, was not a real option. So the LEA was left with this mass condemnation. Teachers must have found it infuriating and insulting.

Example 6. The head of a college studies A-level results carefully each year. If the A-level results which students get in one subject seem to be worse than the results the same students get in other subjects, he displays the data in a staff meeting and asks for explanations. The staff call it 'trial by OHP'. He often seems to have to ask for explanations from mathematics, physics and French departments and he does begin to agree with their point that their subjects are 'more difficult' than other A-level subjects. His problem is: how much more difficult? How much allowance should be made? He suspects that the results are badly below what they should be in one of the departments, even allowing for national differences in the difficulty of some subjects, but he cannot get the department to accept that there is any problem.

The head is trying hard but he simply does not have access to a vital piece of information which is needed to interpret the data: what results can reasonably be expected? He does not know how difficult the different subjects are. This problem thwarts his efforts to use data to monitor outcomes; thwarts his efforts to be fair to both staff and students by looking at evidence, not just acting on hunches; and thwarts his efforts at quality control.

LIVING IN INTERESTING TIMES

The late 1980s and early 1990s were times of great pain for many people, in many countries. There were economic difficulties which were eventually called a recession, the worst feature of which was probably the widespread and long-lasting unemployment.

For teachers these were certainly years of new stresses. Stress has always been a feature of teaching: every year teachers get older, but the students bubble forth as young and inexhaustible as ever. Most teachers manage to respond with vigour and good humour but during the 1980s new kinds of pressures were introduced with a National Curriculum, and a testing system (the SATs) which surpassed comprehension. Then came the Parents' Charter, apparently requiring much which was already routine and unexceptional (e.g. regular reports to parents) but culminating in the publication in national newspapers of examination results, often in the form of 'league tables', i.e. rank-ordered lists showing schools from 'top' (usually schools in wealthy, leafy suburbs) to 'bottom'(usually schools in distressed inner-city areas). Schools at the bottom were excoriated in the press. The league tables were, of course, based on raw data (see Chapter 2) and were therefore widely acknowledged to be of limited value – if not indeed positively misleading – if one wanted to assess the *effectiveness* of schools. Analyses were produced in several LEAs to present fairer information, to move towards fair comparisons.

The most readily available data with which to create fairer comparisons comprised an index of socio-economic status: the percentage of pupils in the school who were eligible for free school meals. Unfortunately, use of this information was a two-edged sword for schools. On the one hand it seemed to provide an excuse for poor examination results, since graphs could show strong correlations between some aggregate index of a school's examination results (e.g. percentage achieving five grades A to C in the examinations at age 16) and a free school meals index. But the excuse could backfire: who would want their children in schools with such a high proportion of students receiving free school meals *when that high proportion seemed to be so strongly correlated with poor examination results*? The insistence of some LEAs and researchers on using these data because they were the only data available may not have been a wise strategy and it perpetuated a myth: that home background is the important determinant of school outcomes. This myth is considered as an instance of the ecological fallacy in Chapter 16.

Of course, many parents have no choice as to where to send their children – travel is expensive.

Morale among staff in inner-city schools must have taken a severe beating with the league tables, even if enrolments kept up. In some schools, enrolments would be damaged and jobs would be lost. Some would argue that while this was unfortunate, it was nevertheless just what was needed. Let the market close down poor schools and then the general standard will rise. Such is the gist of the argument resting on a faith in market forces. The hypothesis is that there was something wrong with low-achieving schools and having pupils transfer to other schools would result in improvements. Teachers would work harder in this competitive environment.

What evidence is there that teachers' lack of effort is a major factor in low achievement in inner-city or any other schools? And even if it were in some instances, then we need to ask what has caused the lack of effort. Are the teaching efforts of teachers who feel threatened by examination pressures actually productive of better examination results and/or more satisfied students and parents? Is there evidence that education can be improved by closing down some schools or creating new types of schools? Moving from one building to another may well have little effect on how one teaches.

We will not know the answers to these questions unless we monitor closely the effectiveness of schools and watch for the effects of changes on the measures of effectiveness. All shades of the political spectrum should support monitoring and experimentation in order to find out the answers to these important questions.

However, from the monitoring we have done in the ALIS project and from data analysed in the Scottish system (Fitz-Gibbon, 1991a; 1991b) there is evidence that:

- it is *departments*, not schools, which vary most;
- almost all schools contain *both* effective and ineffective departments in any one year;
- from year to year, the departments often *change* in effectiveness.

These findings strongly imply that quality, a good education for all students, will be best attained by close monitoring of departments. We need to learn from the most consistently effective departments and take action in the case of consistently underperforming departments. We need to find out, particularly by monitoring schools which undergo changes in management strategies, exactly how much difference can be made in 'whole school effects' – this is still not clear.

SUMMARY

As the world changes, words change too:

- *pupil progress* we now think of as *value added*;
- *equal opportunities* is a topic less often discussed than *quality assurance*;
- *talking things over* has become *staff appraisal*;
- *recognition* is in danger of becoming *performance-related pay*;
- *goals* have become *mission statements*;
- *poaching* is now *healthy competition*;
- *advertising* is now regarded as *good public relations*;
- *hype* is now seen as *high-quality presentation standards*.

But the words do not matter too much. What matters is the underlying reality and we will only get some purchase on that by monitoring the outcomes we care about enough to measure.

PART TWO

Philosophical Approaches

THE POWER OF SCIENCE AND THE WEAKNESS OF POLITICS

Mathematical models, explanations of evolution, close up photographs of Jupiter and Saturn, the prediction and discovery of Uranus, antibiotics and aspirin, the mapping of the human genome, landing men and machinery on the moon. . . . We seem to be doing rather well in science but rather badly in politics and the sphere of social science.

IS COMPLEXITY OR METHODOLOGY THE PROBLEM?

We need to consider whether our lack of success in solving social problems – delinquency, the mass delinquency of war, unemployment, starvation, and more humble problems such as truancy – relates not only to the complexity of the problems but also to methods adopted and ways of thinking. Our mental models may need overhauling. Are we failing to apply the methods which have been successful in science to issues of human affairs?

What are the methods adopted by science with such evident success? The principal factor is that science uses *evidence* as the arbiter, not *authority*.

In Chapter 5 we see the way in which evidence is driving some researchers to question the notion of the type of generalizable findings which 'research' might yield as a guide to action. If unpredictability is the rule, what then is the role of research?

Is the emerging science of 'complexity' a clue to the solution? If schools are complex systems then the problem which confronts us is how to improve complex systems. Further, we find from recent dramatic changes in science – led by physicists, mathematicians and computer scientists – that there may be fundamental reasons for the poor correlations encountered in social science, the lack of success in predicting and explaining social phenomena: it may be unpredictable not just at present given our present methods, but for always.

In Chapter 6 an attempt is made to consider how the modern ideas of complexity fit with philosophical and statistical concepts developed by notable thinkers from a range of backgrounds and experiences – H. A. Simon, W. Edwards Deming, Karl Popper.

Chapter 5

Science and Complexity

In 1979, in an article entitled 'Policy for the unpredictable', Gene Glass suggested that it might not be possible to discover widely applicable research findings (Glass, 1979). He thus was questioning the value of educational research. Education was so complex, he argued, that we might simply have to be content with 'fire-fighting': having monitoring systems in place which could alert us when untoward events were happening.

This was a highly prescient article and fits well with a modern development in science called 'complexity theory'.

Gene Glass arrived at this opinion by the road generally trodden by scientists: close contact with data. He is a highly regarded US researcher and a co-author of the first book on meta-analysis (Glass *et al.*, 1981). Meta-analysis is the term given to procedures for summarizing research findings, and Glass and his colleagues had collected together, and systematically scrutinized, the research findings on numerous topics such as tutoring, computer-based instruction, recovery from surgery, social class and achievement, teaching behaviours and many more.

> I shudder to think of the number of studies we have read and analysed
> in that time. But the experience has been useful and it has left me with
> some impressions about research integration and our field . . . I haven't
> seen a body of literature in which we can account for much more than
> a third of the variability in the results of studies. Many things work,
> and some things work powerfully. The point is that we are unable to
> predict which of several things works well in particular circumstances.
> The variance of success across classrooms, schools, cities, etc. is
> enormous . . . Moreover, of the 33 percent or less of the variance in
> study findings that is explained, most of it is explained by instrumental
> properties *of the research itself* (e.g. the degree of experimental control
> that was exercised, the 'fakeability' of the outcome measures, the
> external validity of the treatment, and the like). Those are the sort of
> variables that may be interesting to research, but they are useless as
> points of leverage to move the real world. (Emphases in the original)
> (Glass, 1979, p. 13)

It is the data which drive theory. Here we have a theory of unpredictability arising from the data – a recognition of the limits of the explanations that social science seems able to achieve. This limit was noted in the first reports back to schools in the ALIS project in 1984, with the diagram in Figure 5.1, although like many researchers I was still hoping that, if we only we could measure important variables, we would be able to explain more of the variation from classroom to classroom.

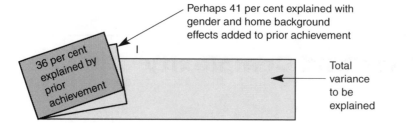

Figure 5.1 *The amount of unexplained variance*

Equally driven by the data, Tymms wrote:

> Many quantitative educational researchers must have felt a sense of
> frustration the first time they sat down to analyse school effectiveness
> data. They will probably have found that the 'best' data available were
> examination data together with some prior cognitive measure and that
> they were able to explain about half the variance of the criterion at the
> pupil level. Such relationships become part of our expectations after
> working in the field for some time, but to anyone meeting it anew and
> coming from a natural science background it seems as though the game
> has just started. . . . Attempts to 'explain' much more of the school or
> pupil level variance are doomed. If there really are chaotic processes at
> work within individual brains in individual lives, in classrooms and in
> schools, it simply will not be possible to contruct regression equations,
> even if they can deal with the structure of the data, that explain much
> more of the variance than we can at the moment. (Tymms, in press)

Glass embraced the notion of unpredictable systems but did not see this as in any
way removing educational research from the realms of rationality and science.
Instead he saw the need to re-conceptualize science:

> We speak too much about Science as prediction, planning, and
> manipulation. And we are prone, when in this frame of mind, to imagine
> educational research as the search for those one or two strings to pull
> that will animate teachers and pupils like so many marionettes . . .
>
> Is the proper challenge of the disciplined study of education the
> creation of a system which adapts, which works reasonably well and
> which, instead of 'optimising' 'satisfices' (to use Herbert Simon's word).
> Should our empirical policy studies be based on the assumption that the
> conditions that make schooling effective are either in practice unknown,
> too numerous or too labile to be controlled by persons at any significant
> distance from the essential nexus of learning, namely a pupil's brain and
> a tutor? (Glass, 1979, p. 14)

MUCH OF NATURAL SCIENCE IS UNPREDICTABLE

As social scientists like Glass and Tymms move away from believing that more
money and greater efforts will make social science more predictable, a new view

has been emerging in the natural sciences. For some decades new procedures and models have been developed by theoretical physicists and mathematicians as the phenomenon remarked on by Poincaré almost a century ago has been investigated:

> It may happen that small differences in the initial conditions produce very great ones in the final phenomena. A small error in the former, will produce an enormous error in the latter. Prediction becomes impossible, and we have the fortuitous phenomenon. (Poincaré, 1908, cited by Davies, 1987, p. 53)

Summarizing part of his book *The Cosmic Blueprint*, first published in 1987, physicist P. C. W. Davies wrote:

> I have been at pains to argue that the steady unfolding of organised complexity in the universe is a fundamental property of nature. I have reviewed some of the important attempts to model complex structures and processes in physics, chemistry, biology, astronomy and ecology. We have seen how spontaneous self-organisation tends to occur in far-from-equilibrium open non-linear systems *with a high degree of feedback*. Such systems, far from being unusual, are actually the norm in nature. . . . We seem to be on the verge of discovering not only wholly new laws of nature, but ways of thinking about nature that depart radically from traditional science. (Davies, 1989, p. 142) (Emphasis added)

In Santa Fe, New Mexico, an institute was created in 1984 by physicists, economists and biologists interested in unpredictability and complexity and the concepts which emerge from this phenomenon (Waldrop, 1992; Lewin, 1993).

The theme of the impossibility of long-term predictions is fundamental in current studies of complex systems. What is clear is that the future is only predictable, at all, in the very short term. This was a point made by Karl Popper many years before the mathematical developments which established that, in certain systems where there is some kind of feedback (also called non-linear dynamic systems), there is a sensitivity to initial conditions, and these initial conditions are always, inevitably, measured with error. The problem with non-linear, complex systems is that the errors, instead of adding up or staying constant, grow very rapidly, making long-term prediction useless.

(A very simple example of a feedback system which becomes chaotic under certain conditions is provided in Appendix 1. The graphs were run on a spreadsheet. 'The system' is no more than a *very* simple equation, yet the outcomes can be chaotic.)

The weather is a good representation of this type of problem. The variables which affect the weather, such as cloud formation, heating, cooling, wind flow, and adiabatic and isothermal lapse rates, are well known and the physics is fairly well understood (better understood than mechanisms of human societies, for example). Nevertheless, to predict the weather for more than a few days in advance is fundamentally impossible even with gigantic amounts of computing power, because the equations which model the processes and can be used for prediction show a great sensitivity to the starting values. Start with one value and you get one kind of weather predicted; start with one very similar, and the predicted weather is quickly entirely different. Indeed, it has been suggested that a minor disturbance such as the flapping of a butterfly's wings could cause a major disturbance in the weather, such as a hurricane (Davies, 1987, p. 52). If the extent to which butterflies were flapping their wings had to be known in order to predict the weather, it is clear the task would be impossible. Because of the 'sensitivity to initial conditions' and the fact that we cannot measure the initial conditions with sufficient accuracy, the weather is seriously unpredictable in the long term.

The lack of predictability does not – and this is perhaps surprising – imply a lack of complete determinism in the system. The lack of predictability is about the lack of the capacity to process information and to know accurately the initial state. In some systems the status of the system would itself require many parameters to specify, which would be simply unknown. But the surprising feature of much work in complexity is that exceedingly simple systems, as long as they contain a feedback loop which makes them non-linear, can produce highly complex, completely random and unpredictable outcomes, although they are fully determined by the simple procedures which define the system. The work on non-linear systems has wrought, in the last few decades, a sea change in science. Physicist P. C. W. Davies wrote of 'nothing less than a brand new start in the description of nature' (Davies, 1987, p. 23).

From books such as *Complexity: the Emerging Science on the Edge of Order and Chaos* (Waldrop, 1992) we gain new insights into how complex systems evolve in response to feedback from the environment. Across many disciplines – mathematics, physics, evolutionary biology, cell biology, economics, archaeology, computing – a coherent set of concepts is emerging. Whether dealing with organisms or organizations, central concepts are those of

- *unpredictability* – the impossibility of prediction under some circumstances;
- *feedback* – the flow of information and consequences from the environment in which a complex organism is surviving;
- *local organization* as opposed to central control;
- *emergence* – the spontaneous development of diverse and effective organizations in conditions which border on chaos.

I will comment more on these shortly, but first I will examine the role of computers in all this.

> In a non-linear system a whole is much more than the sum of its parts, and it cannot be reduced or analysed in terms of simple sub-units acting together. The resulting properties can often be unexpected, complicated and mathematically intractable. (Davies, 1987, p. 25)

The term 'mathematically intractable' seems to sound the death knell for science as normally conducted. If systems are chaotic, full of discontinuities, catastrophes, unevenness and unpredictability, science cannot construct mathematical laws that will predict the future. Mathematical modelling meets its limits. The tools of analysis then become a kind of modelling using computers, a method which is different from the highly successful previous work in science resting on mathematical modelling. Computer modelling can attempt to simulate events in a direct fashion, by rules and procedures rather than equations. Computers are being used to simulate evolution ('artificial life'), to act as learning machines (neural networks) and to model by simulation rather than by mathematics. Tymms has replicated school effectiveness data using a computer program in BASIC (Tymms, in press). Like much else in science it is both enhancing – as we feel that more and more of life becomes comprehensible – and humbling, as our behaviour seems accessible to modelling, even if not to prediction in detail.

UNPREDICTABILITY

Of course, analogies prove nothing. However, they often underpin scientific intuition and lead to advances. The analogies offered here with regard to complexity theory serve only as a heuristic, a 'this might apply' concept, but since education, in particular, is nothing if not a complex system, it would be strange if some of the findings from the new, computer-driven models of complex systems did not apply to education.

A complex system is a system 'describable by a web of informational interactions' (Davies, 1987, p. 159). It is open to the environment and receiving feedback constantly, with the consequence that it is largely unpredictable, in the way of systems which contain feedback loops, be they very simple (Appendix 1) or complex. However, the term unpredictable refers to the details of the system. In some cases the broad boundaries within which it will operate may be definable – just as the climate is predictable even though the weather is not.

These necessary consequences of certain simple assumptions emphasize that complexity can arise from very simple systems and that the future will inevitably be a mystery, a surprise, unpredictable in anything but the very short term.

What does this do for school development plans? This may seem a totally irrelevant question but our mental models are enormously influenced by the state of science and the knowledge that permeates our age. The way people thought in the Middle Ages, when disease, pestilence, hurricanes and rainbows were all frightening and incomprehensible, was very different from the way people think now. It is important, therefore, that we understand and follow the changes that are taking place in the body of knowledge that humankind slowly builds up and can slowly learn to put to use in improving the world. If a strong and insistent message from science is that details of the future are inherently unpredictable and that efficient organisms thrive on the edge of chaos, then the tidy linear planning cycle – set priorities, set targets, plan – may not seem quite so sensible.

So, our new mental images must represent a world of considerable complexity and unpredictability, and we must return again to the question, how can we possibly improve complex systems?

FEEDBACK

Complex systems or 'adaptive agents' are widespread – found in economics, ecology, all living things, as well as in physical and chemical interactions – and they occur when the system itself is open to the environment, when there is a flow of feedback about its own success into the system. What does not seem to have been studied is the effect of *false* feedback. If schools are distracted by misinformation

39

(such as statements by a supposed authority, without evidence, e.g. 'the problem is low expectations on the part of teachers') how does this affect their efficiency and viability? 'An adaptive agent is constantly playing a game with its environment. . . . What actually has to happen to game playing agents to survive and prosper? Two things . . . prediction and feedback (Holland, quoted by Waldrop, 1992, p. 282). Information is needed – and at the local level.

LOCAL ORGANIZATION

Craig Reynolds wrote a computer program to guide the behaviour of mock birds (which he called 'boids') in a computer simulation. He found he could mimic the flocking behaviour of birds by giving each individual bird information and having them use three simple 'local' rules:

- each 'boid' simply flew at the same velocity, as far as possible, as the 'boids' near it;
- each 'boid' tended to move towards the centre of gravity of the flock that it was flying in;
- each 'boid' kept a minimum distance from objects and other 'boids'.

With these three simple rules applied with some random starting parameters, the 'boids' developed flocking behaviour, moving on the screen with the sweep and characteristics of flocking birds, even to the extent of flowing neatly around an obstacle and re-forming as a flock on the other side.

> Instead of writing global, top-down specifications for how the flock should behave, or telling his creatures to follow the lead of one Boss Boid, Reynolds had used only the three simple rules of local boid-to-boid interaction. And *it was precisely that locality that allowed his flock to adapt to changing conditions so organically*. (Waldrop, 1992, p. 279) (Emphasis added)

Does this perspective say something to support the local management of schools and, within schools, the independent management of each department? If schools and departments are locally managed they need local, good information that is relevant to their survival and effectiveness.

EMERGENCE OF ORDER FROM CHAOS

The study of complex systems has been strongly motivated by the need to find what could be called an antidote to the depression induced by the second law of thermodynamics. The second law, which is of the same status as the conservation laws, i.e. not to be violated, predicts increasing disorder (entropy). These predictions from the second law of thermodynamics have been regarded as absolutely fundamental and unavoidable. Indeed, the increase in entropy provides physics with what has been called 'time's arrow'.

Yet order has emerged since the 'big bang', i.e. since the beginning of the observed universe. This seeming contradiction has worried people for many years. Indeed, it seems that Engels wrote in 1940:

> In some way, which it will later be the task of scientific research to demonstrate, the heat radiated into space must be able to become transformed into another form of motion, in which it can once more be stored up and rendered active. (Engels, 1940; cited in Davies, 1987, p. 19)

Thus a social scientist/philosopher recognized the need for some explanation as to how a big bang, radiating energy outwards, heading for more and more disorder, could be squared with the evolution of life forms full of the most incredibly effectively organized systems. The solution has come to be called *emergence*.

Does this phenomenon of emergence cast light on how systems come to be effective? What features need attention? One of the observations in Waldrop's book is as follows: 'When we look at the universe on size scales ranging from quarks to galaxies . . . we find the complex phenomena associated with life only at the scale of molecules. Why?' (Waldrop, 1992, p. 314). The answer given by the young man (Fontana) who asked the question was: first, *variety*, which could have been called 'modularity' – unlike quarks, which can only make protons and neutrons, atoms can be rearranged to make innumerable structures; and second, *reactivity* – structures can interact to form new structures *because they are interconnected*. The level of connectedness seems to be one of the determining factors as to whether a system lives effectively or becomes static on the one hand, or totally chaotic on the other hand. Variety in self-organizing modules which can join into larger structures, the constant interchange of information/feedback, i.e. the reactivity and connectedness – these seem to be important features for effectiveness. Further, the effective organisms (organizations) seem to thrive on the edge of a region of chaos. They are close enough to chaos to be flexible but not so close as to be unable to acquire and process information.

> Evolution thrives in systems with a bottom up organisation, which gives rise to flexibility. . . . But at the same time evolution has to channel the bottom up approach in a way that doesn't destroy the organisation. There has to be a hierarchy of control – with information flowing from the bottom up as well as from the top down. . . . The dynamics of complexity at the edge of chaos seems to be ideal for this kind of behaviour. (Farmer, in Waldrop, 1992)

When these ideas were presented to a seminar, one of the comments evoked was 'Pure Hayek!', and this impression could indeed be a first thought – set up a market and let schools evolve. However, I think that the reality is more complicated. There are markets driven by 'the bottom line' – money – but these are not the only markets; money is not the only motivator (Sen, 1993). But if schools and LEAs are to seek other goals than the maximization of income, they need information, and as yet they are not receiving the information they need on highly important outcomes – students' attitudes, self-esteem, social or unsocial tendencies, addiction behaviours, safety consciousness, social conscience and more. Do we wish schools only to maximize enrolments,whether this is done by an appeal to racism or by what is popularly believed for the moment to be 'good teaching'? Or do we hope for better social engineering?

Essentially, can we choose directions in which to evolve? We can only do this by choosing what to care about enough to measure, measuring it and edging towards the desired outcomes.

Is choice an illusion if the future is determined even if unpredictable? Possibly so – but all we need to assume is that our information processing is sufficiently well developed to enable different futures to be envisaged and some preferred to others.

SUMMARY

If we conceive of education as a highly complex system full of interconnections and feedback loops, then the question becomes 'what do we know about the effectiveness of complex systems?'

'Complexity theory' suggests that important concepts are those of local control, self-organization and emergence, the need for connectedness, the flow of information, efficiency on the edge of chaos and, fundamentally, unpredictability.

If feedback strongly affects the development of complex organizations, then the nature of that feedback must be of utmost concern. What information circulates? Is it good information or misinformation?

This leads to a hypothesis derived from a reading of recent advances in our view of nature: *education will improve when the flow of accurate information on outcomes is increased and the flow of disinformation and unvalidated prescriptions is reduced. The development of monitoring-with-feedback systems is therefore seen as the major priority for school improvement in the coming decades.*

Gene Glass seems to have mapped out the territory some years ago:

> Some general principles are recognisable in how we attempt to deal with unpredictable systems. Such *systems must be monitored diligently*; the actors within them must remain *versatile and flexible*, and the services must be *highly decentralised*. Persons must *command options* instead of eternal truths. In education this style of coping would be *the very antithesis of the style of top-down prescriptive planning* and policy that we researchers imagine ourselves discovering. (Glass, 1979, p. 14) (Emphases added)

Chapter 6

Coping With Complexity

> With the collapse of the notion that the future is scientifically
> predictable the notion of the totally planned society goes down a well.
> (Magee, 1976, p. 100)

Having considered that education is likely to exhibit some aspects of a complex and unpredictable system, we will now look at what some notable thinkers/scientists have been suggesting in connection with strategies for coping with complex systems.

The introduction to this Part espoused *science* as the way to solve problems, and we consider first Popper, the scientists' philosopher. He has sometimes been portrayed as 'right wing' (as in the *Observer* newspaper's report of his death in September 1994). The following is intended to show a little of his complexity and humanity.

KARL POPPER

At the beginning of his lucid exposition of Popper's work, Bryan Magee describes Popper as the scientists' philosopher. Although there have been many philosophers of science, not many scientists have paid a great deal of attention to them, but such is emphatically not the case with Karl Popper. Thus Magee quotes Sir Peter Medawar (Nobel Prize in Medicine): 'I think Popper is incomparably the greatest philosopher of science there has ever been' (Magee, 1976, p. 9). Another Nobel laureate, Sir John Eccles, is quoted as saying 'I have endeavoured to follow Popper in the formulation and in the investigation of fundamental problems in neurobiology', and mathematician/astronomer Sir Hermann Bondi made the incisive statement: 'there is no more to science than its method, and there is no more to its method than Popper has said'.

Karl Popper was born in Austria in 1902. He describes himself as 'what Americans might call a "softy"' – 'The sight of abject poverty in Vienna was one of the main problems which agitated me when I was still a small child . . .' – and states in his autobiography that compassion is one of the strongest emotions he remembers:

> Few people now living in one of the Western democracies know what
> poverty meant at the beginning of this century: men, women and
> children suffering from hunger, cold and hopelessness. But we children
> could not help. We could do no more than ask for a few coppers to give
> to some poor people.
>
> (Popper, 1974, p. 9)

Popper was 12 years old when World War I broke out and records that he was a willing listener to socialist ideas. 'Nothing, I felt, could be more important than to end poverty' (Popper, 1974, p. 12).

Popper's experience of school was none too positive:

> It was during the last terrible years of the War, probably in 1917, at a time when I was suffering from a long illness that I realised very clearly what I had felt in my bones for a considerable time: that in our famous Austrian secondary schools . . . we were wasting our time shockingly, even though our teachers were well educated and tried hard to make the schools the best in the World. That much of their teaching was boring in the extreme – hours and hours of hopeless torture – was not new to me . . . there was just one subject in which we had an interesting and truly inspiring teacher. The subject was mathematics . . . yet when I returned to school after an illness of over two months I found that my class had made hardly any progress, not even in mathematics. This was an eye opener. It made me eager to leave school.
>
> (Popper, 1974, pp. 31–32)

Karl Popper's father was a lawyer with strong intellectual interests – there were 'books everywhere'. He wrote poetry and translated Greek and Latin into German. A picture of Darwin hung in his study.

Karl Popper left school at the age of 16 and enrolled at the University of Vienna without taking the entrance examination. The cost of enrolling was nominal and every student could attend any lecture course. He reports that the University of Vienna had eminent teachers 'but reading their books was an incomparably greater experience than listening to their lectures' (Popper, 1974, p. 39). He did enjoy the outstanding lectures in mathematics, however, and passed important examinations in 1922 at the age of 20. He then went on to train as a primary school teacher in a teachers' training collge whilst also being apprenticed to a cabinet-maker. When he completed the apprenticeship and teachers' training there were no teaching jobs available, so for two years he took up social work, and then secured a job as a teacher.

He continued his studies in psychology but turned increasingly towards methodology, epistemology and philosophy. His thesis was 'On the Problem of Method in the Psychology of Thinking'. On the viva he thought he had failed. He recounts: 'I could hardly believe my ears when I was told that I had passed in both examinations with the highest grade' (Popper, 1974, p. 78). (This indicates problems for advocates of student self-assessment.)

His PhD was obtained in 1928, and in 1929 he obtained further qualifications as a teacher of mathematics and physical science in lower secondary school. He married and settled down as a school teacher, enjoying skiing and mountain climbing with his wife.

During all these years Popper had been searching for a supportable philosophy of knowledge. He had briefly been a Marxist but came to regard that theory, along with the psychological theories of Freud and Adler, as pseudoscientific. 'I had been shocked by the fact that the Marxists (whose central claim was that they were social scientists) and the psychoanalysts of all schools were able to interpret any conceivable event as a verification of their theories' (Popper, 1974, p. 42). He recognized that the demarcation between science and pseudoscience was falsifiability. Pseudoscience did not have answers to the question 'Under what conditions would I admit that my theory is untenable?' He had been hugely impressed by hearing Einstein make clear statements about events which would disprove the theories he was putting forward. 'Falsifiability' became Popper's test of a scientific theory, and he regarded a scientific theory as simply a current hypothesis, always subject to revision if the data demanded it.

These views as to how we know anything are highly relevant to monitoring education, in particular to sorting out misinformation, which will damage education, from accurate information, which will assist it. Pseudoscience has not been supported by empirical testing and may therefore be wrong. Scientific evidence has been tested and is to that degree more likely to be correct.

There has now been much excellent work of a scientific calibre in social science, and the notions of falsifiability underpin it. The tests of reliability and validity, which are essential tests of falsifiability and the adequacy of information, are described in Chapter 10 and are applied to the process of inspection in Chapter 23. Popper regarded his encounter with Marxism as a main event in his intellectual development. 'It taught me the wisdom of the Socratic saying, "I know that I do not know"' (Popper, 1974, p. 36). Perhaps only ex-Marxists should be school inspectors.

Popper studied and wrote out of sheer curiosity. His uncle, Professor of Statistics and Economics at the University of Vienna, introduced him to Herbert Feigl, a famous member of the Vienna Circle before his move to the USA. It was Feigl who told Popper to publish his work. Popper prepared two volumes but was asked for 240 pages. His uncle abstracted these and thus originated the *Logik der Forschung* in 1934, finally published in English in 1959 as *The Logic of Scientific Discovery*.

The *Logik der Forschung* led to many invitations to lecture, including at Bedford and Imperial Colleges, London University, in 1935. As Hitler rose to power, Popper was increasingly in danger. Although he was raised as a Protestant, his family were Jewish. He was offered a position at Cambridge but felt that it was 'meant for a refugee' so he accepted instead a lectureship in New Zealand (Canterbury University College). There he worked to save refugees from Hitler and also wrote *The Poverty of Historicism* and *The Open Society and its Enemies*, books which he regarded as his war work. The latter had as its intended title *False Prophets: Plato – Hegel – Marx*. The essence of 'historicism' is an unjustifiable pretence to knowledge, and he saw this pretence as underlying both Marxism and fascism. Lack of knowledge is dangerous to human life and so is false belief – the pretence to knowledge. We have seen examples in Chapter 4, and Popper had lived through world-shattering examples, with horror.

Hayek invited Popper to the London School of Economics. Arriving there in 1946, he found it a 'marvellous institution. It was small enough for everybody on the staff to know everybody else. The staff, though few, were outstanding, and so were the students . . . eager, mature and extremely appreciative' (Popper, 1974, p. 121).

What guide to monitoring schooling would Sir Karl Popper provide?

> . . . fundamental to Popper's whole philosophy . . . is the realisation that
> *complex structures* – whether intellectual, artistic, social,

administrative or whatever – *are only to be changed by stages, through a critical feedback process of successive adjustments*. The notion that they can be created, or made over, at a stroke, as if from a blueprint, is an illusion which can never be actualised.

(Magee, 1976, p. 67) (Emphases added)

How similar this perspective is to the modern work on complexity: '. . . in the poorly defined, constantly changing environments faced by living systems, *there seems to be only one way to proceed: trial and error,* also known as Darwinian natural selection.' (Langton, quoted by Waldrop, 1992, p. 282)

In describing trial and error using the term 'piecemeal social engineering', Popper could not have chosen a more widely unacceptable terminology. 'Piecemeal' is often used derogatorily, and 'social engineering' is anathema to many. He states in his autobiography that if he is to address an audience he searches his mind for points on which they will *disagree* with him. It is all part of his belief in the need for endless problem-solving, and that means subjecting one's ideas to criticism. (That he was always reluctant to send his works to press may have been related to his expectation of criticism. We can all believe criticism to be good for us but can we learn to like it?)

Popper rejects an approach to the future based on planning. Utopian plans for the future are rejected, with a very clear argument as to why they are dangerous. Utopian plans of a great leader commit that leader to a future which is not in fact under his or her control. When the plans do not work out, then there is a need for scapegoats. Thus begins persecution. Popper's perception of the suffering which can follow from good intentions (like the persecution that followed the initial idealism of Marx) recognizes that the origin of the suffering lies in the error of believing in a future which can be flawlessly designed if only everyone will do their part.

This analysis is provocative and attractive. Reflect on the history of peoples, countries, movements and local events, in and out of schools, and you may well find parallels. These do not establish the hypothesis but, as a heuristic, the danger of utopianism and of an excessive belief in our capacity to plan the future is highlighted. Managers in particular need to dwell on this concept.

Here I would like to use the term *cognitive error*. I suspect that much as we worry about feelings and virtue, large tracts of human suffering actually can be traced to errors in information processing or the effects of misinformation. False beliefs underlie much inhumanity. Perhaps some suffering arises from cruelty, but there may be more hope of correcting cognitive errors than of changing cruel natures. Cognitive errors arise from misinformation, and the mechanism we have developed for identifying such is called science. The price of freedom is not only eternal vigilance but also eternal scientific effort.

So, if we do not plan the future, what do we do to improve society? We solve problems in the present. According to Popper 'The central guiding principle for public policy . . . is "Minimise avoidable suffering" (Magee, 1976, p. 84). The difficult trick here is to find out what is 'avoidable' – which can only be done by collecting information on the effects of actions.

Because (Popper) regards living as first and foremost a process of problem solving he wants societies which are conducive to problem-solving. And because problem-solving calls for the bold propounding of trial solutions which are then subjected to criticism and error-elimination, he wants forms of society which permit of the untrammelled assertion of differing proposals, followed by criticism, followed by the genuine possibility of change in the light of criticism. . . . *A policy is a hypothesis which has to be tested against reality and corrected in the light of experience.* (Magee, 1976, pp. 74–75)

These stages were spelled out by Popper:

$$P_1 \longrightarrow TS \longrightarrow EE \longrightarrow P_2$$

An initial problem (P_1) leads to a trial solution (TS) which will not be perfect and must lead to error elimination (EE), with the result that there is now a new problem (P_2) – an outcome. Life is a series of problem-solving activities. Connor Cruise O'Brian remarked: 'Problems don't have solutions, only outcomes.'

LINKS WITH THE EXPERIENCES OF OTHERS CONCERNED WITH THE DESIGN OF SYSTEMS

When Marvin C. Alkin set up the Centre for the Study of Evaluation at the University of California at Los Angeles (UCLA) in the 1970s, he structured its activities around four evaluation stages:

Needs assessment$\longrightarrow$Programme planning$\longrightarrow$Formative evaluation$\longrightarrow$ Summative evaluation

$$NA \longrightarrow PP \longrightarrow FE \longrightarrow SE$$

In the first three elements we see the same emphasis as in Popper's model: locating problems, proposing solutions and empirical testing. The last term, 'summative evaluation', has an element of finality to it, which may match real-world funding but rarely matches real-world activities. Those left running a programme will know that *ongoing* problem-solving, formative evaluation, will be needed. Since formative evaluation is itself a process of trial and error, it will be complex and, because it must locate problems if it is to be useful, it is a potentially threatening activity, not one which can be comfortably conducted in public. Thus in a study of evaluations conducted of a large-scale federal programme, Alkin *et al.* (1974) found that formative evaluation activities were hidden. Although project directors reported in interviews how much they had appreciated large amounts of problem-solving by evaluators, these evaluation activities were not officially reported. Bland summative evaluation documents did not admit to any false starts or problems encountered. Thus is the myth of tidy management perpetuated.

Herbert A. Simon is a professor of computing and psychology and won a Nobel Prize in Economics. Along with Allen Newell, he is regarded as the originator of the field of artificial intelligence. His classic collection of articles in *Sciences of the Artificial* contains his views on the design of systems or 'artefacts', and we find there the same emphasis as in Popper and Alkin on repeated trial and error. He writes of the 'generate–test cycle'.

> . . . think of the design process as involving, first, the generation of alternatives and, then, the testing of these alternatives against a whole

array of requirements and constraints. There need not be merely a single generate–test cycle, but there can be a whole nested series of such cycles. (Simon, 1988, p. 149)

It is important to note that many of the problems Simon was considering were not messy, human systems confronting social science, but were computer systems; and yet the same trial and error was needed. Theory could not solve the design problems. For example, referring to the development of time-sharing systems on computers, he wrote:

> ... the main route open to the development and improvement of time-sharing systems was to build them and see how they behaved. And this is what was done. They were built, modified, and improved in successive stages. Perhaps theory could have anticipated these experiments and made them unnecessary. In fact it didn't, and I don't know anyone intimately acquainted with these exceedingly complex systems who has very specific ideas as to how it might have done so. *To understand them, the systems had to be constructed, and their behavior observed.* (Simon, 1988, p. 25)

W. Edwards Deming was a statistician who advised industry with such success that he is sometimes credited with changing working practices in Japanese industries in ways that transformed them from the producers of low-quality goods in the 1950s to producers of outstanding quality in the 1980s, giving the country great competitive advantage. He is particularly known for the movement he inspired called 'total quality management' (Deming, 1982; Neave, 1990).

If may not surprise the reader that the trial and error approaches already noted from diverse thinkers in diverse fields are strongly present in Deming's advice. Deming's approach, like that of Popper, Simon and Alkin, focuses on problem-solving.

He drew on the work of another statistician, Shewhart, with 'the Shewhart cycle' (Figure 6.1).

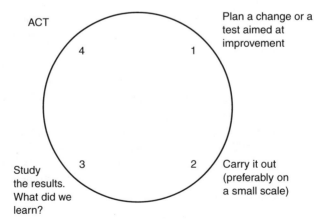

Figure 6.1 *The Shewhart cycle*
Source: Neave (1990)

The ideas were also expressed as a mnemonic, PDSA – Plan Do Study Act.

The 'guru' atmosphere created by many of Deming's followers is a source of some discomfort and suspicion, but nevertheless Deming seems to have touched on many important themes. Furthermore, his followers represent an important counterbalance to a management ethos which emphasizes plans, targets and performance-related pay. Deming explicitly warned against all these currently popular management practices and instead urged

- where there is a problem, management must analyse;
- drive out fear.

This last topic will conclude this chapter.

FEAR AND PROBLEM-SOLVING

A strong message seems to be emerging: in running all but the most simple systems, there is complexity beyond the reach of most theories and predictions. The way forward in such unpredictable circumstances lies with trial and error. Actions must be taken and the outcomes monitored. In particular, this monitoring should uncover problems, for it is by solving the problems that the system is improved.

The people most aware of problems, those who see problems immediately as they arise, are those running the system. But here we have a problem. These are the same people whom managers, politicians and the public may well hold responsible for problems. If there is fear and blame in the system, there will be a tendency not to uncover problems and certainly not to publicize them. If problems (such as truancy, as discussed in Chapter 4) are hidden, then they will not be solved. The system will not improve.

As Campbell (1969) noted years ago, in an important article entitled 'Reforms as Experiments', people need to be allowed to try and fail – and then try again. If their jobs are on the line the first time, then the risks which lead to solutions to problems may not be taken. The system will not improve.

Based on the observation that feedback frequently leads to improvement, an important process to set up in order to promote quality would seem to be a performance indicator system. The notion of having quantitative indicators to track the performance of a system (i.e. performance indicators) is central to notions of quality as put forward by Deming, along with procedures such as 'quality circles'.

CONCLUSION

Major philosophers such as Popper and Russell, statisticians such as Deming and Shewhart, scientists such as Simon and Campbell, and experienced evaluators of social programmes such as Alkin, all espouse the value of a rational scientific approach, the necessity of 'piecemeal social engineering', of data collection, analysis and feedback as a basis for learning by trial and error.

The belief that improvements arise from problem location and problem-solving using empirical approaches is not particularly dramatic. It is simply rational behaviour which should not be in short supply in the modern world (but see Sutherland (1992)).

What are the implications of the plea for empiricism and rationality seen in this chapter along with the observations on the unpredictablity of complex systems and the need for local organization described in the previous chapter? These implications seem to be as follows:

- Improvement begins with locating problems.
- There needs to be regular monitoring of important outcomes so that problems can be located and the effects of trial and error can be discovered – constantly.
- The trial and error needs to be 'piecemeal' so that the effects can be observed, and this implies a fair amount of 'modularity' in the system – so that small changes can be made to the discrete modules which interconnect to form the whole system.
- The results of monitoring need to be fed back to those running the modules of the system.
- The people involved in running the system are the people best placed to improve it – constantly – since they may often be best placed for problem location and have the greatest amount of information relevant to the problem, information above and beyond that provided by the monitoring.
- There is almost certainly a need for confidentiality and security so that problems can be openly explored rather than hidden in fear.

PART THREE

An Up-and-Running Indicator System

It has been suggested in the preceding chapters that complex, evolving systems such as educational institutions need to use good local information, specific to their own local context, to locate problems and test solutions to these problems, in ongoing efforts for improvement. But is a detailed feedback system feasible? Would it cost the earth? Before continuing with general principles for performance monitoring, it may be as well to give a concrete example, in the form of a description of the A-level Information System (ALIS). This provides a kind of existence theorem. It only represents a beginning. Many extensions to its present form will occur, and it is itself subject to a constant search for improvement on the basis of feedback. However, it does exist and has done so for more than a decade, and is being used in one form or another in over 1000 schools or colleges.

The chapter provides a brief history of the ALIS project, followed by some stock-taking.

Chapter 7

The ALIS Project

Why have so many schools and colleges chosen to spend some of their precious and limited disposable income buying into a 'performance monitoring' system called ALIS (the A-level Information System)? (Appendix 2 contains an outline of the structure of the English–Welsh system of education. Advanced Level examinations are taken at age 18 years.) Is it just a gesture of compliance related to the top-down demands for 'quality assurance' or does ALIS provide information which is genuinely useful? Will ALIS continue and grow, and will other similar systems arise? (See Figure 7.1.)

Do lessons learned in creating and running ALIS have a bearing on the design of information systems for other phases of schooling? Can anything be learned from the experience of ALIS about setting up information systems for monitoring other post-16 courses, such as those leading to vocational qualifications?

Will ALIS and other 'indicator systems' enhance the profession of teaching or will the performance indicators produced be used in ways which are ineffective or, worse, unfair? Will ALIS participation improve teachers' 'joy in work' (to use a Deming phrase) or will it demoralize? Will it stimulate and assist improvement efforts?

The evidence is not yet in, but here at least is an up-and-running system pro-

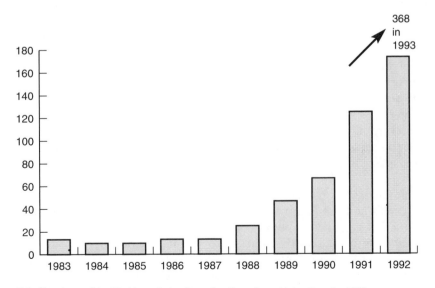

Figure 7.1 *Numbers of institutions (schools and colleges) participating in ALIS.*

viding student-by-student, subject-by-subject data – detailed, local, confidential feedback.

A-LEVELS

The standard reached by students studying A-level subjects is a very high one by international standards. For example, writing of achievement at A-level, Smithers and Robinson summarized the situation as follows:

> Those (few) who remain in education beyond the age of 16 reach a high level of attainment. International studies of achievement in science (which is reasonably similar throughout the world so that comparisons can be made) show that the best four per cent of 18-year-olds in England come behind only Hong Kong and Japan of the 15 countries tested.

(Smithers and Robinson, 1991)

An A-level pass can count as two years' university work in the subject at some of the USA's 'best' universities. In other words, UK teachers are teaching at a standard equivalent to the first half of a university degree in the USA. Perhaps UK teachers are not sufficiently recognized for their high levels of performance, high by both international and absolute standards. Since A-levels have been successful in being highly regarded and perceived as fair, we need to consider whether similar systems are needed which include a wider range of ability – but such considerations are postponed to Chapter 9.

THE ORIGIN OF ALIS: THE COMBSE PROJECT

It was a question from a school governor which led to what eventually became the ALIS project. Back in 1982–1983, a school governor in the UK had little in the way of legal responsibility or clout. Nevertheless, as a concerned parent, this particular governor was active in looking at examination results. He asked me to look at a set of examination results from one department, results which were widely regarded in the school as being yet another in a long series of less than satisfactory A-level results in that particular subject. The school was a large, prestigious comprehensive school and results in other subjects were not seen as a problem. The department concerned consistently argued that the results were low due to the difficulty of the subject and the type of candidates who chose the subject. The governor and others feared that these explanations were insufficient but had difficulty supporting this interpretation.

What the school governor was confronting was the inadequacy of simple raw data. He was looking for comparative data, preferably fair comparisons (see Chapter 2).

It was impossible to give a fair and useful answer with access only to the schools' results and national results, even knowing the nature of the catchment area and the background of the school. What kind of students had chosen to take that particular subject? Had they chosen to stay in school simply as an alternative to unemployment or were they intending to take the subject in a university? Were there differences between examination boards? Looking at the results that the same students obtained in other subjects might help a little but it was highly likely that subjects varied in difficulty. Furthermore, if students were getting worse results in one subject than in another, was this due to exceptionally effective teaching in one subject or was it evidence of worse than usual teaching in the other? What was usual for the kind of students under consideration each year?

There was a clearly a danger of giving a typically useless academic answer – 'more research is needed' – to a pressing practical problem with implications for teachers, students and worried parents. Nor would offering to do some research on these factors be sufficient. Answers were needed for that particular department in that particular school, and as soon as possible.

How can a school interpret examination results? How can a school know whether the results obtained should be considered satisfactory or not, attributed to good teaching, seen as simply a result of the students – 'that was a bad year' – or blamed on the difficulty or leniency of the examination? There was only one way forward, which was to bring together a number of schools, pool their results and at least enable them to see if schools working with similar students were getting similar sets of results, subject by subject. I approached two LEAs for permission and then sent a letter. This letter came to schools from an essentially unknown lecturer who had been at Newcastle for less than four years and had done no teacher training work. I knew only persons in the few schools in which I had been working on cross-age tutoring projects, the area of research to which I felt most committed at the time. (I regarded this move away from experimental studies into survey work as reprehensible. It related to school effectiveness, which was an important area, but the work was really only justified by the need which was clearly demonstrated by the governor's question, and by the conviction that teachers would want the kind of information I planned to collect, as I would have wanted it as a teacher. In other words, I did not at that time have the concepts developed in the chapters on complexity, nor did I realize the potential of what was starting. Teleology may often be a retrospective imposition.)

Despite receiving a letter from an unknown person, 50 per cent of schools responded by sending someone to a meeting. Of the 13 schools present, 12 agreed to participate in what was simply a personal research project, with a sharing of the information back to the school. These were 'comprehensive' schools representing a wide range of social backgrounds. ('Comprehensive' indicates a comprehensive, i.e. non-selective, intake. These particular schools took students from 11 to 18 years of age.) It was decided, at the initial meeting, to concentrate on two subjects, English and mathematics – two of the subjects with the largest enrolments.

Problems were anticipated due to the small numbers of candidates for A-level examinations from the schools likely to become involved. However, it was envisaged that the project would continue on a small scale for about six years and that this longitudinal data would have its own advantages, particularly in providing comparative data across a period which seemed set to include substantial changes in educational practice and examination structures. The examinations at age 16 consisted of Ordinary Level (O-level) examinations for the more able and Certificate of Secondary Education (CSE) examinations for average students, and these were to change to a single examination, the General Certificate of Secondary Education (GCSE), in 1986. Calls for changes to the A-level examination had been persistent for years.

The decision was taken from the beginning to examine school effects subject by subject rather than aggregating to the school level. Apart from the need to look at one subject in particular, it seemed reasonable to suppose that schools might contain some departments which were particularly effective and some which were less effective. Adding up all a school's data to give a single index for a school would obscure such differences.

It also seemed possible that schools could affect examination results more strongly in some subjects than in others. This sensitivity-to-instruction hypothesis could be important in terms of evaluation and accountability: there is no point in holding schools responsible for 'effects' they cannot affect.

The project was called the Confidential, Measurement-Based Self-Evaluation (COMBSE) project.

- **Confidential.** Confidentiality was maintained by having all schools participate under a codename chosen by the school and known only to themselves and the researcher. Although representatives from the schools attended a meeting together each year, and therefore generally knew who was participating in the research, everyone was urged to keep the codenames confidential. One school chose the codename ETON, another COLDITZ and another SHUT, since they feared closure (they are still open: the future is unpredictable.).

- **Measurement-based.** This part of the title flagged the fundamentally non-judgemental position adopted. There was to be no model of 'good practice' against which the schools would be evaluated. There would be measurements, not opinions.

- **Self-evaluation.** Measurement is one thing. The interpretation of the measurements is something else – and would have to be the responsibility of the schools. The methods and techniques of the measurements could be explained but seeking explanations of the results would require the kind of on-site detailed knowledge that would only be available to those actually in the school, doing the work.

So what should be measured? A logical place to start was to consider goals. What were schools striving to provide for A-level candidates? Good examination results? Broadening and educational extramural experiences? A congenial environment? Reasonable motivation to continue into higher education? Since all these were considered legitimate, performance indicators were collected for each of these aspects:

- examination results;
- participation in extramural activities;
- attitudes to school;
- attitudes to subjects studied;
- motivation to continue in higher education.

Having selected some outputs which were considered important, the next task was to collect information on those inputs which might be related to the outputs. These were taken to be

- prior achievement as measured by externally set and graded examinations taken at age 16;
- ability;
- home background (with reservations);
- sex.

In summary, output indicators were assessed because they represented goals of the institution, and inputs were assessed to make comparisons of outputs fair.

A selection of 'process variables' was also assessed in order to see whether any provided any clues as to the outputs. The list started with variables used by Gray *et al.* (1983) and has been added to ever since, first reflecting a long-standing interest in helping (cross-age tutoring and peer tutoring) and then the influence of the Business and Technical Education Council, a body providing vocational courses with strong standards of delivery and resources required for sites to become recognized providers. The list included in 1994 the following:

- presentation of topic by the teacher (chalk and talk);
- exercises (working examples);
- working questions from previous examination papers – with help – under examination conditions (fixed time, no help);
- preparing essays;
- reading;
- class discussions led by the teacher;
- discussions in groups;
- having notes dictated to you;
- making your own notes from lessons;
- using duplicated notes (hand-outs);
- practical work (using apparatus or making things);
- using audio or visual materials;
- making use of IT (computers);
- researching a topic (using a variety of reference material);
- working in pairs;
- presenting your work to the class;
- listening to another student present work in the class;
- giving help to another student;
- receiving help from another student;
- receiving individual help from the teacher;
- producing original work (e.g. devising experiments, writing poetry, designing new projects, composing modelling systems, criticism).

Most of the variables to be assessed could reasonably be collected on a questionnaire to students. Questionnaires are not always appropriate, but interviewing would have been prohibitively expensive even if small samples would have been acceptable (which I doubted), and questionnaires, given to all students would be fine: students taking A-levels are well able to read.

The questionnaire has been changed every year, with changes most frequently relating to the process variables.

In the first year, 1983, schools were sent questionnaires by post to be administered to their own students in mathematics and English (In this first year, the questionnaires did not deal with students' attitudes, so the confidentiality aspect for students did not seem important in that year. Such questions were added as the system developed.) The questionnaires collected data on students' home backgrounds and prior achievement levels, i.e. on inputs. Some process data were also collected by the questionnaire, focused mainly on the use of time: homework, timetabled time and students' reported levels of effort.

Reports were prepared and a meeting was held at the university with school representatives to discuss the main findings of the reports and to clarify the statistical tables. The report enabled schools to compare themselves with schools with similar intakes. These 'league tables' comprised a feature of the report of some interest to schools: they appreciated the use of 'residuals' (once explained) as a fairer method of comparison than percentage pass rates or simple raw grade distributions. In other words, schools were interested in fair performance indicators for outputs, although the term was not in use at the time. The results of some data analysis for the first year of the project have been reported elsewhere (Fitz-Gibbon, 1985) but it is perhaps worth noting that two issues were raised then which now seem, 10 years later, to have finally reached the policy agenda: is the 30 per cent failure rate reasonable and should A-level mathematics be so much more difficult to pass than A-level English?

The following year, 1984, the questionnaire was extensively revised and lengthened and all pupils in the study were given an ability test, the AH6 (Heim et al., 1983). Why was an ability test introduced? Ability testing was very much against the ethos at that time. Figure 7.2 shows the explanation, and is the information currently supplied to interested schools and colleges.

It was in 1984 that a start was made on measuring the outputs other than examination results, such as attitude to the subject (of particular interest to heads of departments), levels of aspiration and attitude to the school (of particular interest to school management teams).

Process data concentrated on the use of time, but data on class sizes were also collected, as was a consideration of what was termed the 'pulling power' of mathematics departments. In response to a direct request from schools, the effects which might be attributable to examination boards were calculated. From only 10 schools and two subjects, five different examination boards were represented. Consequently, the findings were tentative, but this issue was going to become important later, as it continued to worry people: did it matter which examination board was used? (The answer turned out to be no, quite clearly, at least up to 1993.)

The last two years of secondary school are often referred to as the 'sixth form' in the UK and they correspond to the junior and senior years in the USA (See Appendix 2). Since students may leave school completely at 16 and since they may also choose to go to a college or another school, the retention of students in the 'sixth form' is a major concern of schools. In response to questions about their

NOTES CONCERNING THE
ABILITY TEST
(International Test of Developed Abilities: ITDA)

This test is optional and these notes are written to assist schools and colleges in their decision as to whether or not to have students take the ITDA ability test.

What kind of ability test is used?
With the kind permission of Educational Testing Service and the international group studying schools in many nations (IEA) we are using the International Test of Developed Abilities. It consists of a verbal section (comprehension passages) and a numerical section (maths test).

How long does the ability test take?
Fifty minutes of working time and therefore it adds about one hour to the required session for data collecting under examination conditions.

Why was an ability test introduced in 1984?
Participants in 1984 were primarily schools serving students aged 11 to 18 years of age. They were concerned that if they obtained good results at age16 they would appear to be working with more able students than was in fact the case. To provide an alternative measure from which comparisons could be made, an ability test was introduced.

An ability test was also important because it seemed highly likely that the age 16 examinations would change, as indeed they did. By having a test which did not change, we have a baseline against which changes can be assessed.

Are these reasons for using the ability test still valid?
Yes, but they apply more to schools than to colleges since colleges enrol students from a variety of schools.

Are the indicators (residuals) based on the ability test data different to those based on GCSE scores?
Yes, the residuals do differ, sometimes by very little but sometimes considerably, particulary in small groups.

Could the ability test be used to advise students who do not have GCSE scores and/or for whom English is not their first language?
Yes, particularly as we obtain more data, we will be able to make some predictions. Schools and colleges might wish us to produce predicted grades for a variety of courses based on the ITDA given in Year 12.

What is your advice?
Have students take the test if (a) you want residuals based on factors other than GCSEs; (b) you want predictions for students who do not have GCSEs.

Figure 7.2 *Notes provided to schools and colleges regarding the International Test of Developed Abilities*

satisfaction with their 'sixth form' experience, a fair number of students in 1984 had indicated that they wished they had gone to a college rather than staying in the comprehensive school for the last two years. Consequently, three further education (FE) colleges were invited to participate in the study in 1985 and each accepted. (FE colleges offer a wide range of 'vocational' courses as well as 'academic' ones, and are roughly comparable to community colleges in the USA.)

The AH6 had not proved particularly useful in predicting A-levels (the highest correlation was between the verbal score and English, and this was only 0.34), so in 1985 another ability test was used: the Advanced Progressive Matrices (Raven, 1962). In the event this test did not yield better correlations than the AH6, although it was a more pleasant test to administer (better liked by students) and had previously been found useful in identifying gifted students (Fitz-Gibbon, 1974).

The ability testing had to be dropped in the year leading up to the examinations in 1986 due to the researcher's heavy commitments in other areas. Meanwhile, the inadequacy of aggregated data (sometimes called 'means on means' analyses) for use in the study of school effects was being debated, and the need for the kind of student-level data which the COMBSE project had always collected was being discussed, notably at a seminar of the Royal Statistical Society (Aitkin and Longford, 1986), dealing with issues put forward in the USA by Burstein (1980) and using data supplied by John Gray; see also Goldstein (1984), Gray et al. (1986) and Woodhouse and Goldstein (1988). The DES was reported to be interested in school effectiveness data. Contact was made with the DES and a discussion arranged in London at which the project was presented to statisticians and others at the DES. Subsequently, funds were allocated by the DES to enable data collectors to be hired and to cover costs of data processing.

The DES funds enabled the employment of people to collect the data. I had standardized the procedures by using a tape recording to administer the questionnaire and the tests. The tape ensured that all students heard the same information about the project, in the same tone of voice, at the same speed, anywhere in the country, and at any school.

The DES funds also enabled the reinstatement of the ability testing in 1987. With the permission of the publishers the AH6 was reformatted, dividing it into three separately timed sections so that all students attempted each kind of item (verbal, numeric and diagrammatic). Previously, with all items presented in a single paper, some candidates had skipped certain kinds of items. The revision did not, however, significantly improve the test's ability to predict A-level grades.

Being freed from data collection work enabled me to take steps to extend the study. The term 'performance indicator' was coming to be recognized and the proposals for financial delegation were seen as requiring LEAs to change their role and, in particular, to monitor outcomes. Following a meeting of senior staff from seven LEAs (including the two in which were located the schools and colleges already in the project) three more LEAs chose to participate, making a total of five LEAs. The LEAs requested that the study be extended to the major A-level subjects and also to include one subject with a small enrolment to meet the interests of one of the authorities in increasing the effectiveness of a resource-based, independent learning project called 'Supported Self Study'.

A request for a further small grant from the DES was successful.

The sixth year, 1988, saw what I described at the time as an 'enormous' increase in the scope of the project (not anticipating what was later to happen): from two to five LEAs, from 12 to 50 institutions, and including not just two A-level subjects but 11, namely: biology, chemistry, economics, English, French, general studies, geography, German, history, mathematics, physics.

The commitment of the LEAs to the project was shown by their allocation of funds to cover the cost of data collection and analysis and by the fact that two LEAs seconded teachers to the project full-time for a term. Some LEAs new to the project allocated funds without which it would have been impossible to include their schools. The DES funds allowed the project to continue in the original sample.

I was still anxious to find an ability test which was a reasonably good predictor of A-level grades. In 1988 the International Test of Developed Abilities (ITDA) became available to us through the good offices of Professor Bryan Dockrell, visiting Professor at the University of Newcastle-upon-Tyne, and Frances Ottobre of the International Association for Educational Assessment (IAEA). The ITDA was being developed under the auspices of the IAEA. The intention was to have a high-ability test in several languages which could be used for pre-university students around the world. The Educational Testing Service, Princeton, New Jersey, undertook a research project, funded by the US College Board, equating the ITDA to the US Scholastic Aptitude Test (Ottobre and Turnbull, 1987). The ITDA proved to be rather better than either of the ability tests used previously, particularly in the prediction of science and mathematics, with correlations up to 0.58. It was not expected that an *ability* test would ever correlate as highly with A-level grades as would the measure of prior *achievement*. Like predicts like. The A-level examination demands lengthy essays, problem-solving, descriptive and analytical writing and a considerable fund of information committed to memory. Ability alone is not enough to get students through A-level: effort and application and a considerable set of aptitudes which may not be tapped by ability tests probably figure in A-level performance and also in the performance on examinations at age 16.

In 1988, since some LEAs were by now paying for the project, the confidentiality aspect had changed: LEA personnel as well as school and college management teams might see the data and ask to know which codenames represented which institutions. In order to signal this change, the project name was changed from COMBSE to ALIS: the A-level Information System.

The reporting back to schools had undergone several changes. After the first year of the project, the reports changed from one single report to one for each subject. In 1988, to get the examination results out quickly, the reports were split into three: exams, attitudes and processes. This meant the production of 33 unique reports (three for each of the 11 A-level subjects now analysed) each year and 50 copies of each. In addition, the comments which students had written down in response to open-ended questions were typed up to insure anonymity and provided to headteachers. Originally these were read through before being posted out, to delete the proper names and really scurrilous remarks, but eventually we had to just rely on headteachers to use the information wisely.

THE DEPARTMENT OF EDUCATION AND SCIENCE

The two years of DES support had amounted to a mere £7000 in total but had been vital at the time to encourage the system to continue. Unfortunately, attempts to obtain further funding from the DES ran counter to the market ethos, which was rapidly permeating the London levels of the education sector. After a morning's dialogue with VIPs (heads of statistics, economics, performance indicators, for example) I was told 'You have such a good project, why don't you go for venture capital and set up as a consultant?' Clearly, the speaker was unaware of the then current definition of a consultant: 'A man, in a suit, travelling north'.[1] A consultant was certainly not a granny from the North East. I looked hard at the economist, hoping he might remark that venture capitalists might not be too keen to risk their money on the belief that schools and colleges would pay to be monitored. However, he said nothing and it was also clear that the DES was itself piloting performance indicators and would not fund what it itself kindly described as a 'more sophisticated' system.

The main thought in my mind about the DES suggestion that we 'go private' was that universities exist to contribute to knowledge, and I felt that the development of ALIS *was* a research project. Education is an applied discipline like engineering. Developing ALIS was like developing an engine in engineering – it needed research, design, trials and improvements. There were some practical issues, too – mainframe computer costs would go up if the project were commercial; there might have to be different arrangements for software use; and tax reclaims would be affected.

What would a wise policy response have been?

If the DES personnel had been working in a system in which they could be wise, they would have said not just 'You have such a good system; see if it will survive in the marketplace', but rather 'You have a good system up and running. We need to ensure it is evaluated so that we can see if it provides a way in which we can improve education.' The best methodology would then have been to identify about 80 schools which could be paired on the basis of some key characteristics such as size of sixth form, GCSE results, and possibly urban or rural location. Then a coin could be tossed for each pair of schools, and ALIS offered to one of the pair on the basis of the coin toss. This would ensure a random sample of schools offered ALIS and a random sample not offered ALIS. For the next four years the schools should all have been followed, with inspections and qualitative data collection as well as monitoring of examination results student by student. The difference would be that the ALIS schools would get the information fed back and all the extra information which ALIS provides on attitudes and processes.

In short, the DES should have offered to conduct a proper 'clinical' trial of ALIS (see Chapter 3). Such a trial requires random assignment to make sure the schools being compared are as equivalent as possible. If schools and colleges volunteer to take part in ALIS they are already different in some way from schools and colleges which do not volunteer.

In retrospect I have to admit that the suggestion to go private was perhaps not as unreasonable as I felt it was at the time. Performance indicators could become an industry and be ethically run but the research ethos might suffer.

LEAS TO THE RESCUE

When the DES would not fund the work, I turned to the local LEAs, and for a couple of years they paid for data collection; eventually, five LEAs shared the cost of a post at the university. Given a belief in the necessity for modular, hierarchical systems to manage complex tasks like education, this approach to the LEAs was right and proper. It was helped by the *Local Management of Schools* report commissioned from Coopers & Lybrand by the DES, which assigned to LEAs the role of monitoring (Coopers & Lybrand, 1988). The DES circular which came out at about the same time (Department of Education and Science, 1988) also assigned a monitoring role to LEAs.

> The Secretary of State will expect schemes submitted to him for approval
> to include the following elements: . . . the monitoring and evaluation
> procedures to be applied under the scheme, including the measures
> the LEA proposes to use to evaluate the performance of schools.
> (Department of Education and Science, 1988, p. 31)

We ran conferences targeted at LEAs, but school and college staff attended more than LEA staff. However, a few LEAs recognized the value to schools and colleges and worked with alacrity and highly effectively – organizing INSETs with us, organizing data collection, and subsidising participation where possible. The foresight of a few individuals, like those in the North East who had been the earliest supporters, was probably critically important to the successful development of the project in areas outside the North East.

For several years we required schools and colleges to join through their LEA rather than on their own account, but eventually we had to develop invoicing procedures for separate schools and colleges. Institutions did not want to wait until they could persuade their LEA to join and sometimes preferred, anyway, to have the data for their own internal use without any question of its being used elsewhere.

STAFFING

Up till 1988 I was the general ALIS factotum. Then a grant from the university research committee for research on cross-age tutoring in urban schools made the situation clearly desperate: more people were needed to run the ALIS project. It was the greatest of good fortunes that Peter Tymms was available and that we have been able to work together almost ever since, even during his two-year sojourn at Moray House, which prestigious institution cleverly offered a permanent post before the University of Newcastle finally did. I was able to persuade another former student, Mike Lacy, to run the project in 1990, and since then have been able to take on research associates, including Christopher Egdell, who started in the 1990–91 academic year.

Thanks, ironically, to the recession we have been able to employ highly skilled people – mathematicians, statisticians, computer scientists, engineers – who would not normally look for jobs in education. They are needed if we are to become more efficient and therefore accessible to more schools and colleges. Almost no course in social science or education equips people for the kinds of work we now need to run indicator systems of the sizes of our current projects. We are moving to the use of a relational database management system for the data, and can see years of development which could be undertaken to streamline more, and provide more data in more attractive and economical ways.

Some events have been important growth points. Many of these are particular to a region of the country and often the work of one person who has recognized ALIS as a desirable system. Frequently, people leaving the North East for jobs elsewhere have taken ALIS with them – a kind of cultural diffusion by person.

Particularly important have been contacts with professional teacher associations. The Association of Principals of Sixth Form Colleges (APVIC) set up an ALIS-APVIC steering committee, which has given vital advice and support, produced newsletters and runs an annual conference with us. The Secondary Heads Association (SHA) asked us to run a cheaper, examinations-only, version of ALIS which we did, providing in its first year (1993) data to over 350 schools and colleges, 14 per cent from the independent sector. The National Association of Head Teachers (NAHT) is working with us on a Year 11 information system and performance indicators for primary schools. We value these appreciations from users above everything.

One of the main areas needing constant development is the feedback system. Indicator systems have to use computers. The software and printing facilities on computers therefore heavily influence the output from indicator systems. Regression lines (explained in Chapter 14) became popular, particularly due to the good work of Dr Kevin Conway at Greenhead College, who devised a system of tracking students against a regression line. It has a few flaws but, nevertheless, he caused many people to think of ways to use data, and that was important.

Chapter 6 extolled the value of problem solving to improve systems. We turn now to the first step in problem solving: locating the problems. But firstly, the problem which led to the creation of ALIS is re-considered.

TAKING STOCK – AND PROBLEM-SOLVING

What of the school whose questions started the whole project? The data did show that there was a problem, even after account had been taken of the students they were working with and the difficulty of the subject. This recognition was the beginning of starting to seek solutions. How they solved the problem was a matter for the school. There was no glare of publicity or severe measures, but the problem was effectively addressed.

The account above, up until 1988, followed closely one presented at the 1989 annual meeting of the American Educational Research Association. The following is taken directly from that paper. It is presented to show that we were aware of deficiencies in the system. It is one thing to be aware and another to set deficiencies right. Much of the subsequent history of ALIS represents attempts to deal with the problems identified.

> There are some notable limitations to the system as presently implemented and these need to be considered from the outset.
>
> First, the project provided a set of Performance Indicators, a database but did not provide a person to ensure the data were understood or used. One meeting a year was not enough for this purpose especially when there were no other pressures towards paying attention to the indicators.
>
> Another possible hindrance was the nature of the reports: they were heavy and indigestible. . . . There was a good deal of information

and much of it appeared complicated at first sight. . . . The mathematics department heads might have taken the report home for light reading but the English department heads largely ignored it (Williamson and Fitz-Gibbon, 1990). The single best-recalled part of the reports appeared to be the verbatim comments from students (suitably edited to maintain anonymity) which were only included in two of the five years of the project. Numbers were less memorable.

In short, there was *nobody asking any questions about the performance indicators, nobody assisting schools in their interpretation each year, and the reports were stodgy.*

As indicated in the extract, we were aware that the information provided was not being fully utilized and there were problems in the presentation of the largely statistical feedback.

Nobody was asking questions. Who should have been asking questions? Although some LEAs were immediate leaders, the overall response was disappointing, especially in view of the fact that LEAs had clearly been assigned a role in monitoring schools by the Coopers & Lybrand report (Coopers & Lybrand, 1988) and by the DES circular 9/88 (Department of Education and Science, 1988). Perhaps the problem was that LEAs thought they were monitoring because their advisors felt they knew their schools. After all, if advisors were in and out of schools fairly often, then they presumably knew schools as well as HMI. In other words, LEAs were simply ready to believe what many people still believe: that chatting and looking around is a sufficient way of monitoring schools. Few LEAs had a research and statistics branch of any size and, perhaps because of lack of advice from researchers and statisticians, few LEAs investigated more than raw data. (The exceptions that have come to our attention have been London (now disbanded), Cleveland, Bradford, Nottingham, Birmingham and Staffordshire.)

The growth in ALIS came, then, not from 'above' – the LEAs who had been told to monitor – but from schools and colleges themselves.

Four key events probably had an impact and certainly seemed to make most educators add the new term 'value added' to their vocabulary (along with 'vire'):

- The publication by the Department of Education (formerly the DES) of School Performance Tables, commonly known as 'league tables', showing raw examination results.
- The funding of schools based on student numbers – thus setting schools in competition. (Michael Duffy swore he'd seen notices in school grounds saying 'Trepassers will be enrolled'.)
- The SATs – Standardised Assessment Tasks to be given at the ages of 7, 11, 14 and 16 years (more on these in Chapter 8).
- The removal of colleges of FE and sixth form colleges from LEA ('incorporation').

What was the impact of all this introduction of market forces? Not every economist was in favour. Professor Sen of Oxford explained to the British Association meetings in 1993 that whilst some men had greatness thrust upon them, Adam Smith had smallness thrust upon him. The market was not always an effective or appropriate mechanism and Adam Smith never said it was.

For good or ill, league tables raised the stakes attendant on examination results and the awareness of and interest in 'valued added' mushroomed. Now questions *were* being asked and perhaps that was a major influence in the growth of ALIS in these years.

Then HMI was re-constituted within the Office of Standards in Education. OFSTED seemed, from the legislation which spawned it, to have been brought into being to seek out failing schools (see Chapter 23). This too may have increased the interest shown by schools in having good data. Should one be grateful to OFSTED for frightening people into being interested in data, or regret their offensiveness to the profession? Much depends on the net impact and that, tyically, is not being assessed.

Nobody was assisting schools in their interpretation each year. For a few years we insisted that schools and colleges joining ALIS should have a presentation to all staff before data were collected and then another after data were received. This was certainly ideal. It seemed important that staff had opportunities to make suggestions about the project, to challenge what we were doing and to seek explanations of anything that our steadily improving reports still did not make clear. Fairly frequently, staff started out not nearly as keen as management on the whole idea, but then began to appreciate the fairness of the system and to see that we were trying to help the profession, not distress it. The quality and interesting features of the data and the analyses began to be recognized and good data were seen as protection against poor data or mere opinion. It was a considerable pleasure to see statistical terminology such as 'regression' and 'residuals' become part of the working vocabulary of many teachers, not just in the mathematics departments.

The sessions held in schools, colleges and LEAs throughout the UK were a great source of motivation but as the project grew the demands began to be more than we could cope with. It was our very good fortune that one of the earliest LEA persons to show an interest in the ALIS project was David Elsom, who had been a deputy principal at a college and, being an economist, had tried to make sense of the examination grades yielded subject by subject in the college. Having attempted this, he immediately recognized the value of the ALIS database and jumped on a train going to Edinburgh one day to discuss the project with us. Since then he has been one of our providers of INSET,[2] tremendously appreciated. We are now building a team of INSET providers through training conferences and by making material available. It takes time, but seems very necessary.

The reports were stodgy. This was a great advantage in the early years, for the reports could be counted on to put off governors, press and politicians and thus inform the profession without threat. Now that more and more persons understand the reports (supported by the 'explanation booklet') and have seen how the indicators fluctuate from year to year, early anxieties may have diminished. The results of accurate data are so much less clear cut (and more realistic) than the results of inaccurate rumours and opinions.

However, we are working on more readily accessible forms of feedback, particularly graphical. The ALIS disk programmed by Christopher Egdell has been widely welcomed. Given GCSE grades, it will give A-level predictions in 43 subjects and throw up regression and 'chances' graphs from a menu.

We have conducted a small number of experiments to inform our own procedures and find that:

- invitations to participate in research seem to be related to positive attitudes to ALIS (Tymms and Fitz-Gibbon, 1995);

- sending additional graphs or sending no additional material resulted in more positive attitudes than sending additional tables;

- simplifying the process reports had no apparent impact on attitudes (Tymms, 1995).

We have sought research funds for experiments on types of feedback and the effects of networking – putting departments in ALIS in touch with one another in various ways for mutual support and the 'constant improvement' that Deming urges. Unfortunately, experiments seem not to win the approval of reviewers for the Economic and Social Research Council (ESRC), who do not display any appreciation for their value as a guide to action. Two applications containing experiments were turned down. Two applications to do more observational work or follow-up surveys have, on the other hand, been successful. One problem with the peer review system is that the volunteers who run it are not responsible for the outcomes of their advice. Perhaps ESRC should introduce some teams whose work is assessed in terms of 10-year outcomes and compared with the random funding of a selection of projects which pass a basic screening.

There is one last question. Why were we the first to develop such a system? Only now, 10 years later, are others matching up age 16 and age 18 examinations. Early work on the link between examinations at age 16 and at age 18 had actually been undertaken by M. F. Al Bayatti in a PhD completed in 1979 working under the supervision of J. R. Green in the Department of Statistics, University of Liverpool (Al Bayatti and Green, 1986), but that was largely ignored and they had trouble getting it published. Perhaps it was too sophisticated to attract attention in education. I deliberately used a linear relationship, although I reported that a curvilinear one (fourth power) would produce slightly more accurate results. The simplicity and transparency of the system seemed important if it was to be acceptable. A similar consideration applies to the use of important new software developed by Professor Harvey Goldstein at the London Institute (multilevel modelling). We were among the first to attend his workshops and have used the technique for research but have not used it in the feedback for several reasons, transparency being one and another being a reservation detailed in Chapter 14.

Still, it is quite amazing that this obvious way of studying and evaluating education had not been applied earlier. One possible reason might be that A-levels were seen as elitist and irrelevant by some researchers. The possibility of learning from them did not seem attractive. However, they were, and still are, at the time of writing, a major gateway to the professions and of enormous importance in the lives of some students. They deserved to be well studied.

Information system modules

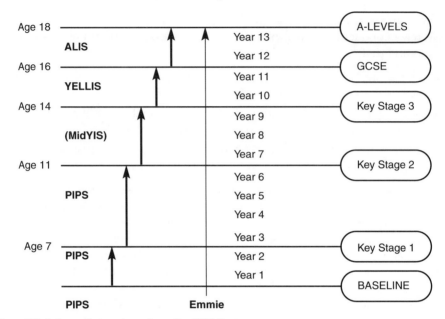

Figure 7.3 *Information systems from the CEM Centre*

FURTHER DEVELOPMENTS

Gradually, other systems have been developed to the point where we can now offer to monitor the entire range of educational provision (Figure 7.3). All systems continue to undergo development even as they are in use. The underpinning research and initial development have been accomplished with outstanding support from some LEAs, Training and Enterprise Councils, the Secondary Heads' Association, the National Association of Head Teachers, the Research Committee of the University of Newcastle-upon-Tyne and individual schools and colleges. Particularly to those individuals who, in those various organizations, saw the development of monitoring with feedback as valuable and gained support for it, we all owe a great debt of thanks.

NOTES

1 The south of England is predominantly Conservative voting, and the north is mainly Labour voting. The north often feels disadvantaged. For example, Paul Davies, the famous physicist who left the University of Newcastle-upon-Tyne for Australia, taking a pay cut but gaining better working conditions, published data showing that science grants decreased with distance from London.
2 INSET = *In service* education of teachers, i.e. staff development meetings. It is distinguished from initial teacher training, which is *pre-service*.

PART FOUR

Measurements for Monitoring Systems

> I've been asked to teach *all* of the philosophical and social foundations
> of Education in 10 weeks! Ten weeks! Five would be alright, but ten!
> (Professor of Education)

This Part starts with a chapter on 'assessment' – the measurement of achievement by tests and so forth. It is not only because of the current controversy surrounding tests in the UK (illustrated in Chapter 8) that a book on monitoring needs a chapter on assessment. What students learn represents one of those major outcomes that we care about enough to measure, so assessment is an integral part of monitoring.

In Chapter 9, an 'assessment transcript' is proposed and justified by reference to some knowledge in social science. This illustrates the way in which social science can be of some help in taking steps towards systems that work – in this case by setting up a system which can learn.

In Chapter 10, assessment in vocational education is considered, with a viewpoint which might be considered controversial by those to whom the notion of general ability is anathema, regardless of its usefulness in describing the world as it seems to be.

A central theme in this book is that we measure that which we care about enough to bother measuring. Consequently we need to measure students' attitudes as one of the major outcomes of education. Hence there is an introductory chapter on measuring attitudes (Chapter 11).

The measurement of events, processes or actions will generally be more difficult than the measurement of mental states, such as achievements or attitudes. How can the ongoing stream of events and processes be captured, and which processes are important? Chapter 12 illustrates the difficulties but also the usefulness of students' reports of teaching and learning processes.

Chapter 13 looks at the standard ways of ensuring quality in measurements of any kind, whether the measures be ratings, practicals, inspections, attitude measures, examinations or whatever. The techniques are well established. In a sense, this chapter is a whirlwind tour of measurement concepts.

Are 'whirlwind tours' useful? One study (Reder and Anderson, 1980) found that reading summaries of articles led to longer retention than reading the actual articles. There may be something to be said for brief summaries rather than the exhaustive treatments that are considered so academically desirable.

Chapter 8

Measuring Achievement: Problems and Conflicts

In the summer of 1993, the tests which were to be given to all 14-year-olds (Key Stage 3) were almost completely boycotted by teachers.

> At 1 pm last Monday, after months of trying to head off a teachers' boycott of the first national tests for 14-year-olds in English, mathematics and science, John Patten, the beleaguered education secretary, was finally forced to admit defeat. Out of 600,000 pupils only a few thousand pupils in a handful of schools put pen to paper. The tests were a flop.
>
> (*Sunday Times*, 13 June 1993, p. 11)

WARRING FACTIONS

In the UK assessment has become an area of politicized controversy.

At the time of writing, we have seen the proposed introduction of Standardized Assessment Tasks (SATs) for ages 7, 11, 14 and 16. Tests are to be conducted and marked by teachers themselves and the intention seems to be that the results will be published in 'league tables' which rank order schools. Here is an account, transcribed from a radio broadcast from 1993, of the impact of the publication of 'league tables' of LEAs drawn up on the basis of a pilot of SATs for Key Stage 1 (i.e. for 7-year-olds).

BBC Interviewer . . . lists of primary school scores in tests of 7-year-olds were given to the press. Local authorities were ranked in order, from Richmond at the top to Bradford at the bottom. The Labour council in Bradford hardly knew what hit it.

Bradford Councillor We were lampooned and all sorts of . . . very menacing suggestions were made about the nature of Bradford and the people within it. I feel that we were slandered. We had tabloid papers ringing us up asking was this anything to do with the number of Asian or black people in the city. We had all sorts of people crawling their way around schools looking for horror stories. We are not hiding from evaluating progression and all the other things that need to be done in schools, but we were told quite clearly, and we believe that these tests were wrong.

BBC Interviewer Councillor Ralph Barry, the Vice Chairman of Bradford's Education Committee, might be expected to react to Bradford's position at the bottom of the primary schools' table by complaining 'We was robbed', but he is not alone. Dr Diane Shorrocks of the School of Education at Leeds University wrote the official evaluation of last year's tests of 7-year-olds, and concluded that the results were 'undependable' largely because of differences in the stringency with which local authorities applied the tests. Bradford was rigorous in grading its children, others were not, and Bradford paid the price. Dr Shorrocks submitted her conclusions, including the word 'undependable', to the government's advisers at the beginning of December. Two weeks later, in spite of her reservations, they published the table of results. So how did she react when she opened her newspaper and saw it?

Diane Shorrocks   I think I and the whole team were rather surprised.

BBC Interviewer   Surprised?

DS   Surprised.

BBC Interviewer   Had you expected the figures to be published?

DS   We had not. I wasn't aware – the whole system was always referred to as an unreported run for quite a long time. It's my view – it's my impression – that local authorities also thought it was going to be an unreported run. The only sense in which it was going to be reported was that it was going to be reported to the individual children's parents.

BBC Interviewer   Do you think it was fair that those tables were published in the way that they were?

DS   I think I would raise question marks about fairness. In the first instance, because the local authorities had not expected them to be published and, certainly, if I were in the shoes of the government, I think I would want to make certain that any information I gave was as accurately based as possible, if only that, when results are published in subsequent years, we want those to be taken seriously.

BBC Interviewer   And this information wasn't dependable in your view?

DS   We raised, as a result of very detailed analysis, very detailed data gathering, significant questions about the dependability of the outcomes in 1991.

BBC Interviewer   For primary school teachers in Bradford, publication proved an ordeal. Children at Caroline Illingworth's school had done well in the tests for Standard Assessment Tasks known as SATs, and she was horrified to see Bradford come last.

Caroline Illingworth   Well, the first thing that went through my mind was I don't believe that that's the case. I don't believe that if any authority followed the guidelines and did it properly that we could have results like this. I immediately thought something is wrong somewhere. I was very shocked when I thought of all the hard work that had gone into the testing by my own staff and by all the staff within Bradford, and I knew that there was something wrong somewhere along the line with the table.

BBC Interviewer   What did the teacher in your school, who had actually carried out the testing, say to you?

CI   'I don't believe it.' She just looked at the table and said 'I just don't believe this. How can we be the worst authority? How can we when we haven't got poor children, when we do what we should be doing within the school? I don't understand how we have been given this position.'

BBC Interviewer   What was her mood?

CI   Very despondent.

BBC Interviewer   What was yours?

CI   Very angry. I was angry because I knew we had performed the SATs as well as we could do. I knew that in my school, as in other schools, the children had done well. They had enjoyed the SATs. We had made it very enjoyable for them, at the same time we had done it rigorously. I was very angry that by doing something like this, even though we don't agree with testing at this age, I don't think anybody in education does, we'd done our best. Because we'd done our best, we were being pilloried for it.

(The interviewer then turned to Baroness Blatch, the Education Minister.)

BBC Interviewer   Why are those figures published at all when the official evaluation had said that the aggregates were undependable?

Baroness Blatch   No, no, no. The important thing is that the SATs are in very early stages and we know that 1991 was particularly problematic for teachers who had to implement it. 1992 has been much smoother. We said that we would put out the aggregates, which is what we did. We said we would not put it out school by school and, therefore, parents would not have the difficulty of comparing a school with another school or, indeed, a child with another child because of the difficulties of it being a first run. *We now are much more confident about the quality of that information and, therefore, it will be put out school by school eventually.* (Emphasis added)

PUBLICATION OF ASSESSMENT RESULTS

From Baroness Blatch's remarks the intention is clear: once the tests are of sufficient 'quality' they will be published school by school. Is this a strategy which will improve education? Is this a system effectively designed to achieve its goals? This threat of publication may be causing most of the continuing strife between the government and teachers. The 1993 Key Stage 3 tests collapsed and the 1994 tests also seem set to collapse, with continuing opposition from the National Union of Teachers and a survey of 800 secondary schools indicating that only a third conducted any tests and far fewer were reporting the results.

Why are schools so opposed to league tables? There are many reasons. League tables of raw results are clearly unfair, taking no account of the kind of students in the school. Schools serving less able children, no matter how hard they try, will not do well in a league table of raw results. Even if 'value added' league tables were proposed, the profession would be unlikely to want them published. The examination results do not tell the whole story of a school's quality. They do not take into account the quality of life for its students – extracurricular activities, sports, music, debates – the quality of the relationships between teachers and students, and students' enjoyment of lessons, love of learning, and aspirations.

Schools do, however, want value-added data – and data on all sorts of other important outcomes – to use internally to inform practice. These data, however, have to be student by student, class by class, and subject by subject to be of use. Whole school aggregates are of almost no use for improvement purposes. The information needed is fine-grained and far too sensitive to publish, since some will relate to the work of individual teachers. *No profession does personnel work in public.* No profession should be asked to, least of all teaching, which represents one of the most open of all professions. Almost all its students are submitted for external examinations over which teachers have no control. Schools can be visited and have always been inspected. In short, *teaching is not a profession which resists accountability but the system has to be a fair one.*

The danger is that the standardized assessment systems which Baroness Blatch clearly wanted will be required at all the key stages but the data will be either corrupted or unavailable because of the insistence on publication and league tables.

There are complicated issues. It may be that actual or potential parents need some access to, say, three-year averages for subject groupings, such as science, humanities and languages. As long as we keep a fair system of external examinations, such data will be available and the system will evolve towards some working accommodations between the reasonable refusal to have personnel work conducted in public and the equally reasonable demand for open systems of information.

Given the ongoing conflicts it is important for the profession, the politicians and the public to consider carefully how one of the main outcomes of education, namely achievement, is to be assessed. These problems are discussed in this chapter but a way forward is held over to the next chapter.

PROBLEMS OF INTERNALLY ADMINISTERED TESTS IN THE CONTEXT OF PUBLICATION

Unfortunately for teachers, the 'left' talks of 'trusting teachers with assessment' and the 'right' probably hopes to avoid the cost of external marking. Between the two, teachers have found themselves saddled with having to come up with grades for their own students, not just internally, for reports to the students and their parents, but for external publication as school data.

There are many problems surrounding internal assessment, especially when exacerbated by the threat of publication.

Corruptibility

One problem which no one seems willing to discuss is how on earth such a system can be operated on a basis of personal honesty. The proposal for SATs has been that teachers give the tests, teachers mark the tests of their own students, teachers report the marks, and publication follows, in league tables in the local press, school by school, so that the teachers' work may be judged. Surely there is a flaw in this design? How will anyone know who is cheating? Deming said 'Wherever there is fear we get the wrong figures.' There *will* be fear. Schools are now funded on a formula driven by student numbers. Jobs will be on the line as well as professional pride and self-esteem. If teachers are marking their own students, how strictly will they mark when a nearby school has just published a peculiarly rosy picture of the achievement of *their* students?

One teacher's outcome is another teacher's baseline for value added

Whilst the teachers of Key Stage 1 may wish to show good SAT results in order to avoid the kind of damage that Bradford suffered, the teachers responsible for Key Stage 2 may imagine that it is better that the SAT results for their intake underestimate the students so that it is easier for them to show value added (good progress) at the next key stage. These conflicting preferences could result in disputes, pressures, trading agreements – all destructive of professional approaches but all understandable in a system which introduces fear not only by publication but also by inspection (a topic postponed to Chapter 23).

Internal assessment endangers teacher–student relationships

Another problem is the danger of setting up a destructive relationship between teachers and students, one too fraught, in which the teacher is both coach and umpire. In the USA there have been riots in connection with teacher-given grades.

But it is not the dramatic riots that should concern us most. Rather it is the silent, widespread fear which could arise; students suffering a possible bias against which they have little redress; the dreadful situation for parents – should they or should they not complain if they feel a teacher is unfair? If they complain, things might go worse for their child; if they do not, the unfairness is unchallenged.

Another way in which internal assessment damages relationships is that it deters some students from praising their teachers. To do so might be seen as favour seeking. Equally, it can deter complaints. Either way, the tensions inherent in having teachers responsible for assessment interfere with feedback between teachers and students and alter relationships.

The danger of destructive labelling

Students will recognize that the grades 'type' them. Statements like 'Level 1 idiot' may become a playground term of abuse. Parents will be upset by grades which rank-order their children in levels and make this the subject of public report. Even though the results of SATs would only be published in school averages, the very publication and the stress put on teachers will exaggerate the importance of these key stage tests. The parents of students who produce low grades could feel blamed for letting down the school even though they have done all they can.

The unavoidable bias in internal assessment

There could be prejudice – against the poor or against the rich, against the attractive or the unattractive, against one ethnic group or another, against one religious group or another, against one gender or the other, against one particular child or another. We cannot pretend this might not happen. We can quite easily set up systems which avoid it, with properly conducted external assessment, keeping markers unaware of whose papers they are marking, i.e. what is known as 'blind marking'. This 'blindness' is the only way in which to avoid bias in any assessments which require judgements to be made.

It may be argued that the moderation procedures ensure equivalent standards and would check against bias, but even a massive, very expensive investigation would not be effective. Moderators can only check roughly the general standard of grades. They cannot re-mark all pages to check for bias against a particular child. Moderators may indeed constitute a conspiracy of the professionals against the laity – a protection mechanism. *Given the possibility of bias, the only way to remove it is by adopting procedures which make it impossible. Quality must be built into the system.*

The danger of a switch to inauthentic assessments

If the SATs became totally objective, right-or-wrong tests, such as the multiple choice tests which can be marked by machines, this would solve several problems: there would be less of a workload for teachers, and they would be incorruptible short of open cheating; they would remove the teacher from conflict with the student or parent about the grade, since the grade would no longer be dependent upon the teachers' judgements. Given these many benefits – not to be denigrated – the secret, speeded, multiple choice objectively marked tests *which the US is beginning to mistrust* may be proposed as a solution for the internal marking of the SATs.

Why are the tests mistrusted in the US? One reason is that such tests have not been closely tied to any syllabus, so their secret content may be unrelated to what has been taught. However, this could be avoided by agreement on the curriculum.

The major problem is the backwash effect of such tests on teaching, what Shavelson describes below as the dysfunctional impact. Multiple choice tests may encourage the teaching of multiple choice answering techniques – not a particularly authentic life skill. Here Shavelson describes preparation for a speeded multiple choice examination:

> I came face to face with the dysfunctional impact of testing: my
> daughter was preparing for the Scholastic Aptitude Test – a
> standardised, multiple choice, time-limited test taken at the end of high
> school. Choice among colleges hinged on how well she did. She studied
> test after test, learning decontextualised vocabulary and tricks to speed
> up responding on the quantitative sections. Only when a colleague from
> Australia remarked that it seemed like a terrible waste of Karin's time to
> be studying stuff that would be of no use to her beyond the aptitude
> test did the absurdity of the whole thing dawn on me. She spent untold
> hours reviewing for the SATs, while ignoring her calculus, physics,
> English and other academic work. Contrast this to Australia, a country
> like ours in local curriculum control, where seniors take exams in
> subject matters such as physics, mathematics, geology, and English. In
> preparing for the exams in Australia, studying means studying
> something of substance.

> (Shavelson, 1990)

This quotation illustrates why, in the US, millions of dollars are being put into attempts to obtain what they call 'authentic, high-stakes, curriculum-embedded tests' – and which we have always called, simply, *examinations* (see Appendix 3).

Internal assessment places an unreasonable workload on teachers

Internal assessment is often unpaid extra work for teachers. It represents an attempt to get assessment on the cheap at the expense of teachers' time.

A positive point: Internal assessment can provide valuable feedback for teachers

Teachers can certainly learn from conducting and marking SATs (Gipps and Murphy, 1993) and do have a genuine professional interest – yet how do we reconcile this with the need to protect teachers and students from a destructive system? Perhaps the issue at stake is the use to be made of the data. There will be a return to these issues in the next chapter.

WHAT PREVENTS A MOVE TO ENTIRELY EXTERNALLY ASSESSED KEY STAGES?

One answer to the above question is professional advice from educators.

Problems with professional advice

One reason politicians give for ignoring professional advice, especially that from the university sector, is that they can find advice pointing them in diverse directions; the profession itself is far from united and therefore quite useless. They have a point.

To illustrate some of the diverse positions espoused by educationalists it is worth quoting one of the much admired writers on education, John Holt:

> Our chief concern should not be to improve testing, but to find ways to eliminate it. (Holt, 1969, p. 51)

> . . . there are two main reasons why we test children: the first is to threaten them into doing what we want done, and the second is to give us a basis for handing out rewards and penalties on which the education system – like all coercive systems – must operate. . . . The economy of the school, like that of most societies, operates on greed and fear; tests arouse the fear and satisfy the greed. (Holt, 1969, p. 52)

There would not appear to be much of a dialogue possible when such a viewpoint is adopted. It has a certain appeal and this against-any-testing attitude may be fairly widespread. Anyone proposing examinations, assessment, performance indicators or accountability will encounter this attitude and will wonder what to do about it. Some choose to ignore it, believing it to be of little practical consequence, since the examination system is intact and most teachers accept the need for assessment.

Paul Black gave the anti-assessment viewpoint the following treatment:

> There are critics of course who say that any argument that sees value in more systematic assessment must be linked to a sausage machine model

of education. To assert the inevitability of such a link is about as reasonable as asserting that to make regular measurements of the weight of a recently born baby is to reduce the baby to the status of a battery chicken. (Black, 1988, p. 34)

This analogy fits in with the idea that when we really care about what is happening, we measure it. Unfortunately arguments by analogy establish little.

A system without external examinations

Trying hard to eschew analogies, what can be said about the disparagement of systematic testing? One approach is to look for examples of systems without examinations. For many years there were few systems of external assessment in the US and the quality of education delivered in inner-city and suburban schools differed hugely. In ghetto schools, perfectly adequate teenagers came through the system unable to read; many 'switched off' from school. Members of staff frequently resorted to setting easy work and either chatting amiably or striding around with threats of caning to get through the day. There was no feedback to staff on their effectiveness on any criterion other than keeping the students contained in four walls for each 50-minute period. No one ever tested what was taught, so it did not matter what was taught. Students' perceptions of the effort involved in studying were unrealistically low. Routinely, the algebra course was only partially covered; the geometry course was rarely finished by the end of the year. Students would get into universities on special criteria for minority students, but if they wanted to study mathematics or science they were in deep trouble because they were so far behind.

If this lack of desire for achievement (a situation fostered by the indifference of a system which did not care enough to measure what was taught) had resulted in happy, motivated, unstressed students and relaxed teachers, perhaps it would have been all right. But that was far from the case.

A position only slightly less negative than John Holt's was taken by two influential professors:

> It is our contention that much is to be gained from teachers having a
> central role in the assessment of their own pupils. . . . the longer
> emphasis is placed on external systems of assessment, divorced and
> remote from schools, classrooms and teachers, the longer will the
> unhelpful divide between teaching, learning and assessment be
> perpetuated.
>
> (No citation (please see foreword for explanation))

This quotation says very little while casting emotional aspersions by the use of words like 'divorced' and 'remote' – without acknowledging that examination boards consult widely on syllabuses and involve practising teachers at every stage. And what is meant, in the quotation, by the terms 'a central role' and 'emphasis'? What exactly is recommended: that all assessment should be internal, that there should be no external examinations, or there should be a compromise?

Nevertheless, if there are problems with examinations, they need to be tackled. There is criticism of 'end-tests'. Arguments such as the following are made against end-of-course examinations or 'end-tests': examinations only measure the ability to do well in examinations; examinations can be passed by item-spotting; a three-hour examination cannot represent a term's work; many students are distressed by examinations and cannot demonstrate their true levels of competence; examinations measure rote-knowledge, not understanding; examinations such as the A-level examinations lead to the adoption of outdated, poor, didactic teaching methods; examinations are developed to be reliable when what is more important is that they are valid; examinations are norm-referenced but it is criterion-referenced assessments which are needed; examinations promote competition and control.

In contrast, the arguments made to promote examinations include the following: examinations set standards; examinations provide accountability; examinations provide parents with information on which to base their choice of school in a competitive market; examinations ensure that a syllabus is taught; examinations enable us to provide assessment which is free of gender, ethnic, social class and religious bias; examinations can be monitored for their fairness, reliability and validity; examinations motivate students; examinations promote good teacher–student relations.

Since these issues seem to return as frequently as the issue of flogging, some of these conflicting views need looking at more closely, although not with any real hope of reconciling the opposing camps.

Examinations as coercive

One role of assessment is motivation – swotting for the test. The anti-testing perspective seems to involve an idealized view, a Rousseau-like pretence that everyone simply, naturally works. Adolescents have many competing claims on their time. If they are to have a chance to learn to make choices and manage their time, in those adolescent years, then they need to have demands made on them in schools, demands which compete adequately with other interests.

The backwash and rote-learning arguments against examinations

In an attempt to check opinion against evidence, and responding to widely held beliefs that 'didactic teaching' would be prevalent in examination classes to a greater extent than in non-examination or even non-assessed classes, Scarth and Hammersley (1988) undertook extensive observations of hundreds of lessons and failed to find strong support for this common belief. Ibrahim's (1992) work and the ALIS project are demonstrating that even in heavily examination-dominated A-level teaching, teachers adopt a wide range of teaching behaviours.

However, regardless of the proportions of teachers who do or do not adopt didactic strategies when pressured by examinations, the origin of the belief is worth pursuing. The implication is that didactic teaching (called 'direct instruction' by those more neutral towards it) is adopted by teachers as a way of getting students through examinations. There are at least four possibilities which need to be considered in evaluating this contention. These possibilities lead to a two-by-two situation: either examinations are samples of useful behaviour (i.e. they are 'authentic') or they are not, and either didactic teaching does or does not promote

	DIDACTIC TEACHING...	
EXAMS ARE:	...does help in the exam	...does not help in the exam
Authentic	A	B
Inauthentic	C	D

Figure 8.1 *Didactic teaching and authentic assessment*

high examination scores. The cells are labelled A, B, C and D in Figure 8.1. If didactic teaching helps students to do well in examinations (i.e. if cells A or C apply) then it is only fair to students to use it. In this case, if it is thought that there is something inherently wrong in didactic teaching, then the response needed is to change the examinations so that didactic teaching does not benefit those students who receive it.

There is a nice irony here. The worst form of didactic teaching might be typified as feeding in information rather than teaching for understanding. It seems likely that, because of the limited capacity of short-term or unorganized memory, such a strategy could only be effective with small bodies of knowledge tested promptly after learning. Yet this approach of frequent 'continuous assessment' is often advocated by those opposed to long end-tests and worried about didactic teaching. It may well be precisely the long final examination, the culmination of two years' work, which is the type of examination in which rote-learning will be least likely to be effective. If you are going to be examined on two years' work, you need to understand it. Memorizing will not get you very far. Long examinations may be exactly what we need to promote if we wish our schools and colleges to be 'educating minds' rather than 'educating memories' (Perkins and Salomon, 1989).

H. A. Simon summarizes the situation regarding learning with understanding thus:

> When something has been learned by rote, it can be regurgitated more or less literally, but it cannot be used as a cognitive tool. Laboratory experiments have shown that material can usually be learned more rapidly with understanding than by rote, is retained over longer periods of time, and can be transferred better to new tasks. In spite of the great pragmatic importance of the distinction between rote and meaningful learning, the difference between them is not thoroughly understood in information processing terms. Partly it is a matter of indexing: meaningful material is indexed in such a way that it can be accessed readily when it is relevant. Partly it is a matter of redundancy: meaningful material is stored redundantly, so that if any fraction of it is forgotten, it can be reconstructed from the remainder. Partly it is a matter of representation: meaningful material is stored in the form of procedures rather than 'passive' data, or if it is stored as data, it is represented in such a way that general problem-solving processes and

other procedures can readily make use of it. All of these are aspects of understanding and meaningfulness that need further exploration.

(Simon, 1988, pp. 119–20)

From Simon's description one could formulate the hypothesis that active learning – *using* the material that is to be learned, acquiring procedures and developing understanding by working with the material in meaningful ways – would promote retention. Recent research suggests precisely this. Cohen *et al.* (1992) studied retention of knowledge of cognitive psychology 11 years after students had taken courses which included both examinations and project work. They noted that their work 'provides some evidence for the importance of coursework in the form of essays and projects since performance in course work, rather than in examinations, emerged as a predictor of long term retention.'

If coursework shows an influence on long-term retention, not to use it in two-year A-level courses would seem unwise. However, the stereotype of A-level examinations drawing only on rote-learning seems somewhat unlikely. A learning-with-understanding approach would seem more likely to pay off, given the strong component of an examination at the end of the course.

Research on learning of the kind to which Simon (1988) and Cohen *et al.* (1992) refer should inform the construction of examinations. We can formulate testable hypotheses: regardless of the particular kind of examination, if it is sufficiently long (about three hours minimum, say) and comprehensive (covering at least one year's instruction of six hours per week) then the best strategy for doing well will be to work towards understanding the work (e.g. by applying it in projects or teaching it to others), not to cram and memorize (e.g. by drill and regurgitate exercises).

Of course the four cells are oversimplifications, as is the term didactic. If we were concerned here with research, the approach would be to seek better definitions and to quantify: what proportion of various examinations is authentic; what proportion of variance in outcomes seems to be associated with the use or non-use of didactic teaching? Those calling for 'the collection of evidence about the intended and unintended effects of assessments on the ways teachers and students spend their time and think about the goals of education' (Linn *et al.*, 1991, p. 17) are surely correct.

On the whole, assertions about the effects of examinations have rarely been empirically checked and the effects remain as areas of controversy and opinion. Controlled experiments on such system-wide variables would be difficult to organize but we could doubtless learn something from the ongoing development of the system.

SUMMARY: THE VIRTUES OF AN EXAMINATION SYSTEM

Some of the aggravation surrounding assessment has been illustrated and we have considered issues which need to be sorted out if the education system is to have the basic data on achievement needed for accountability to society, the development of knowledge (subjects), and the production of a motivating and peaceful framework for staff and students.

Perhaps the virtues of the UK type of examinations need emphasizing.

Teacher–student relationships

- External examinations remove teachers from confrontations with students.

- Teachers become coaches rather than judges.

- Cajoling the teacher will not work. The giving of presents to the teacher is common in some cultures, and in others the same sense of obligation to the student can be induced by rewarding the teacher with smiles or compliments, or just by simply being attractive. It is important that students sense that apples for the teacher, whether material or symbolic, cannot obviate the need to perform in the examination. Equally, though, the other side of the coin is that the difficult student will be judged on his or her performance, without prejudice. This represents the opportunity for a fresh start; it is analogous to the required closing of juvenile records by the police.

Protection from the winds of fashion and experts

An examination system frees teachers from being bullied as to how to teach: they can find their own methods, suiting their own strengths and weaknesses. As long as their students' progress is reasonable and levels of student satisfaction are good, teachers can manage their own professional needs.

Delivery standards for teachers

The demands of a syllabus help to ensure that teachers deliver the full content, and produce a desire for achievement.

Clear goals for students

Students know that there is a body of skills and knowledge which they must acquire.

Finally, if those who are against the use of examinations can create effective systems without them, in reasonably ordinary circumstances, they should do so and let their alternative be evaluated.

Having never been without external examinations, many educationalists in the UK have failed to appreciate their virtues.

Perhaps, though, formal testing *is* inappropriate in English and the arts. We should consider having a national testing programme that covers only the subjects in which there are clear facts and skills and something in the way of progression: maths, sciences, foreign languages, design and technology and applied disciplines like accountancy. It is certainly worth considering having several other subjects treated as cultural and recreational, studied for their own intrinsic interest. Any debate on testing may need to separate the opinion-based subjects from the knowledge-based subjects.

Chapter 9

Assessment: Some 'Solutions' Including an Assessment Transcript

The purpose of this chapter is to suggest some solutions to the problems explored in Chapter 8. However, the solutions themselves are not as important as the attempt to (a) ground the proposed solutions in existing knowledge, and (b) create solutions which are themselves methods whereby we can go on learning and therefore eventually develop better solutions.

Arguments were presented in Chapter 8 in favour of externally set and marked, end-of-course examinations. Evidence was also presented in favour of coursework as a means of promoting learning for understanding and long-term retention. The issue, then, should not be how to choose between the two but how to provide motivating assessment systems whilst all the while learning more about the impacts of assessment.

THE ASSESSMENT TRANSCRIPT: A SOLUTION FOR WARRING FACTIONS

We no longer live in the era of the quill pen, when people could be forgiven for wanting only one grade per child because all record keeping was by hand. With computers, we can actually handle large amounts of information quite easily. Multiple outcomes are feasible.

In this context, and taking into account the areas of controversy which need the illumination of information, a suggested form is provided in Figure 9.1, and the rationale behind this design is the subject of this chapter.

The assessment transcript represents a means of recording achievement on courses, academic or vocational. It is narrower than a 'record of achievement' in the sense that the term has been used by, for example, Broadfoot (1988), because it deals with formally measured and recorded outcomes from formally constituted, timetabled courses, not processes or ratings or extra-timetable activities.

The discussion of the assessment transcript can be based on a number of propositions for which there is support. Some of these represent strong findings, particularly in psychology, but the extent to which the arguments are correct is not as important as the method: that proposed innovations should be based on some evidence, not arise out of the blue. The propositions, which will be discussed in turn, are:

- Proposition 1. The content taught is a crucial influence on what students know, understand and can do – therefore record content.
- Proposition 2. Achievement takes time – therefore record time.
- Proposition 3. The grade awarded will depend upon the method of assessment as well as on the students' learning.

STUDENT TRANSCRIPT

GNVQ Level III

Last Name:

Address(es):

First Name(s):

Date of Birth:

Postcode(s):

Begin date	Centre	Topic { module / unit / course }	Hrs.	Internally Assessed Grades					Externally Assessed Grades					GPA
mth and yr / Duration in months				Practical	Coursework	Project	Exam	GPA	Practical	Coursework	Project	Exam	GPA	

GPA

Figure 9.1 *An assessment transcript*

- Proposition 4. Different people need different information – therefore record details.

- Proposition 5. Society has a right to know whether grades have been awarded internally or externally, regardless of moderation procedures – therefore record this routinely.

The propositions almost all have the ring of many 'findings' in social science: they seem obvious. In a way, we all 'know' them to be true. But acceptable as these propositions are, their implications are nevertheless often neglected.

Proposition 1. The content taught is a crucial influence on what students know, understand and can do – therefore record content

You may think this is obvious, but in the literature on school effects and school effectiveness there is little reference to the curriculum. The focus is on the effectiveness of the 'delivery'. School effects are even averaged out across all subjects, so that the differences that exist in the effectiveness in different subject areas are ignored. The implication is that any timetabled, assessed course is interchangeable with any other. *What* is delivered receives less attention than relative student progress as reflected by grades.

This lack of consideration of *what* is taught is evident in the school performance tables published at considerable expense in the national press. The percentage of students achieving A to C grades or passes is recorded in these 'league tables' with no differentiation by subject despite the evidence that some subjects are more difficult (or more severely graded) than others.

When the USSR launched 'Sputnik', the first object ever to reach the critical velocity which kept it orbiting the earth rather than falling back to earth, this shook the USA badly, for the USA had assumed it was the world leader in science and technology. Funds were quickly ploughed into new science and mathematics curricula. After some years of work on several different curricula, the question was posed as to which worked best.

Walker and Schaffarzik (1974) studied this question, collecting comparative data across several implementations of several curricula, and then came to the rather unexciting but well-based conclusion that students learned, in science at least, what they were taught and did not learn what they were not taught. To ask which curriculum was 'best', therefore, you had to know what was worth learning and then look at each curriculum in terms of **'content inclusion and emphasis'** – what was taught and how much time (emphasis) was placed on it. Unfortunately, there were only one-off evaluations conducted of these projects. There was no monitoring system in place so that comparisons of learning and motivation in non-project classrooms were not available. Had there been, we might have learned more from Harvard Project Physics, the 'New Maths', projects and all the other projects. The same comment applies to the UK equivalent: the Nuffield projects. A monitoring system would have provided a framework for evaluation which could have guided implementation and development as well as monitoring outcomes.

Figure 9.2 *Content inclusion and emphasis*

Preece (1983) suggested that what is studied is the critical factor in achievement. Variations in *how* the topic is studied (e.g. the quality of teaching or presentation) are, he argued, minor in their impact on achievement, compared with whether or not a student has in fact studied a particular topic.

Consequently, the topic studied, the syllabus followed and in particular the syllabus delivered in the classroom, are critical factors in what students end up knowing or not knowing. This viewpoint was also a conclusion from a study of innovative science projects in the US (Figure 9.2).

The topic column in the assessment transcript should therefore be backed up with reference to particular syllabuses as followed in the centre (school or college) when the student took the particular 'module', 'unit' or 'course'. This is simply a matter of documentation – but nationally the designation of syllabuses is not yet straightforward.

There needs to be some consistency in the terminology used for courses. For example, does 'design' equate at all with 'design and technology'? Do employers understand the content of either? Some central information service needs to be available. How are employers, admissions officers and students to find out about these features? They could use libraries, but complex systems should be flexible and efficient. If a syllabus needs changing, it should not have to wait for a print run. There should be an agreed set of broad area titles to be recorded on assessment transcripts, a central registry of syllabuses, and electronic access to the information on electronic networks and information highways.

In short, the content is probably as important as the grade received, yet there are many different syllabuses which can make it difficult to know what the content was.

The principle of 'content inclusion and emphasis' is linked to 'delivery standards'. The syllabus on offer indicates what teachers will teach and serves as an 'entitlement' for students. This seems obvious in the UK but it is not at all clear in the US what teachers are teaching – hence the issue of 'delivery standards'.

The principle that students learn what they are taught applies in many if not all subjects. It apparently does not apply in reading competence. In the absence of schooling over the long summer holiday, middle-class children are found to improve their reading but inner-city children decline. Thus any comparisons must compare like with like, and this means subject with subject in assessment, monitoring and evaluations. Some subjects show greater sensitivity to instruction than other subjects, i.e. how they are taught or for how long has more influence on the learning outcomes of some subjects than of other subjects.

Proposition 2. Achievement takes time – therefore record time

Two kinds of time should be routinely recorded for courses; duration and contact hours. Time represents costs, both to student and to the institution providing instruction.

Consequently, on the assessment transcript there is a column for 'duration in months', so that we know the elapsed time for the course, and also a column for 'hours', to indicate the contact hours involved during the elapsed time.

The availability of such data can enable institutions to monitor the impact of time distributions (if any) on course outcomes. Do some students succeed better in less time-pressured courses and is the provision of such courses a way to meet the needs of those students? By altering the elapsed time, will this keep more students achieving to desirable levels?

Schools and colleges may wish to collect information on the effectiveness of specific courses' timetables with differing amounts of elapsed and contact time, relating the findings to the costs of provision.

Proposition 3. The grade awarded will depend upon the method of assessment as well as on the students' learning – therefore record method

Different methods of assessment will yield different results from the same students. Thus to expect that coursework grades will place students in the same rank order as grades based on written tests is contrary to experience. Different methods of assessment measure different kinds of achievement and students differ in their aptitudes. Some are better at one kind of work and others at another.

There are research-based reasons for making the distinction between methods of assessment. There is fairly extensive 'multi-trait, multi-method' literature initiated by an article by Campbell and Fiske (1959) and showing that how one assesses has a very large impact on the results obtained. Indeed – and this is somewhat embarrassing for social science – there are many situations in which *how* the assessment is made – the *method* – has a greater impact on the outcome than *what* is assessed – *the trait* that is measured. For example, a report of the Scottish Examination Board found that when reading and writing skills were assessed by either a portfolio approach or an externally marked paper, the results were more

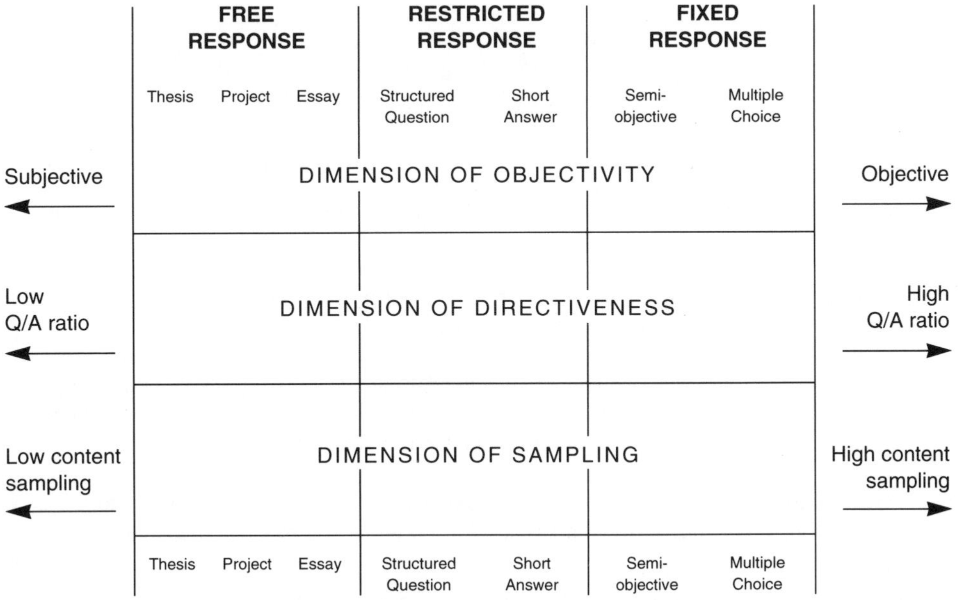

Figure 9.3 *Diagrammatic comparison of test types*

strongly correlated by type of assessment than by whether reading or writing was being assessed (Fitz-Gibbon, 1991, pp. 39–40). This challenges the idea that the concept of 'writing skill' can be defined independently of the method of assessment to be used.

Different methods of assessment measure different aspects of performance and therefore yield different results. One frequently reported finding is that girls tend to score higher marks on essays than boys but lower marks on multiple choice items.

Massey (1977) in a report for the Cambridge Examination Board suggested that types of assessment varied along three dimensions – objectivity, directiveness and sampling. Multiple choice items can be highly objective: they leave little in the way of options for the candidates and can be used to sample the syllabus extensively. Essays, on the other hand, may be subjective, may leave decisions to the candidate and may not sample the entire syllabus. Each type of assessment has its virtues and limitations, and a full assessment programme should probably include a considerable variety of methods (Figure 9.3).

It will be important, however, not to create too fine a set of divisions, both to avoid information overload and to avoid redundancy incurred by the use of methods the results of which relate so closely as not to justify separate reporting.

The four methods shown in Figure 9.4 would be adequate for the assessment of many subjects. Each is quite different and therefore needs to be separately reported.

Other kinds of assessment could be suggested but these are four which seem important. Each kind of assessment addresses a different kind of motivation, a different kind of aptitude on the part of the student, and a different way of running a course. There is often strength in variety, and rather than dictating that all courses should be of a certain kind, it would seem preferable to provide courses of a variety of kinds.

Coursework often has to be assessed by teachers rather than by external examiners. This causes problems, since it has to be acknowledged that if assessment is to be used for accountability then teachers cannot be the assessors, even

---

- Many subjects have associated practical skills – therefore we need **practical examinations** or skill assessments.

- **Coursework**, or 'continuous assessment', can cover a wider range of content than can examinations, and is sometimes preferred by teachers and students.

- **Projects** are motivating, allowing deep reflection and painstaking effort, and provide experience of planning and meeting deadlines – not to mention gaining help from others. Projects allow integration of knowledge, understanding and skills.

- **Examinations** can be fair, authentic assessments on agreed syllabuses. The blind assessment which they provide is needed for the protection of equal opportunities and quality assurance.

Figure 9.4 *Major modes of assessment*

with highly expensive moderation procedures. Yet there are good reasons to use coursework. By providing regular feedback to students there is often enhanced learning and better pacing of the learning effort throughout the course. Furthermore, as mentioned in Chapter 8, a study of how much students remembered up to 11 years after taking a course showed that the amount of long-term retention of information was better predicted by coursework grades than by external examination grades. This suggests that students working well throughout the course will retain the information better than students who simply make a last-minute short-term effort for the examination. Cost-effectiveness considerations alone would suggest the need for coursework – to lead to a better preserved investment in learning.

However, current enthusiasm for totally coursework-based courses sometimes wears off as people find that a straightforward examination at the end of a course is actually efficient, in terms of the teachers'/lecturers' time, as well as being productive in terms of the students' learning. Some students, however, will avoid courses which rely on end examinations. These self-selection mechanisms will make the interpretation of the data difficult in the future, but this is a price we may be willing to pay for a system which benefits from the motivational aspects of providing students with choice and feedback. *The important point is that the origin of recorded grades should be recorded on the assessment transcript.*

Proposition 4. Different people need different information – therefore record details

As soon as we assess two or more components, the issue arises as to how the grades should be summarized for the course. This is an issue that has been the source of many controversies about the recording of information in records of achievement, examination transcripts and certificates. One possible approach is to *let the end-user decide*.

Controversies about the percentage of a grade which should be attributed to coursework and examinations are unnecessary – there is no need to add the two kinds of measures in any proportions or with any weights. Sometimes examination boards even try to make the two grades produce more or less the same rank order, by shifting groups of grades up or down, or by using other procedures falling under the general title of 'moderating'. This should be strenuously resisted. *The grades should be awarded independently of each other*, preferably blind to the candidate's other grades.

It is sometimes feared that if examination grades are reported separately, the coursework grades will be ignored. Employers, for example, might be more interested in the examination grades than in the teacher-given coursework grades. However, the coursework grades may actually be more relevant to an employment situation than the examination grades. After a few years of having both kinds of data available, it may be possible to show the predictive validity of each kind of assessment. Rather than hide this information by adding non-commensurates together and dividing by X, we should keep separate methods of assessment separately recorded and let end-users be the ones who decide the kind of assessment to which they wish to pay attention. This is not only democratic, but is also intelligent. It is the setting up of systems which allows us to learn from the data as they are collected in the system.

Proposition 5. Society has a right to know whether grades have been awarded internally or externally, regardless of moderation procedures – therefore record this routinely

When grades are externally awarded – i.e. work is externally assessed – there are some common standards across institutions and there is the potential for preventing bias for or against some candidates. We need to know the internal or external origin of grades.

When there are no external grades, institutions can begin to drift apart in standards, which may well be the case with universities. Coleman (1994) reported a study of levels of achievement in French, showing that outputs at some institutions could be lower than the input elsewhere. The external moderation system in universities is equivalent to what used to be the 'CSE mode 3' system (as UK teachers will recall) and is coming under increasing attack (Howarth, 1993).

In summary, the eight columns in Figure 9.1, under the heading 'internally and externally assessed', are there to record the way in which the course has been assessed. *There is no implication that each column has to be filled in for each course.* Thus, if a course is totally internally assessed, then all grades will be recorded in the first four columns. If it is a totally externally assessed, examination-only kind of course, there will simply be one grade in the last of the eight columns.

The column headed GPA represents grade point average. There is always the temptation to average grades, and people will do so, whether or not it makes sense, so columns are provided. *We do not yet know*, in the context of our particular examining and assessment systems, whether or not it makes sense, because we have not collected the relevant data. Figure 9.1 represents the kind of form on which relevant data can be collected, so that in the future we will have some evidence as to whether we need to look at the separate components or whether, for some purposes, it is sufficient to look at the overall grade point average. Probably different users will have different needs and make different decisions.

CONCLUSIONS: THINKING OF ASSESSMENT IN TERMS OF A WHOLE SYSTEM

As with all issues regarding the functioning of a complex system, we must think in terms of the whole system. Thus we have to think of assessment as producing not just the *intended* outcomes of grades which guide decisions by employers, higher education selectors, students themselves etc. but also the non-cognitive, *concomitant* outcomes of an assessment system – the motivation of students, the evoked interest and attitudes towards the subjects studied. We have to worry about the effect of testing on teaching, what has sometimes been called the backwash effect of examinations. We have to consider the effect of an assessment system on those who do *not* participate in it – such as students who are not catered for by external examinations. We have to think of the impact of an assessment system on teachers: will league tables lead to corrupted data?

Arguments have been advanced, often with reference to existing research, to support the design of the assessment transcript shown in Figure 9.1. Were such

```
A   S   S   E   S   S   M   E   N   T
    o   u       t   t
    c   b       a   u
    i   j       f   d
    e   e       f   e
    t   c           n
    y   t           t
                    s
```

Figure 9.5 *Mnemonic, drawing attention to the four main stake holders*

details to be regularly recorded, on, say, individual student records, there would be a basis from which the system could learn.

With some embarrassment (for these tricks are slightly corny), I offer a mnemonic. Since the stakeholders can all be labelled with words beginning with S, we have the mnemonic shown in Figure 9.5.

This mnemonic draws attention to the four main stakeholders:

- society;
- subject taught;
- staff (meaning teaching staff in schools and colleges);
- students.

One way to evaluate the importance of a component in a complex system is to ask what will happen in the system if the component does not work. What if the system does not work for any of these stakeholders?

- If the needs of *society* to create an appropriate workforce and to avoid creating a disaffected underclass are not met, then the system is in trouble. If certification is given for learning or skills which are inadequate, problems are built into the system.
- Despite the current fashion to blur subject boundaries, there are demands which relate to the structure of what is taught, whether that is integrated humanities, history, combined science or physics. The disciplines which are studied are constantly developing and also have their own specific demands. If the needs of the *subjects* are neglected, the curriculum can be trivialized, out of date or ineffective. And, as can be seen from the arguments regarding English, each area of the curriculum, if not each subject, will have its own issues, not necessarily shared with other subjects. We need to contemplate the possibility that assessment systems may need to be subject-specific.
- If *staff* leave, switch off or stop trying, or if effective teachers are no longer attracted to the profession, the system is in trouble. Equally, if staff refuse to co-operate, the system collapses.
- If *students* cannot or will not cope with a curriculum, the system is in trouble.

It sometimes seems that the task of teachers can be summed up as *motivating and matching* – motivating students to work and matching the tasks day by day to the ability of the student to accomplish the task. This complex and challenging job has to be accomplished within the assessment framework, the syllabuses and the grading systems – and in the context of students' lives, in which there may be powerful currents running, out of reach of teachers.

On one point, however, I think the situation is clear: assessment systems must be informed by teachers and accepted by teachers. In plans to redesign assessment, teachers should be regarded as prime 'customers' for two reasons.

One is that if teachers do not accept it, it is unlikely to succeed. Thus teachers in Scotland, working with parents, rejected the proposed model of teacher-given and teacher-marked tests and obtained drastic changes, including not having the data published. Teachers of English in the UK in 1993 refused to go along with a style of testing that seemed to them to ruin the subject and which would have produced a set-back in ways of teaching, losing many years of what they saw as progress.

The point is not whether they were right or wrong. The point in each case is that teachers had the power to scupper proposals because those proposals depended upon teachers to implement them.

There is a second and equally important reason why teachers are central to the design of systems of assessment. This relates to the motto which is often said to underpin the 'free market' economies: 'The customer is right.' One reason why this attitude often produces better goods and products than other attitudes (such as 'We're the experts and we'll decide what customers need') is that the customer frequently *knows more* about the full complexity of the job than any 'experts'. Teachers know what it takes to run a classroom and create achievement, in their own circumstances, in an ever-changing world in which the classroom also undergoes change. Their advice is therefore ignored at great risk, not because they occupy some special rank as 'professionals', but *because they have better information than others*, information derived from their daily experience of making the classroom work. This recognition that the 'worker' knows most about his or her job is part of many modern approaches to management. Like most rules it cannot be applied without exception, but extreme caution is wise if the rule is violated.

Chapter 10

Assessing Vocational Courses

Why should the assessment of vocational courses be any different from the assessment of academic courses? It probably should not. The differences between vocational courses (e.g. engineering versus caring) and between the 'academic' courses (such as physics and art at A-level) are probably as great as any difference between vocational and academic courses in general, and the same principles of assessment apply. The distinction between the academic and vocational is itself a blurred one and possibly unhelpful. Setting up a syllabus, a course and assessments of various kinds (practical, coursework, projects and examinations) is just as applicable to vocational courses as to any other. Indeed, music could be regarded as vocational, and there is a well-functioning set of external assessments to certify achievements in music. All the arguments about the danger of internal assessments being unfair in not maintaining consistent standards and with respect to potential bias against individuals apply to vocational courses as much as to any other courses.

The problem with assessment in the vocational area seems to be an unwillingness to put in the funds required for quality external assessments, and therefore vocational courses have often been internally assessed. Students themselves recognize the problems. In comments on questionnaires used in monitoring a vocational course (the BTEC Business and Finance National Diploma), students wrote:

> . . . many teachers have favourites, therefore I believe marking is done
> due to favouritism.

> Is a distinction here worth the same as a distinction at other places?

The monitoring of standards is essential for fairness and also for any computations of value added. If some courses are, say, severely graded, this could look like courses providing poor value added – students would appear to be achieving less. Conversely, high grades can be questioned: are they a result of effective teaching or lenient grading? Without the kind of standards which only an external system can securely deliver, value added cannot be evaluated.

CORRELATES OF OUTCOMES ON VOCATIONAL COURSES

It has been suggested that prior achievement measures do not correlate well with achievement on vocational courses (Adult Commission, 1993). However, the extent to which prior achievement correlates with grades from vocational courses is partly affected by the lack of standardization in the vocational courses themselves.

There are suggestions that vocational course results should *not* show strong correlations with prior achievement. There are probably three reasons for this belief that a lack of correlation with prior achievement is not a problem, but is, rather, desirable. One is the belief that vocational courses can be assessed on criterion-referenced scales. A second reason is the belief that prior academic achievement is irrelevant to vocational achievement – the content is different. A third reason might be the belief that students' motivation is transformed by the methods of teaching adopted on vocational courses.

CRITERION-REFERENCED TESTS AND 'COMPETENCES'

The textbook example of a 'pure' criterion-referenced test (CRT) is the driving test. Criteria are set: you drive without crashing and you look in the mirror and so on. If you meet the criteria, you pass the test, regardless of how many others passed that day, regardless of whether or not your instructor is known to the examiner, and regardless of who you are, what you look like, your age etc. Fair, objective, clearly defined criteria are there to ensure that the system is fair. And perhaps it works for driving tests (though there are constant rumours about some norm-referencing, about not having 100 per cent pass rates each month, so that towards the end of the month (it is asserted) some examiners may adjust their standards). But even the driving test assessment of fairly definable skills is not purely criterion referenced. Standards will be set according to criteria external to the assessment process – extrinsic criteria. In some systems, where the car is likely to be essential to a wage earner, the criteria are less stringent: a multiple choice test will get you a licence. Cost and impact of the assessment also come into its design. They will be factors in the design of anything but the most trivial assessment tasks.

It seems reasonable to say that if you want to know whether or not someone can drive a car, you should test them on driving a car, not give them a test of intelligence or even a test of perceptual style. The test of the skill (a sample of actual driving) *will* tell you whether or not someone has a minimal competence – it will answer a 'can do'/'can't do' question of the kind advocated in criterion-referenced systems. But is that good enough? Will that approach produce the highest quality when applied in vocational testing situations? Let us pursue the driving test example. The 'can do'/'can't do' question can be answered, but if you were an employer of bus drivers you would want to employ the safest, most trustworthy and skilled driver – people's lives are at stake. Would the driving test assess this kind of long-term quality? Would a small sample of someone's driving, even on an advanced test of skills, predict accident rates, for example? It seems not, whereas seemingly irrelevant tests of perceptual style and selective attention do. Indeed, paper and pencil tests of intelligence have been found to predict accidents and traffic offences (Conger *et al.*, 1966; Smith and Kirkham, 1982).

The problem is that short tests of competence are not necessarily predictive of long-term performance. Certainly, the assessment of some minimal level of 'mastery' simply hides information. Almost any skill can be performed with a greater or lesser degree of competence, and, furthermore, subsequent performance will bring into play other factors which cannot be tested in a limited time, since, like concentration or long-term commitment, they are extensive in time and sensitive to contexts which cannot be simulated.

The best way to predict for individuals will always be to monitor on the job.

Meanwhile, in selecting for important jobs, general aptitudes are almost certainly important. The often-decried habit of employers of looking at examination grades when hiring for jobs which seem unrelated to examinations may actually be born of experience and insight which researchers have not had to develop, free as they generally are of the responsibility for running any enterprise.

Generally ability, as reflected in scores on many school tests and examinations, is very widely, positively correlated with many kinds of outcomes.

THE USEFULNESS OF THE CONCEPT OF GENERAL ABILITY

Those who continue to doubt the existence of general ability may like to consider this clear statement from Perkins and Salomon:

> There can be little doubt that some aspects of cognitive skill are quite general: IQ and g for general intelligence measure a side of human intellectual functioning that correlates with effective performance *over a wide range of academic and non-academic tasks*. For this aspect of cognitive skill, the answer is in, and favours generality (Perkins and Salomon, 1989, p. 16). (Emphasis added)

Any remaining doubters should refer to Barrett and Depinet (1991). In an extensive survey of the literature, they took issue with key points made by McClelland (1973), and concluded that, contrary to McClelland's assertions:

- Achievement in school, as measured by grades for academic school work, does predict subsequent success in a wide variety of occupations.
- Intelligence tests and aptitude tests also predict job success.
- Although the prediction does not prove a causal relationship, no other mediating variable has been found to 'explain' the observed relationships between achievement, aptitudes and job success. Social class, for example, does not contribute anywhere near as much to the prediction as do the cognitive variables.
- Aptitude tests generally show the same predictive validities for minorities as for others.
- Testing for 'competences' does not provide better prediction of job success than aptitude and achievement tests.

They conclude:

> The evidence has not shown that competences can surpass cognitive ability test in predicting any important occupational behaviour. . . . Since 1983, the evidence increasingly shows that cognitive ability tests do predict job performance in a wide variety of occupations. . . . If McClelland's concept of competences is to make a contribution to the field of psychology, he must present empirical data to support his contention. (Barrett and Depinet, 1991, p. 1021)

There are several consequences arising from these kinds of findings:

- End-tests in vocational areas *should* correlate with general aptitude. If they do not, perhaps they are not sampling widely enough or not differentiating the outcomes sufficiently.

- Aptitude tests and/or achievement tests can be used as baseline data for looking at relative progress (value added) for vocational courses.

- End-tests must be long enough and varied enough to produce variation in outcomes, i.e. differentiated outcomes. Pass–fail-type criteria are arbitrarily defined dichotomies which hide information and should not be used.

If we do not learn to assess vocational areas in ways which help to give jobs to those who will do them best, it will cost us dearly in terms of lost productivity, stress on the job and effectiveness. Indeed, for one situation in which data were available (federal government jobs, prior to promotion), two US researchers estimated the costs:

> Meta analysis of the cumulative research on various predictors of job performance shows that for entry-level jobs there is no predictor with validity equal to that of ability which has mean validity of .53. . . . For federal entry-level jobs, substitution of an alternative predictor would cost from $3.12 billion (job tryout) to $15.89 billion per year (age).
>
> (Hunter and Hunter, 1984)

When we have in place a transcript system of the kind proposed in the previous chapter, the kind of data needed for such assessments in the UK will gradually become available.

THE THEORETICAL ISSUE WITH PRACTICAL IMPLICATIONS: THE ISSUE OF TRANSFER

Closely related to the notion of general ability is a newly named construct: 'core skills'. The claim is that core skills apply across all courses and can be separated from knowledge of content of the course. They are deemed to be important because, once acquired, they can be applied to other courses. This raises an issue familiar to psychologists: transfer. The issue of transfer is of major concern at a time when there are calls for testing for 'core competences' or when there are calls for tests of basic skills: reading, writing and mathematics.

Can skills be taught and tested out of context? For example, is a substantial amount of sheer knowledge an essential part of problem-solving or can problem-solving be learned in any context and then generalized and transferred? A recent review of the topic (Perkins and Salomon, 1989) presented the research in a lucid style. Their answer to the question 'are cognitive skills context-bound?' is best summarized in their own words:

> As the psychological tale has unfolded, the answer to the questions looks to be, 'Yes and no.' The tale is one of neglected complexities. Early advocacy of general cognitive skills overlooked the importance of a rich knowledge base, took it for granted that general heuristics would make ready contact with a person's knowledge base, and had few worries

about transfer, which was supposed to happen more or less spontaneously. Mistakes all three, these oversights led to considerable scepticism about general cognitive skills, the view that cognitive skills in the main were context bound, and interesting developments in the psychology of expertise as well as artificial intelligence work on expert systems. But more recent results suggest that this trend had its blind spots too, in neglecting how general heuristics help when experts face atypical problems in a domain, how general heuristics function in contextualised ways to access and deploy domain specific knowledge, and how lack of conditions needed for transfer, rather than domain specificity, is to blame for many cases of failure of transfer. These more recent results point towards the synthesis that we now think might be fleshed out. (Perkins and Salomon, 1989, p. 23)

Research on transfer and how it can be promoted must, and undoubtedly will, continue but the answers will almost certainly not be of the kind 'transfer does or does not occur' but that it does to a certain extent under certain circumstances and is probably strongly affected by ability factors. The synthesis spoken of by Perkins and Salomon will be quantifications and qualifications: how much and under what circumstances.

(We encounter here a general problem in social science: the posing of questions in terms of 'Is it A or B?' when in fact the question should be 'how much is there of A and how much of B and what of their interactions and the contexts in which there are stable findings?' *Until social science adds quantification routinely to its discussions it will continue to debate false dichotomies.*)

In a forthright article which has to be considered brave in these days when university academics are supposed to be looking for contracts all the time and are therefore tempted to tailor their comments to the wishes of sponsors, Alison Wolf wrote of 'current fashion' in assessment:

Current proposals originate . . . in a speech by the then secretary of
State Kenneth Baker in 1989 in which he proposed the following 'core
skills':
– communication written and oral
– numeracy
– personal relations – team working and leadership
– familiarity with technology
– familiarity with system
– familiarity with changing social contexts – especially foreign language
   knowledge
After listing his half dozen, Mr. Baker made three specific proposals
which . . . have defined and permeated the core skills debate ever since.
. . . *in spite of encompassing unrecognised, major and irresolvable
problems.*

(Wolf, 1991)

Wolf traced the adoption of the ideas by the Confederation of British Industries, the National Curriculum Council and the National Council for Vocational Qualifications, and quoted the most powerful person in this current trend:

> If the learning requirements are stated as outcomes, they can also be stated independently of any particular subject, discipline or occupation. Thus the specification of core skills . . . can stand independent of, and outside, any syllabus.

This is an example of the saying-will-make-it-so syndrome. All that is needed for transfer, apparently, is that the 'requirements are stated as outcomes' – and transfer will be available to make these generic skills assessible. The chief executive of the National Council for Vocational Qualifications wrote an entire book on the issues of assessment. There was no discussion of the research on transfer. Many public figures seem to feel that ignorance of social science research is excusable, no matter how relevant such research is to the issues with which they are grappling.

Smithers (1994) wrote a highly critical report on vocational courses, based on wide-ranging interviews and site visits in the UK and Europe. He recommended 'that the assessment of (vocational courses) should include written examinations as well as assessments of practical skills, independently set with marks externally verified.' (In crediting various persons as sources of information he had to note on two occasions that the person concerned did not wish to be named for fear of losing grants. This issue of the role of universities is considered in Chapter 25, where we see that Smithers is not alone in having a concern for the diminishing independence of these institutions.)

Meanwhile, his recommendation seems eminently sensible. Enough is known, especially in organizations like the Business and Technical Education Council (BTEC), to proceed with the design of examinations which encourage understanding ('educate minds', as Perkins and Salomon put it) and there is little in the way of evidence to show that examinations as used in the UK require poor teaching practices; rather, there is evidence that a wide variety of practices produces reasonable results in the academic area. The application of a wide variety of assessment methods, as recommended in Chapter 9, can yield information which can guide future planning in the area of 'vocational' assessment no less than in 'academic' assessment.

Chapter 13 introduces some standard concepts which must underpin quality in assessment procedures of any kind – whether the 'assessments' be examinations, judgements, inspectors' ratings, performance tests or whatever.

Chapter 11

Measuring Attitudes

In this chapter we are concerned with two questions: should we try to measure students' attitudes and, if so, can this in fact be done in any reliable and valid way?

SHOULD WE ATTEMPT TO MEASURE STUDENTS' ATTITUDES?

We should try to do this, for several reasons. Measurement gives messages. If we only measure achievement, then the message is that only achievement results matter. Important as achievement is, there are other outcomes that we care about enough to measure. Teachers expend considerable effort to make lessons enjoyable as well as effective. They like students to develop a liking for the subject, not only to do well in it. They want the time in school to be a broadening, high-quality experience. They hope that students like school and speak well of it. Since we care about these things, we should try to measure them, to monitor them lightly and efficiently.

Furthermore, sometimes a decision is made to change from one syllabus to another, or from one examination to another. Since the grading is fairly well normed and kept equivalent, there may be no improvement in achievement, but teachers in the department will be happy with the change if it results in improvements in students' attitudes. This improvement may be the only good outcome to arise from a syllabus change.

Yet another reason to measure attitudes is this: teachers may in fact have more effect on attitudes than on achievement. Thus in the ALIS data, the types of teaching and learning activities employed seem regularly to be more closely related to whether or not students like the subject than to the amount of progress they make. Why should this be? I suspect it is an effect of the examination system. Given that they are working in the framework of a set syllabus, with textbooks and predictable examinations, teachers will all tend to teach the content, and cover the syllabus. In this situation student achievement may be fairly robust, determined largely by the student. But some kinds of teaching may motivate and interest the students, regardless of their impact on achievement.

There is one further important point to consider before concluding this section. The correlation between positive student attitudes and high student progress is quite weak, with correlations of about 0.2. In other words, positive attitudes and good achievement levels are *not* closely associated. This means that the rationale for caring about attitudes is not that we want students to like the subject so that they will do well. It is, more reasonably: 'We want students to like the subject so that they, and we as teachers, will enjoy a high quality of life.'

HOW TO OBTAIN INDICATORS OF STUDENTS' ATTITUDES

If you want to know what students think of a school or college, how do you find out? One obvious way is to ask them – all of them. This need not be too expensive if you use a questionnaire. However, there are problems with this. One major difficulty with questionnaires is that of non-response (you send out 3000 and get back 300). Other problems are the reliability and validity of the items (Chapter 13).

Non-response can be dealt with in a monitoring system by assembling all the students under examination conditions and requesting that they complete the questionnaire. Some will be absent and need follow-up, mail-back questionnaires, but response rates of 80 and 90 per cent can easily be achieved, and often 100 per cent with vigorous follow-up.

Reliability and validity are dealt with by established procedures and by constant effort and revision. One approach to measuring attitudes, for example, is to create a series of items relating to one particular attitude. Some of these may be simple statements with obvious face validity. For example, if you are measuring 'attitude to the institution', one item might be 'I liked school/college this year'. Students respond on a scale ranging from 'strongly disagree' to 'strongly agree'. Other items relating to the same attitude can be drawn from interviews with students, e.g. 'In this school/college you are treated more like an adult'. Again, the respondent agrees or disagrees. Does this item belong on the 'attitude to the institution' scale? You find out only when you have some data and check it out statistically. If students who are positive on one item are positive on another (i.e. if the items are strongly correlated) they are measuring similar things and can be used in making up a scale. The general approach is to start with face validity and to check out the pilot data statistically to see that the intercorrelations among items are sufficiently high.

Why aim for a 100 per cent sample, i.e. the whole 'population'? One might consider saving paper and expense by using only a 20 per cent sample. You would want to obtain a random representative sample of students, however, and this turns out to almost certainly be more trouble than asking all students to complete a questionnaire. First, you have to know how to draw a representative sample. If it is to be representative of every subject being assessed, you have to know students' timetables, examination entries etc. Has it to be gender balanced? Aptitudes might affect attitudes, so you have to know aptitudes or achievement levels. Even if you manage to design an acceptable sample, you then have to find the particular students or send the questionnaire. Mailed questionnaires suffer from low response rates, so you need to follow up. If the school is to administer the questionnaire, individual students have to be located and pulled out of classes. Sampling is more trouble than going for 100 per cent. And, in any case, no matter how carefully the sample is drawn, nothing less than 100 per cent will seem acceptable to staff. A 20 per cent sample of a class of 30, for example, is a mere six students. 'Which six?', teachers would want to know – and rightly so. Education is delivered in small groups and therefore sampling fractions should be large, preferably 100 per cent.

What about the items, i.e. the individual questions in the questionnaire? Aren't they inadequate measures? It depends. The appropriate methodology is to produce several items for each aspect you wish to measure. For example, measurement of attitude to biology might have six items and attitude to the institution might have another six items. These groups of items can be used to form attitude scales, using long-established techniques. (For an excellent illustration of the development of an attitude-to-school measure, see Epstein and McPartland (1976).)

Even so, students are responding to set questions, which do not elicit their personal feelings. Therefore, open-ended items should be included in the questionnaire, e.g. 'How do you feel about having decided to study at this college?', which give students a chance to tell you things you have not thought to ask. These items must then be typed up and fed back to the school without students' names. The questionnaire responses must be confidential.

This all seems reasonable, and the questions of reliability and validity can be addressed because the entire process is open to inspection and can be replicated from year to year, and from school to school. This possibility of close replication is vital, since raw data are not informative. You need to see your data in context year by year.

HOW NOT TO OBTAIN INDICATORS OF STUDENTS' ATTITUDES

Let us consider an alternative to the use of questionnaires which has been canvassed by a highly notable professor:

> The first step after a suitably meaty question has been formed would be for a small group (or small groups) of advisers or inspectors to meet to discuss their understanding of what was involved. . . . Fairly soon after these discussions had begun they would need to spend time in schools pursuing the answer to their chosen question. Classroom observation, discussions with pupils and staff and other forms of qualitative data gathering would probably all be relevant. It would not do to be too prescriptive in the first instance. The quality of the accounting would doubtless improve as the participants become more experienced.
>
> At the end of each day's visit the team would reassemble briefly to exchange thoughts and perceptions. After the first school had been visited the team would have collected some relevant evidence but not be in a good position to interpret it. This could only follow after at least one other 'comparable' school had been visited. When this had been completed, however, the team would be in a position to make its first, albeit tentative judgements. Did school A or school B have the higher proportion of for example, 'satisfied' pupils? And, if so, what proportion, roughly speaking?
>
> The judges would not of course be expected to be in exact agreement but would need to cluster round the same answers. If, for example, two members of a group of four concluded that 'about half' the pupils in a school were satisfied one thought it was 'well over half' and one 'well under half' this would probably be acceptable; but a bigger gap would be a sign that more discussion, agreement and, possibly, evidence was

required. The judgement would be delivered to a school not just as a single figure but in the context of some of the 'supporting evidence' as well. To be of direct use to a school's subsequent efforts to improve its performance this 'supporting evidence' would need to provide pointers to areas that required attention. These would almost certainly differ from school to school.

This long extract has been quoted to represent a clear and honest attempt to describe the kind of methodology which underlies the inspection process.

There are substantial problems with this methodology and they need to be recognized and researched if inspection is to continue to draw on the public purse. This is an issue pursued in Chapter 23. Here let us focus on the simple question of the proposed way of assessing the proportion of satisfied students, and summarize a few of the inadequacies of the proposed interview/inspection-type methodology as a way of assessing student satisfaction:

- It *costs* a great deal more than does the collection and analysis of questionnaires for all students.

- The *reliability* of the procedures would need studying and this would require excessive amounts of time. If different interviewers had different effects, establishing reliability would be well nigh impossible – it is indeed very difficult to standardize people and/or their behaviour.

- The *validity* of the procedure is questionable because of the influence of the powerful adult figure on the students' responses (known technically as the 'demand characteristics' of the situation), because of students' needs to give socially desirable responses and the differential impact that different interviewers might have ('interviewer effects').

- The *size of sample needed* would have to be estimated from the evidence of reliability and might well turn out to be too large to bear, given the associated expense.

All in all, a simple questionnaire seems to be the method of choice if you want to know what students think. Even with a well-developed and well-tested questionnaire there are precautions needed. The use of audio tapes to standardize instructions is desirable and, if students cannot read, audio tapes can be used to administer the questionnaire.

In the next chapter, the measurement of teaching and learning processes is considered.

Chapter 12

Measuring Processes

Once outcomes have been measured – such as students' satisfaction with their courses and their performance on those courses – the next question to arise is 'why are some courses getting better outcomes than others?' Is there anything to be learned from the teaching groups which are obtaining particularly good outcomes?

This is one of the main reasons for the inclusion of various process measures since the inception of the ALIS project. Guided partly by Carroll's model of school learning (Carroll, 1963), the early process variables concentrated on use of time: homework, timetabled time and students' reported levels of effort. Then, when attempting to assess teaching and learning processes in classrooms, a set of questions was added about the frequency with which various activities were undertaken. Some of these derived from a study of school effects in Scotland (Gray et al., 1983). A major concern in this chapter is to indicate the extent to which such data are reliable, valid and useful.

The focus adopted here is that of measuring teaching and learning processes, but clearly 'processes' could involve anything which happens in schools, or even anything that impacts on what happens, such as legislative effects.

Many researchers in school effectiveness have focused on processes taking place outside the classroom – management features, for example. However, Porter commented:

> The disagreements and confusion surrounding the concept of good
> teaching pale in comparison with the disagreements and ambiguities
> surrounding the concept of effective leadership.
>
> (Porter, 1991, p. 27)

There is also the curriculum to consider – who is offered what courses?

If *what* is taught is important but *how well* it is taught has only a trivial impact, then much of the work on 'school effectiveness' may be studying short-term effects which quickly disappear from the system and have no long-term consequences.

If such is the case, then school effectiveness researchers and those monitoring education should give greater consideration to measures of 'yield' in various areas of the curriculum rather than continuing with the current emphasis on relative performance or value added. (By 'yield' is meant the proportion of an age group that obtained some form of credit in an area, e.g. 'percent gaining credits in sciences' (Howson, 1987a; 1987b).)

In a meta-analysis (a quantitative summary of many research studies), Wang et al. (1993) concluded that learning is influenced by proximal rather than distal variables – it is what happens in classroom which affects outcomes, not the building or how it is run, who owns it etc. This is a rather sweeping generalization but it serves as some justification for the decision to concentrate on classroom processes.

Further support for that early decision can be found in Porter (1991). Although I disagree with the focus of the article on providing indicators 'to serve the information needs and interests of policy makers and the public' (Porter, 1991, p. 23) the following conclusions arrived at by Porter are welcome:

- School process indicators must be defined separately by subject matter area and level of schooling (p. 23).

- School process indicators must be capable of estimating change over time. This requires stability both in the indicators and in their technical definitions. A continuously changing indicator system would not be capable of tracking reform efforts (p. 24).

- Measures of indicators must be taken under standard conditions (p. 24).

- Indicators must be defined in ways that allow information to be collected, cleaned, analysed and reported in a timely fashion (p. 25).

However, Porter turns to *teachers' self-reports* for a source of evidence, although he recognizes that self-report for the published indicators he envisages may be a problem. Indeed, in the ALIS project the need for economy of effort as well as validity led to the collection of process data *directly from students*.

The extent to which anything can be learned from students' reports is considered in the remaining part of this chapter. Further discussion of the need for process variables can be found in Chapter 17.

LEARNING FROM PROCESS INDICATORS BASED ON STUDENTS' REPORTS OF CLASSROOM ACTIVITIES

This idea of learning from surveys is essentially seductive and dangerous, as explained in Chapters 2 and 3. As an example, take a teaching activity. We found that, for four years running, students who reported frequently being set essays in chemistry had both better achievement (higher residuals) and more positive attitudes. Were the essays *causing* these outcomes? Or were the essays a sign of a hard-working teacher, willing to mark essays every fortnight? Or did classes that were willing to work hard, and were committed to the course, write good essays and therefore have more essays assigned? If, on the other hand, the teacher set essays and they were all poor, perhaps it would not encourage frequent setting of essays.

In short, a cause–effect relationship between a process and an outcome cannot be deduced simply from the fact that they are associated, i.e. they seem to be correlated. Basically, the association should be seen as generating three hypotheses, each of which would need further investigation (Figure 12.1).

Thus, for the example above setting essays in chemistry, we might postulate the causal links shown in Figure 12.2 and described above: perhaps frequently set essays caused high achievement, or perhaps high achievement caused the frequent setting of essays, or perhaps a pattern of motivation caused both essay-setting and

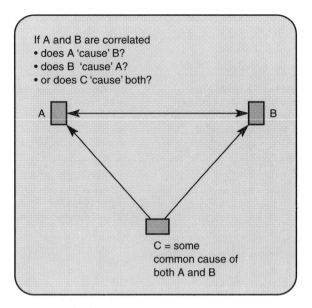

Figure 12.1 *Relationships between process and outcome variables: the problem of causality*

high achievement. The test would be to set essays frequently to some classes and to set them less frequently to others, i.e. an experiment.

The confusion between correlation and causation has led to many overstated research 'findings' in school effectiveness research. Thus lists of 'correlates of effective schools' have been produced as though they were blueprints and seeking to implement them would lead to an effective school.

Table 12.1 from Scheerens (1992) is typical. The comments are the author's, designed to point out that the list would be pretty useless even if the causal relationships happened to be true. (Another value of experimental research is that it

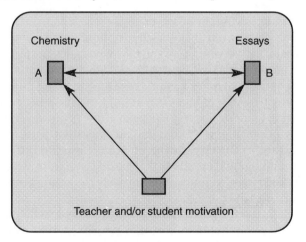

Figure 12.2 *Relationships between setting essays and performance in chemistry: the problem of causality*

forces the researcher to operationalize the intervention – to spell out exactly what has to be done to implement the 'treatment': the 'intervention'.)

Table 12:1 *Comments on the famous 'Correlates of effective schools'*

Correlates of effective schools (found in some but not all studies)	Comment. Even if the relationship was causal...
Emphasis on acquiring basic skills	Are basic skills and only basic skills the criterion for effectiveness?
Strong educational leadership	What balance exactly should there be between decisive and democratic (or dictatorial and dithering)? What does 'strong' mean? Good PR? Spins a good story? Or is this just another 'motivation to achieve'?
Frequent testing	How frequent? Are results fed back? Internal or external? Teach to the test and basic skills again?
High expectations of pupil attainment	The literature on expectations is a minefield and the concept is often used simply to blame teachers, without evidence
An orderly and secure environment	Is anyone campaigning for a disorderly and insecure environment?

WHICH 'PROCESSES' SHOULD BE MEASURED?

We return, however, to the point that if a monitoring system throws up very good results in some classes, the question will inevitably be 'what is going on in those classes?' We need some measures if only to generate hypotheses, being careful not to claim that associations demonstrate causation.

In the remainder of this chapter some evidence will be presented regarding the use of students' reports of the frequency of use of teaching and learning activities.

One problem in having an observer in the classroom is that the observer has an impact on the class, even if he or she is simply a grey, non-powerful, humble researcher. An alternative way to investigate what goes on in classrooms is to ask students. Their answers will not be totally reliable, but then no data are totally reliable. Their perceptions may be coloured by their own preferences (girls tend to report less frequent setting of essays than boys, perhaps because of boys' distaste for essays and girls liking of essays (Hodgson, 1994)). However, if students' reports were completely unreliable, we would find no consistent patterns from year to year, and that is contrary to the experience of ALIS. Described, then, in the next few paragraphs are findings which show that asking students what goes on in classrooms provides evidence which stands up well to scrutiny, even though it yields some surprises.

In Figure 12.3, the frequency with which various teaching and learning activities were reported by students in the ALIS project in 1993 is shown. The shaded area indicates the average frequencies reported across 43 A-level subjects. These showed peaks of highly frequent use for the following activities: 'exercises',

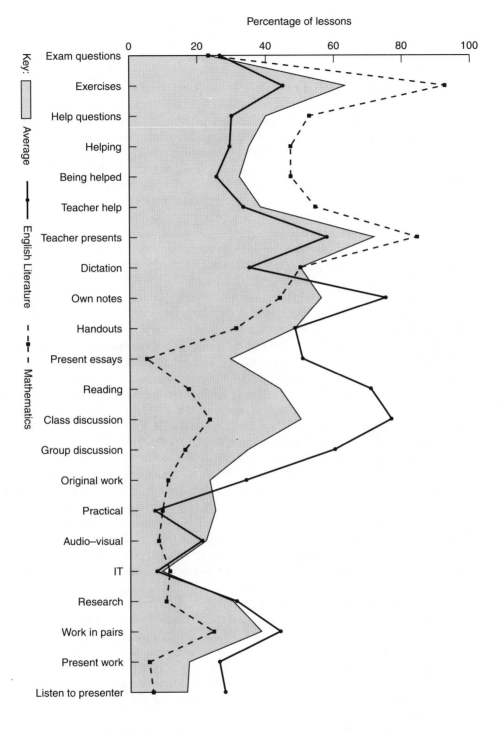

Figure 12.3 *The profile of perceived learning activities for Mathematics and English Literature*

'teacher presenting work to the class', 'making one's own notes', 'use of hand-outs' and 'class discussions'. Superimposed on this background data are the frequencies reported by students in A-level English literature and A-level mathematics. As might be expected, mathematics showed a peak approaching 'every lesson' on 'exercises'. 'Teacher presenting work to the class' was reported 'almost every lesson' on average. 'Preparation of essays' in mathematics was reported as 'never to almost never', which seemed reasonable. In English, the peaks were related to 'making one's own notes' and 'class discussion', with 'reading' and 'group discussions' also showing high reported frequencies of use.

There were significant differences between the profile of activities reported for English and that reported for mathematics. The mathematics groups reported a considerable amount of 'helping each other' and 'receiving help from each other', both of which might be considered 'active learning' in that this help would involve discussing the topic, problem-solving and using initiative. In English, there was a large amount of 'class discussion', 'group discussion' and the production of 'essays' and 'original work'. These latter activities might be also considered student centred and indicative of active learning.

In short, the two subjects – mathematics and English literature – both seemed to incorporate active learning but in different ways. Furthermore, it is a fairly reasonable hypothesis that *how you teach depends on what subject you teach*.

One way to check the validity of data is to see if expected differences actually are illustrated by the data. The course in A-level English *language* is often seen as providing more scope for teachers to employ active learning strategies than does the A-level in English *literature*. The English language A-level is seen as promoting active learning, the development of skills and a more student-centred approach. Does this expected difference show up in the data? In Figure 12.4 we see the activities profiles for English language and English literature. They were practically coincident. Was this indicative of a failure of the method of measuring? Surprising as this finding was, when a colleague active in researching English teaching was consulted, he was not surprised. He had videotaped English literature and English language lessons taught by the same teacher and found very similar methods of teaching being employed. Teachers were themselves almost unaware of this lack of difference but, when shown the videotapes, agreed that there was little distinction between the way English language was taught as opposed to English literature. The method of looking at activity profiles seemed to have been validated but the finding was surprising to all concerned.

A further test was undertaken, looking at a vocational course. The course in Business and Finance had been run under the conditions required by the Business and Technical Education Council (BTEC), which required project work and a certain level of resourcing for computing needs etc. Assessment had to include students' original work. In Figure 12.5 data from the BTEC course are plotted along with those from three A-level courses covering similar content: Accounting, Economics and Business Studies. In many of the activities shown, there was a considerable difference in the reported frequency of use of a particular activity. Perhaps one of the most surprising findings related to the use of information technology, where fewer than 15 per cent of BTEC students reported 'never or almost never' using information technology, whereas for the A-level courses the percentages

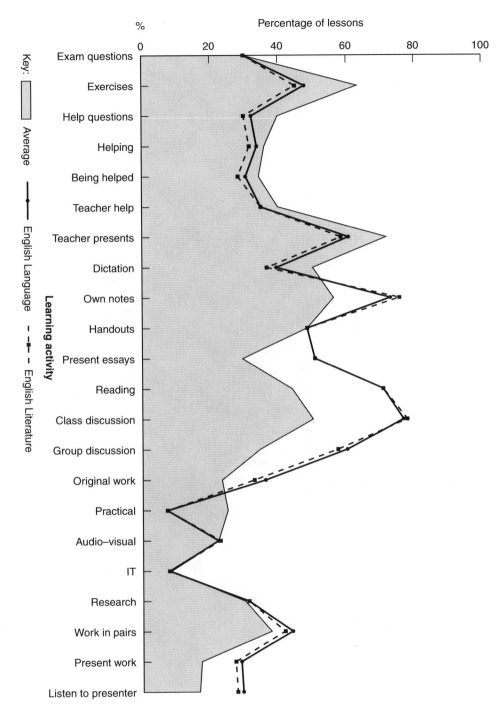

Figure 12.4 *The profile of perceived learning activities for English Language and English Literature*

Key:

▨ Average

━●━ English Language

━■━ English Literature

Learning activity

% Percentage of lessons

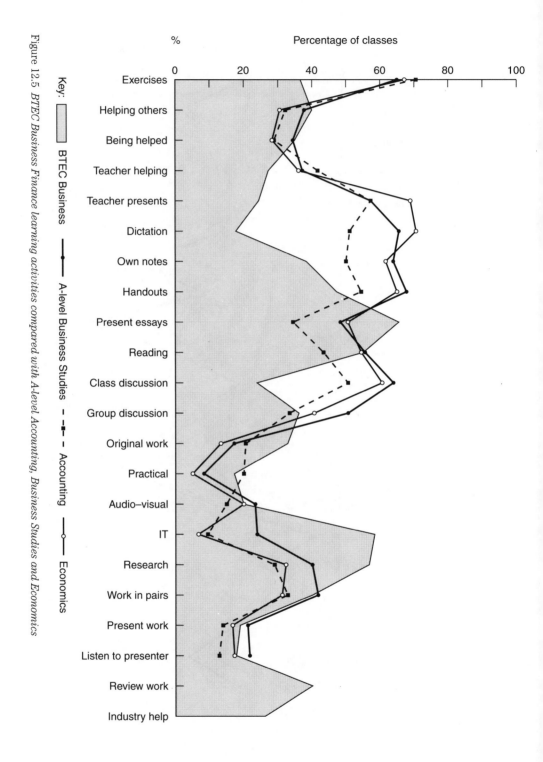

Figure 12.5 *BTEC Business Finance learning activities compared with A-level Accounting, Business Studies and Economics*

ranged from 60 per cent to almost 80 per cent. Was there a shortage of information technology available for A-level? Was there a lack of training of staff in the use of information technology for A-level? Was there a backwash effect from assessment which in the BTEC course demanded the use of information technology because of project work, whereas in the A-level course no such modernizing was demanded, so that pen and quill accounting could get you through an A-level course in Accounting? There was also evidence of greater amounts of interaction and active learning on the part of students on the BTEC courses. Fewer than 5 per cent reported 'never working in pairs' and 'never presenting their work to the class', whereas the percentages in the A-level subjects who reported never using these active learning methods averaged between 40 per cent and 50 per cent.

What we see here, then, is that the frequencies reported on questionnaires completed by students did seem to pick up differences of the kind that were expected.

Classroom processes can be economically monitored by questionnaires to students. Chapter 17 considers further the use of process data and the need to collect it.

Chapter 13

Assessing the Quality of Measurements

Measurements, of whatever kind, are of high quality if they can withstand various challenges; if they can withstand efforts to falsify them. This is Popper's falsifiability philosophy in action and is also standard procedure in the social sciences. (These measurement-testing challenges are less emphasized in the physical sciences, perhaps because the things measured are easier to operationalize and the variables of concern are more easily isolated.) The concepts apply to any kind of measurement, such as examinations, attitude questionnaires or judgements – whether made by school inspectors or skating judges. Note the term 'operationalize' – to put into operation. Measurements require a set of procedures. In social science these may include selecting of test items, setting up the conditions for the administration of the tests, and agreeing procedures for assigning marks. Standardization of the conditions under which data are collected may often be vital.

So what are the challenges that any measurement should be able to withstand with reasonable aplomb? The two fundamental ones are reliability and validity, both being sometimes subsumed under the general heading of generalizability.

How can reliability be challenged? If we can show that the measurement procedures, when applied to the same thing, yield inconsistent results, then there is a problem with the reliability of the measurement. This is a serious problem because we are left wondering which value, of the several inconsistent values, should be used.

How can validity be challenged? If we can show that the measurements are not measuring that which they purport to measure but are probably measuring something else, then there is a problem with validity. This too is serious. Measurements will not be useful if they are not measuring what we want them to measure.

Neither of these criteria should be considered pass/fail dichotomies. Measurements are more or less reliable and more or less valid, not absolutely reliable or absolutely valid. Furthermore, measurements in social science cannot be certified like a voltmeter. The conditions of use and the purposes enter into the question of reliability and validity.

For measurements to be considered to have 'quality' they must be adequate in terms of reliability and validity. Otherwise they are uninterpretable or misleading.

'Quality is suitability for purpose' – so we also have to ask if the measurements fail on other grounds, e.g. are they too costly or do they have bad consequences? The latter criterion has always been called 'reactivity'.

These procedures for assessing the quality of measurements will be applied in Chapter 23 to school inspections. In this chapter they are summarized in Figure 13.1. The figure summarizes what is often taught in a term's work on measurement

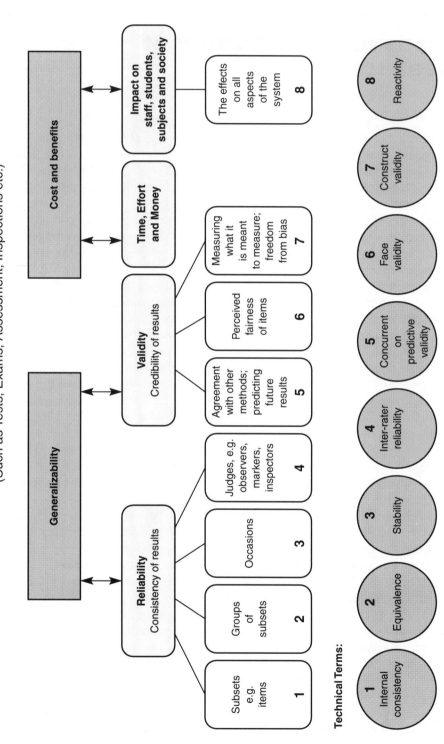

Figure 13.1 *Criteria for evaluating the quality of measurements*

in psychology or education, and details can be found in measurement textbooks from those disciplines. The ideas were applied to performance indicators by Fitz-Gibbon (1992).

QUALITY OF THE PROCEDURES USED BY EXAMINATION BOARDS

The high value we can place on the work of UK examination boards has been discussed elsewhere (Chapter 9 and Appendix 3). Here a criticism must be voiced.

Admirable as the examination boards are, they use a procedure which lacks face validity and is possibly biased. Because the marking of examinations which contain authentic tasks (such as essays) involves the use of judgement, the procedures that protect judges from bias should be used. First and foremost, it is necessary to keep the judge from knowing any information which is irrelevant and might bias his or her judgements. This is sometimes called keeping the judge or rater 'blind'. Bias could arise from reading essays from the following:

- James Edward Carrington – famous private school.
- Murlidhar Deshingkar – inner-city comprehensive school.
- Katie O'Flanagan – Catholic secondary school.

Bias could be based on:

- gender;
- ethnicity;
- social class;
- religion.

These divisions are known to carry prejudices and the only way to avoid any chance of bias is to have the names of the candidate and the school removed, i.e. to make the assessment procedure blind. The board in Northern Ireland is the only one which does this. Boards in Scotland do at least ensure that the scripts from a school do not all go to a single marker. Why don't examination boards follow this fair methodology? They say that numbers would get mixed up – but those selling

---

I have frequently marked papers from Eton . . . I have also marked papers from the inner city comprehensives to which Professor Fitz-Gibbon refers and am able to reassure him (sic) that the criteria applied . . . are identical.

. . . my mind set is such that I expect Eton's work to be good . . .
Eton's procedures, the meeting of deadlines and staff responses are without exception exactly what they should be.

I do know that the assessment was and is a good deal fairer than that of university and polytechnic degree examinations.

Figure 13.2 *Responses to letters in* The Times *about names on examination scripts*

raffle tickets manage. They say that handwriting counts for more – maybe, but handwriting is a little more under the candidate's control than gender, social class and ethnicity, and nor does religion seem much under control.

I wrote a letter to *The Times* on this topic. The printed replies are shown in Figure 13.2 and demonstrate eloquently the case for unconscious prejudices – and illustrate the insouciant presumptions of many who run the country. They argue only from an appeal to personal experience, not even asking for evidence. The examination system can only be completely fair if names are removed from scripts prior to marking.

We face a world in which jobs may be scarce, in which the work of schools may continue to be under public scrutiny and in which all societies contain groups between which hostilities can develop. The existence of the fairest possible system of assessing achievement must be a fundamental demand placed on education. Reliability, validity and the thoroughgoing fairness of blind external assessments and high-quality indicators are not optional extras but a foundation of fairness on which social justice and communal peace can be built.

PART FIVE

Basic Statistical Procedures for Monitoring

The popular expression 'The simpler the better' has its parallel in science in the principle called 'Occam's Razor': if there is a simple model it is to be preferred to a more complex model, other things being equal. Fortunately, the statistics needed for educational monitoring are frequently very simple and entirely accessible. This makes for an open and understood system which will be particularly valuable in the early years of monitoring.

In Chapter 14 simple procedures for value added analyses are described. In Chapter 15 a less simple analysis (relative ratings) is considered because it has the virtue of requiring only one set of examination results and is therefore very useful. It provides a sophisticated way of making adjustments for the differences in difficulty of various examinations even when you have no auxiliary measures. Finally, in Chapter 16 a problem called the ecological fallacy is illustrated because the belief that socio-economic status has strong effects on achievement is partly a result of this statistical problem.

Chapter 14

Value Added

'Value added' is the term which is now frequently applied to measures which are also called 'progress', 'effectiveness' or 'performance' (as in performance indicator). But all these terms are misleading, since they impose an interpretation on the measurement when the fact is that the interpretation is not clear. In the monitoring projects, we prefer to use the statistical term 'residual'. Although technical, it is precise and does not pre-empt or ignore the problem of interpretation. As was described in Chapter 2, a residual is what is left over after you have taken account of one or more relevant factors. However, since the term value added is now so widely used in the UK, it is used here, although with reservation.

The interest in value added has developed nationally in response to school performance tables published each year by the Department for Education and generally referred to as 'league tables'. The tables show, for each school, raw examination results summarized by such indicators as the percentage of students obtaining five subjects at grades A to C (five 'good passes') or the percentage attaining at least one pass. These tables enable newspapers to publish lists of schools rank-ordered by examination results from high to low. These are raw data (type 1 data). It seems likely that most people recognise that the examination results are affected by the kinds of students in the school as well as by the standards of teaching or the school's 'effectiveness'. The issues surrounding the publication of data, whether raw or value added, are taken up in Chapter 24.

In this chapter we will work from the assumption, widely accepted in research, that the data for each student must be the starting point of any analysis. We will therefore be referring always to value added for each student within a subject/department. Once we have value added measures (residuals) for each student, then these measures can easily be averaged to give departmental indicators of value added, and could be averaged to give 'whole school indicators' if this were sensible. The student data can also be averaged for each sex, for different ethnic groups or groups defined by which primary school was attended or by home-background characteristics. In other words, once you have good individual measures for each student, many further analyses become possible.

HOW TO CALCULATE VALUE ADDED

There are four commonly used ways to calculate the progress made by a pupil, the 'value added' as it is called now in the UK. These are:

- simple subtraction;
- simple regression;

- multiple regression;
- multi-level modelling regression.

Each of these methods will be briefly described and then applied, by way of illustration, to the value added between GCSE and A-level.

Simple subtraction

This method can only be used if the final outcome is measured in the same way as the input. If the number of GCSEs is the outcome measure, then a student who had four at the age of 16 and stayed on to take more GCSEs and make the total seven passes could obviously be said to have a value added of three passes (i.e. output - input = 3). However, this is just an item of raw data, and is difficult to interpret. Furthermore, it tends to be a gross, undifferentiated measure – passed or not – rather than a measure which includes an indicator of the quality of the pass. In the absence of comparisons with similar students in other schools, it says little about the quality of the education provided.

Rather than a simple 'gain score', i.e. 'output - input', it is more informative to look at 'output *taking account* of input'. This can be done by combining data from many similar schools or colleges, thus enabling fair comparisons to be made by the use of simple or multiple regression.

In simple regression, account is taken of just one feature which relates to the outcome measure. Multiple regression deals with more than one feature. (There are several types of regression which need not be of concern. Suffice it to say that the type referred to here is known as ordinary least squares regression.)

Simple regression analysis

The piece of information needed for value added for a student is the extent to which the student did better or worse than might reasonably be expected. What 'might reasonably be expected' is results in line with those from similar students in other schools. The students should be similar in terms of prior achievement, preferably, since this will be the best predictor of subsequent achievement. If prior achievement is not available, then some other cognitive measure must be used, such as a test of aptitude or developed abilities. There are good reasons for simply using prior achievement in the prediction of grades, the major one being that prior achievement is the best predictor of grades and therefore can provide the fairest comparisons.

But even after deciding to use prior achievement, there are questions remaining about the particular measure of prior achievement. Figure 14.1 gives an example of the type of decisions that had to be made in choosing how to use GCSE results to predict A-level results. It provides an illustration of an important point: before a value added system can be put into operation, some exploration and empirical evidence is needed. Value added systems need time to be developed in response to data.

The general approach is to:

1. collect data on prior achievement;
2. collect data on subsequent achievement by the same students;

The choice of predictors for A-level results

How shall we relate A-level results to GCSE results? Shall we use biology to predict biology, French to predict French? It is a matter of general principle that the longer any test, the more reliable and valid it is – but only providing that no bias enters into the measurements. Relating this general principle to GCSE scores would suggest taking into consideration all the students' GCSE scores, not just those in one particular subject. You might at first doubt that mathematics, for example, is a good predictor of A-level English but, in fact, that turns out to be the case. In fact, in some early data in the project, the major difference found between students who passed A-level English as opposed to failing it was their mathematics score at age 16. In fact, achievements in all subjects are positively correlated. Should we then sum up all the points that students have gained at GCSE? To do so would be to run the danger of introducing a bias in the data due to the fact that how many subjects a student takes at age 16 is not necessarily a reflection only of the student's aptitude. The number of subjects taken at age 16 reflects very much the policy of the school in which that student was studying. In some schools students take only five subjects and concentrate immediately on A-levels, in other schools students regularly take eight subjects, whilst in others they might be allowed to take ten or even more GCSE subjects. It will be a matter of looking at the data to see if this potential bias, this irrelevant factor, reduces the accuracy of the prediction made – if a total GCSE (sum of points) score is as good a predictor as the average GCSE score. The data show clearly that the average GCSE score is the better predictor.

Figure 14.1 *The choice of predictors for A-level results*

3. relate the two;

4. use the relationship to obtain, retrospectively, the achievement which might reasonably have been expected from each student, i.e. the 'predicted grade' for each student (which is roughly equivalent to the average grade achieved by similar students in the whole sample).

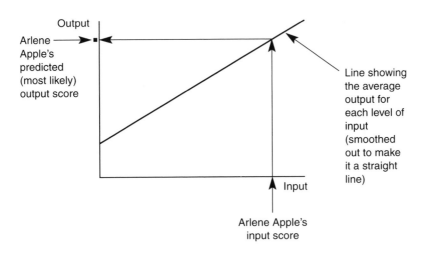

Figure 14.2 *What achievement is it reasonable to expect, i.e. how do we arrive, statistically, at a predicted grade?*

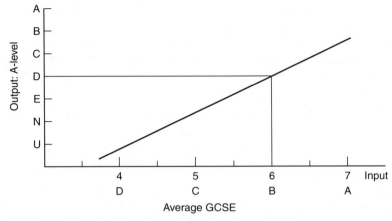

Figure 14.3 *Regression of mathematics at A-level on average GCSE score*

Figure 14.2 shows this procedure of finding a predicted grade if the relationship between the prior and subsequent achievement is represented by a line. The horizontal axis represents the input (which could be an aptitude test or a prior achievement measure) and the output is on the vertical axis (the examination result or final assessment result you are interested in). The critical information needed is the line which shows how to get the predicted grade. This line is called the regression line. How this line is arrived at in practice is not important here. It can be thought of, as on the diagram, as roughly representing the average output for students whose prior achievement places them at a particular position on the input axis. (In statistical packages it is simply the regression line and this is worked out for you. Statistical packages will also calculate and save the 'predicted' value for each student.)

It might be helpful to look at a concrete example. In the mathematics graph in Figure 14.3, a student entering with an average of grade B was likely to come out

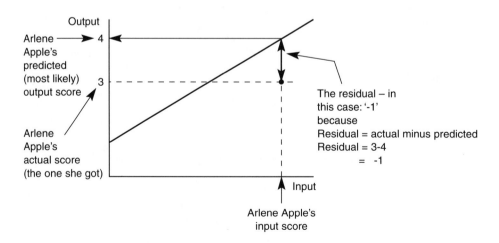

Figure 14.4 *A negative residual*

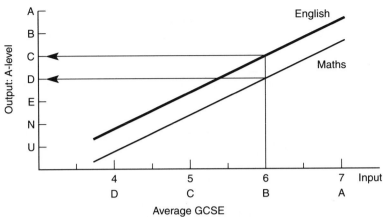

Figure 14.5 *Showing English apparently a grade 'easier' than Mathematics*

with a D grade on A-level mathematics. This D grade would be called the predicted grade for this student. Note that the prediction was made on the basis of two pieces of information:

- the particular student's average-GCSE score;
- the general pattern of the relationship between average GCSE scores and A-level scores in the data for that particular examination that year – as summarized in the 'regression' line, the line of best fit.

If a student gets a higher grade than predicted, and in fact about half of the students will get higher grades than predicted, it is said that the student has a 'positive residual'. The residual is defined as the difference between the grade the student actually got and the grade which would be predicted on the basis of the regression line. If a student achieves a grade lower than that predicted, then the student has a negative residual as shown in Figure 14.4.

It has been noted that the residuals are frequently referred to as value added measures, but it would clearly be more accurate to refer to them as *relative* value added. Every one of the students has obtained some kind of grade in an A-level examination which represents, surely, value added over their GCSE scores. However, some have obtained more value added than others as shown by their residuals. The habit has developed of referring to value added in terms of doing better than the competition; just keeping up with the average progress is called zero value added (a score equal to the predicted grade).

Now we have a way of making reasonable predictions, of setting reasonable expectations for performance.

We also have a way of comparing the apparent difficulty of various examinations. When we find, for example, that mathematics A-level yields grades on average a grade lower than English A-level, then we can see that that information needs to be taken into account in looking at the results in schools and colleges (Figure 14.5).

Using regression lines to examine students' results Many teachers find it helpful to plot their entire class's results on such a graph, and then consider who did particularly well in terms of progress (those highest above the line) and who were less successful for some reason or another (i.e. those below the line) (Figure 14.6). To give an example which was cited by the Audit Commission (1993), biology teachers at one school noticed that the negative residuals were often obtained by students who were not taking A-level chemistry. Perhaps there were concepts in biology which needed some concepts from chemistry. This is a good example of using data to generate hypotheses, to look for ways to improve – the essence of Deming's approach to quality (Chapter 6).

In general, it is of considerable interest in the department to see with which students there has been considerable success, and with which less success. The data can be looked at to find clues as to possible explanations. Sometimes no clues will become apparent; at other times, perhaps after a year or two, hunches (hypotheses) may arise.

Individual student residuals will always be fairly large in a system as complex as, and with the uncertainties of measurement that are inevitable in, education. The examinations themselves will yield scores that depend on how well the teacher spotted the items in that particular year, on how many students were ill, and on how many were in top form. Students can misread questions, and markers can mismark answers. Nobody pretends that grades are totally accurate. Their strength lies, first, in their being reasonably accurate – were they not, the correlations and consistencies we see would not occur – and second, in there being no fairer way to access achievement. (Further discussion of the value and fairness of examinations can be found in Chapter 8.)

Before moving on to consider further the ways in which to interpret the value added residuals, perhaps a word about the accuracy of the statistical model is

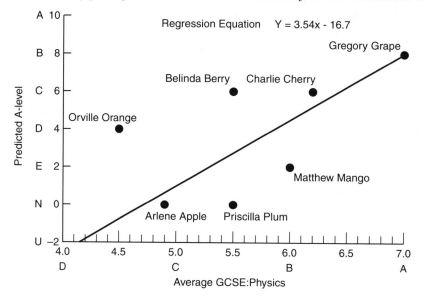

Figure 14.6 *Students' results placed on a regression graph*

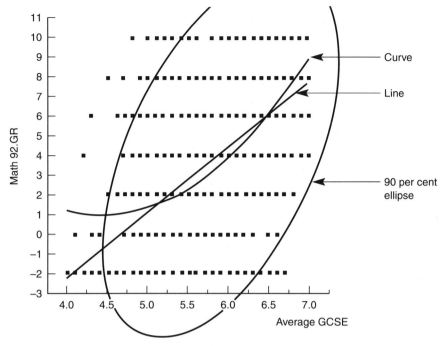

Figure 14.7 *Is the line appropriate or is a curve needed?*

needed. People generally ask two questions: is the straight line an adequate representation and is it reasonable to treat the scales as continuous when the grades are in fact discrete? The straight line is a very good approximation, although a line with a slight curve is a slight improvement. These statements are illustrated in Figure 14.7. The improvement is so slight that it seemed more important, as the system developed, to use the simplest model – the straight line. Given the uncertainties in any of the measures, the gain in accuracy obtained by using a curve was negligible in practical terms. As for the issue of discrete grades, there is a method called logistical regression which can be applied in place of the simple linear regression generally used. The residuals produced by this alternative method, which treats grades as indivisible quantities, correlate very highly indeed (better than 0.99) in our experience with the simpler residuals described here. In other words, the problem is not worth worrying about.

Once we have a residual for each student, we can sum up the residuals and take the average residual as an indicator for the department. *It is important to recognize that the average residual for a department will fluctuate from year to year*. The fluctuation will be quite substantial if the number of students is small. Teachers readily recognize this, particularly when the data have been first presented not as a simple statistic of effectiveness but in the form of a student-by-student list showing each student's actual grade, predicted grade and residual. The data from which the average residual was calculated have thus been seen and are available for alterations if reasonable. For example, it might arguably be sensible to exclude some of the results and recalculate the average residual. Results might be excluded for odd cases such as a student who joined the class only shortly before the examination, or a student who was absent for most of the year.

How should the fluctuations from year to year be interpreted?

Using value added information (Note: this section uses some terminology from statistics which will only be familiar to those who have completed a basic introduction to statistics. Most of it is still accessible to the general reader.)

Value added indicators for each department should simply be used for light monitoring – keeping an eye on the apparent effectiveness of each department. The fluctuation to be expected from year to year has been emphasized.

One way to keep an eye on the performance indicator provided by value added measures is to produce graphs like the one in Figure 14.8 based on real data. The darkest line joins up the residuals for each year, from 1989 to 1993. The symmetrical outer lines indicate the limits which are generally regarded as statistically acceptable. As long as the indicator (the average residual) stays within the limits it is not 'significantly' different from zero. The limits are set by the size of the sample (the number of students) and the variability. Large homogeneous samples will have narrow limits but limits will be broader if the number of students is smaller and/or the variations in the results are greater.

Since the variability does not alter very much in A-level grades, the limits largely reflect the sizes of the groups, i.e. the number of students. In the graph shown, the limits suggest that geography started out with a large number and obtained a significantly negative residual. Groups then became smaller in 1990 and 1991 and the residual improved. In 1992 and 1993 the groups were about the same size as in 1989 and the residual stayed within the acceptable limits (though only just in 1993).

Graphs of this kind are named 'Shewhart graphs' after the statistician who first used them, and they feature prominently in Deming's work on total quality management (e.g. Neave, 1990, p. 79; Deming, 1982, p. 337). They can now be found in many statistical packages. However, it is important that they are drawn on the basis of data from a large number of institutions, not using only the data in one institution. The graphs are also known as 'statistical process control' graphs, and governors who come from industry may recognize them.

The drawing of the confidence limits might seem to be critical to the interpretation of the graphs. The problem is that no one knows where these limits should be drawn. One approach used in industry is to draw the limits at *three* standard deviations either side of zero – quite wide so that almost all residuals will fall within the limits. If the limits are drawn at *two* standard deviations, then an indicator which falls outside the limits can be said to be 'significantly' different from prediction (i.e. from zero) in statistical terms using the 0.05 level, which is traditional. (The upper and lower confidence limits are just a simpler way of representing the more familiar 95 per cent confidence limits on the mean.)

The fact which cannot be escaped is that we will only learn how to interpret these indicators with experience – so schools and colleges participating in monitoring systems will probably know before statisticians. A school might recall, for example, that one year it had an exchange teacher who did not know the A-level system, and everyone felt the examination results suffered as a result. If this was 1991 in

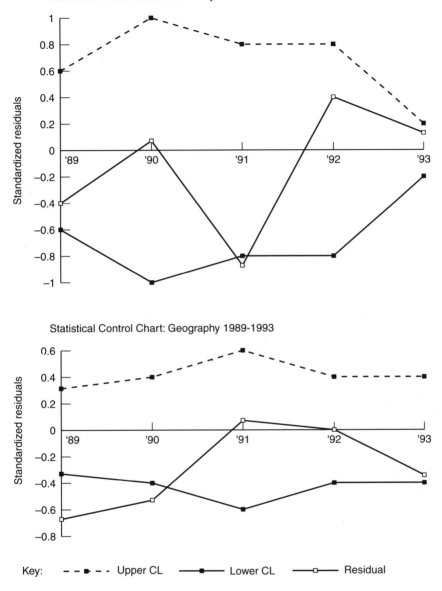

Figure 14.8 *Shewhart statistical process control charts showing the variation in average departmental residuals across four years for a chemistry department and a geography department*

Notes: CL = Confidence Limit
The residuals for the chemistry department went outside the confidence limits on one occasion, in 1991. Three out of the five residuals were positive on average. The residuals for the geography department were outside the limits for the first two years but then improved to be in line with expectations (i.e. close to zero) for the next two years. 1993 saw another low result, near to the confidence limit.

chemistry, then the observation seems to support the use of the confidence limits shown on the chart in Figure 14.8 – there was an explanation for the indicator going out of the 'acceptable' range between the confidence limits (sometimes called control limits). To aid this learning from experience we have suggested that schools keep a record for each year of the teachers, the textbooks, the examination board, the student list (or key characters from the list), the timetabling – whatever the school feels might vary from year to year and relate to the results.

Multiple regression

Research studies into school effectiveness often take into account many more factors than prior achievement. The data show that these other factors frequently add only a small amount to the accuracy of the prediction equations. Moreover, multiple regression is a maximizing procedure: even putting in random variables can improve prediction in a multiple regression equation because the mechanism for the selection of the variables to be included capitalizes on chance variation, the kind of chance correlations that arise in any body of data. It is, therefore, dangerous to include too many predictors in a regression equation. To see whether the process has produced reasonably stable equations, cross-validation – applying the regression line to a new set of data – is the ideal test.

However, one need not make *a priori* judgements in this matter, nor decide finally to use only simple regression or only one kind of multiple regression. In the ALIS project we produce a variety of tables of residuals based on both simple and multiple regression. Schools can see whether or not the indicators are much the same as different sets of variables are taken into account. For 1994 data, the extent to which the various indicators were correlated can be seen from Table 14.1. On the whole, the answer obtained from taking account of prior achievement is sufficient. Other factors add little, in general. Further discussion concerning what should be taken into account can be found in Chapter 18. The factor most frequently thought of is home background, and Chapter 16 needs to be read as background for the discussion in Chapter 18.

Multilevel modelling

Anyone following the research on school effectiveness will have encountered the term 'multilevel modelling'. The term refers to the analysis of data which is structured at several levels, such as:

- the level of the *student*, e.g. the individual student's home background as indexed, for example, by the occupational status of the student's parent(s);
- the level of the *classroom*, e.g. the proportion of the class with parents in 'professional' occupations;
- the level of the *department*, e.g. average occupational status of the parents of the students in a whole department;
- the level of the *school*, e.g. average status of all the parents of the school;
- the level of the *LEA*, e.g. average occupational status in the LEA.

There may be effects on achievement due to home background of the individual

Table 14.1 *Correlations of residuals from regressions using average GCSE score (AV.GCSE) as the only predictor with the residuals arising from regressions including other variables*

	AV.GCSE plus SEX	AV.GCSE plus ITDA	AV.GCSE, plus ITDA, SEX and Parent's occupational status	ITDA alone
Chemistry	0.98	0.93	0.91	0.80
Geography	0.99	0.90	0.81	0.66
French	0.99	0.93	0.90	0.82
Mathematics	0.99	0.95	0.93	0.90

Notes: Data from ALIS 1994.
ITDA = International Test of Developed Abilities (a measure of aptitude)

student but there may also be effects due to the composition of the class – the proportion of professional parents, for example. Hence there is a need for measurement at several levels and for statistical models which allow these multiple levels to be properly taken into account. Multilevel modelling allows for 'compositional effects'.

Another reason for using multilevel modelling is to take into account that students in one classroom will tend to have results more alike than if they had been the same students but scattered into different classrooms, i.e. to take account of grouping effects if there are any (known statistically as intraclass correlation).

When these various levels are taken into account, the random variation which can be expected (and which is often called the 'error' or 'confidence') can be more accurately assessed.

There were three main centres in the early development of multilevel modelling software. These comprised Stephen Raudenbush and Antony Bryk in Chicago, Murray Aitken and Nick Longford, formerly at the University of Lancaster, and Harvey Goldstein and John Rasbash at the University of London Institute of Education. The decision by Goldstein to design the multilevel modelling software for use on IBM PC compatibles and to imbed it in Nanostat, a statistical package similar to MINITAB, was probably a wise one, making the package very attractive to users. This work has been supported by the Economic and Social Research Council and regular workshops are held in London. People attend these workshops not simply from education but from economics, medicine, social policy, etc. The existence of these cutting-edge statistical procedures arising out of work in educational research can be expected to raise the status of educational research and attract competent researchers into the discipline.

Multilevel modelling is a tool which has long been needed. There was a time when there was no solution to the problem that if you were working with the classroom as a unit of treatment you were nevertheless encouraged to use the student as the unit of analysis. The need to separate out effects at the various levels and model the data, taking account of the non-random assignment of students and classes, and of the dependence induced by this structure in the data, was acute.

In explaining achievement it may be necessary to consider the effects on the individual students of their own abilities, aptitudes, interests, gender, home background, etc., and also the cumulative effect of the peer group on the student. The nature of the peer group could be partially represented by the average socio-economic status in the class, the general ability level of the students with whom they are taught, the proportion of girls in the class, etc. Multilevel modelling allows for this multilevel structure in the data to be taken into account. It makes allowance for the fact that students in one class are not a random selection of students but are likely to be more like each other than students in different classes in different schools – both because they came to be in one class and because they will be taught as a group and share many interactions as a group which can be expected to give them some common characteristics. Because the data are more realistically modelled, multilevel modelling should be able to detect differences which other methods of analysis overlook. However, this is a research function more than a monitoring function.

In the ALIS project, the data analysis has relied on simple regression procedures rather than using multilevel models. One reason for this was that the multilevel models were not available when the project started, and it is important in a monitoring system to keep the methodology constant over several years so that the data are comparable from year to year. However, even though we will incorporate residuals based on multilevel modelling, as just one more indicator, there are important reasons for not using multilevel modelling exclusively.

Multilevel modelling is a form of inferential statistics. It regards data as samples – the data from a classroom, for example, are regarded as being a random representative sample of the classroom's data, not *all the data* ('the population'). In monitoring, however, we have always aimed to collect *all the data*, not just a sample. We aim for 100 per cent coverage because teachers teach every student and want data on every student. Also, classes are small, so that a 20 per cent sample, for example, might be no more than six students – too small to provide a reliable indicator. For these reasons and for simplicity, so that the system is transparent, we have provided simple value added measures based on simple regression.

A final and important reason for caution in using multilevel modelling is that it will take the residuals of the kind we provide (ordinary least squares residuals based on the whole sample) and make adjustments to the data to 'shrink' the estimates towards the average. The smaller the classroom group the more extreme its average residual, for example, the more the average residual is shrunk towards zero. An inner-city school obtaining a good result will find it shrunk towards zero on the statistical basis that such a result is unreliable. In statistical terms this is very reasonable and is sometimes referred to as a Bayesian approach. Each individual classroom is evaluated in the context of the whole data. Whilst this shrinkage seems justifiable in statistical terms, for samples, if a teacher had obtained a very good set of results with a small group of students, he or she would certainly not want the results to be adjusted downwards.

In short, the argument can certainly be made that the results we look at in an indicator system every year are, for that year, not a sample of the data but a description of the population of data for the participating schools and colleges. Adjusting the data is not entirely defensible when you view the data as population data and when the feedback is based on close to 100 per cent of results. This argument was accepted by Raudenbush:

> Although the shrinkage estimates are generally more accurate than estimates without shrinkage . . . they are also biased. Suppose a school serving students with low prior achievement were especially effective. In this case, it would have its score 'pulled' toward the expected value of schools with children having low prior achievement. That is, it would have its effectiveness score 'pulled' downward, in the 'socially' expected direction, demonstrating a kind of statistical self-fulfilling prophecy! (On the other hand a similar school doing very badly would be pulled up.)
>
> (Quoted in Fitz-Gibbon (1991b), p. 79)

However, the use of multilevel modelling for research purposes and to draw more general conclusions from the data is certainly wise. Furthermore, we need experience of feedback which includes multilevel modelling residuals. It could be that they provide a better guide to what is happening in the school. Even so, the issue only becomes important in small samples. As the size of a department approaches 30 or more, the difference between a multilevel residual and the simple regression one will be negligible.

Another reason for not using multilevel modelling, and a very important one, is that it removes the procedures from the understanding of most of the participants in the information system. Whilst many people are willing to use inflation rates, exchange rates, cost of living indices, etc. without knowing the origins of these indicators and without thoroughly understanding them, these are general national indicators which are not tied to the performance of small groups of individuals in the way that educational indicators for schools and classrooms are. Given the sensitivity of the educational indicators which are, in the ALIS project, produced at the level of the school or classroom, which is sometimes even at the level of the individual teacher, it is very important that the profession can see exactly how the indicators are calculated and be able to make adjustments if justified.

This principle of the transparency of the procedures is particularly important in the early years of an information system, before it has built up a measure of trust and experience among its users. We have also seen that politicians are extremely wary about moving away from simple raw data, fearful lest statisticians remove the evidence that parents and politicians need in order to judge the schools. By making the data accessible to every numerically competent teacher in every school, the accusation of tampering with the data can be deflected.

SUMMARY

Value added measures can be calculated using relatively straightforward and well-understood statistical procedures. The calculation of error terms is easily done and the entire process is within the competence of most mathematics departments using statistical packages. What a department needs is the regression equation based on a sufficiently large and representative sample from schools around the country. The understanding and interpretation of such value added measures is accessible to staff in any discipline, particularly when presented in the form of graphical representations.

Value added measures require measurements at two points in time: a baseline (at time 1) against which an outcome (at time 2) can be assessed to yield a 'value added' index. Such a statistic is better referred to by its technical name: a residual. It represents what is left over after the baseline measures have been taken into account. The residual is clearly not a pure measure of 'effectiveness' or 'value added' but contains error and all the aspects which affect the outcome but have not been measured. The use of multiple regression to take more factors into account was described. It should be noted that social science rarely finds that more than about half the variation in outcomes can be accounted for by prior measures.

The average residual for a department is a fair performance indicator, representing the type 3 data described in Chapter 2. Ways to track these indicators over time using Shewhart graphs (statistical process control graphs) were described.

Reasons for the use of multilevel modelling in research, more than in monitoring systems, were suggested.

Chapter 15

Relative Ratings: Assessing the Relative Performance of Departments Using a Single Set of Examination Data

'One in 87 is a twin' sighed the gentleman from the Scottish Examinations Board (SEB): 'Same surname, same date of birth'. He was discussing just one of the many sources of problems attendant on the matching of examination results from two occasions. In Scotland, almost all students take 'Standard Grade' at about 16 and many take Highers a year later. Moreover, these external examinations are administered by the same board, the SEB. Yet value added measures were not produced because of the problems in matching the data, student by student. Instead, the SEB, with ideas from Kelly and Lawley (Kelly, 1976), created an alternative procedure for giving schools feedback on the performance of their departments: relative ratings.

Relative ratings require more explanation than regression approaches, because the technique is not as simple and has not been widely used.

School departments often compare the results obtained by their students with the results the same students obtain in other examinations taken at the same time. Thus performance in, say, mathematics might be compared with the performance of the same students in English, physics etc. When the concurrent set of examination scores is the only information available, such comparisons are the only method of evaluating the results for a department. A problem with this approach is that examination subjects are actually of differing difficulties. Thus grades in English will tend to be higher than those in mathematics. This pattern appears in results from practically all examination boards in England, Ireland, Wales and Scotland. The differing difficulties of the subjects present a complication in evaluating examination scores using a concurrent set of results.

Following a paper by Kelly (1976), which contained an appendix by Lawley, a method was developed of re-scaling the examination results to obtain 'correction factors'. A set of Kelly–Lawley correction factors for 1993 GCSE results is shown in Table 15.1.

For each subject the correction factor tells you how much to add on to get the grade that would have been awarded had the examinations all been of equivalent difficulty. Thus from Table 15.1 we see that chemistry was most difficult, because the amount to be added was largest (0.7), whereas English language was slightly easy, and should have 0.5 subtracted from the grade.

Table 15.1 *Kelly/Lawley correction factors for GCSEs; YELLIS 1993 sample of 70 schools*

Alphabetically by subject			Rank ordered from easy to difficult		
Subject	no. of students	Correction*	Subject	no. of students	Correction*
Biology	866	0.16	E. language	8135	−0.53
Business	1745	0.15	E. literature	6555	−0.41
Chemistry	961	0.73	CDT	3443	−0.30
CDT	3443	−0.30	Information tech.	1142	−0.16
Economics	120	−0.06	H. Economics	1373	−0.09
E. language	8135	−0.53	Economics	120	−0.06
E. literature	6555	−0.41	Religious Studies	1218	0.04
French	3647	0.47	History	3011	0.08
Geography	3125	0.28	Business	1745	0.15
German	1040	0.34	Biology	866	0.16
History	3011	0.08	Double science	4285	0.21
H. Economics	1373	−0.09	Single science	2067	0.24
Information tech.	1142	−0.16	Geography	3125	0.28
Mathematics	7330	0.33	Mathematics	7330	0.33
Physics	888	0.33	Physics	888	0.33
Religious studies	1218	0.04	Spanish	356	0.34
Single science	2067	0.24	German	1040	0.34
Double science	4285	0.21	French	3647	0.47
Spanish	356	0.34	Chemistry	961	0.73

*Add the correction factor to the grade (expressed on the scale A = 7, B = 6 etc.).
Thus French was about 1 grade harder than English language, since you subtract 0.53 from English language and add 0.47 to French.

ASSESSING SUBJECT DIFFICULTY USING THE RELATIVE RATINGS APPROACH

But how was the difficulty of subjects assessed? For value added approaches difficulty can be determined by looking at the expected grades for the same level of academic aptitude (as indexed by prior achievement, for example) but what can be done when all that is available is one set of examination results, i.e. there is no measure of academic aptitude? The approach is to consider each student's average grade to be an indicator of the student's academic aptitude. But the average grade would depend upon the difficulty of the subjects taken – so we have a circular problem. We want a measure of difficulty but we need to adjust the grades on the basis of difficulty in order to get it.

The solution to such a circular problem is iteration, applied to a matrix equation, a procedure best left to mathematicians. Suffice it to say that the difficulties are estimated by assuming a general ability factor, which is derived solely from the examination grades.

The procedure provides correction terms for each of the subjects on the basis of all the results available for that year. These correction terms can be seen as indicating which subjects were difficult and which easy (or, equivalently, which were graded severely and which were graded leniently).

There is another step in the calculation of 'relative ratings' as used in Scotland. The same iterative procedure which produces the correction terms on the basis of all the available data is then used within each school to compare the results achieved in the various subjects. Within the school a school-based correction term is arrived at which indicates the apparent difficulty of the subject in that school. The 'relative rating' which in Scotland is reported back to schools in tables each year is the difference between the two correction terms.

If, for example, mathematics in a school appears difficult, but no more difficult than it appears in the whole sample, then its relative rating would be close to zero. If, on the other hand, mathematics in a school appeared easy, whereas in the whole sample it appeared difficult, the school would have a large positive relative rating, indicating that for some reason it was getting better than expected results in mathematics *compared to the results the same students were obtaining in other subjects in school when these subjects had been equated for difficulty.*

Whenever there are no good prior predictors which would allow a value added approach to be used, relative ratings can be particularly valuable.

In summary, relative ratings answer the question of effectiveness in one subject by considering how well students at a particular school did in their other subjects. 'How well did students in my particular subject achieve in comparison with how well they did in other subjects, taught by my colleagues?' The question is answered after taking account of subject difficulties found in the large body of data from hundreds of other schools.

EVALUATION OF RELATIVE RATINGS

Relative ratings were a useful solution to the problem of the lack of use of examination data as information to schools on the performance of their departments.

There appear to be three major problems with relative ratings but none is serious enough to undermine their careful use. First is the issue of the behavioural impact. The statistical comparison made in relative ratings is between departments within the same school. Relative ratings for departments sum to zero within a school, either as weighted or unweighted elements depending upon the computation chosen. This summing to zero implies that a department only does well in comparison with others in the school who do less well. One department's good news is another's bad news. The behavioural implications of this indicator are unfortunate: departments within a school are in competition. To some extent this cannot be avoided when the only source of information about students' abilities is their concurrent performance.

To get a high relative rating, the physics teacher, for example, should hope students do poorly in mathematics. If the physics department is obtaining particularly good results it is likely to make the mathematics department look bad and vice versa. This element of competition between departments could be unfortunate in its impact on teachers in a school. One would hope to find, for example, mathematics and physics teachers to some extent planning collaboratively and working to make each subject support the other subject. The existence of a relative rating indicator system could possibly put such collaboration in jeopardy and increase the competition to have students spend more of their time on one teacher's subject than on other subjects. However, with careful use by school management, this element of competition could presumably be avoided.

A second problem is the lack of transparency of the system. It would be difficult for a school to check the computation of the relative ratings whereas, with the regression approach, most teachers can learn to check the data and thoroughly understand the origins of the indicators.

The third problem is very much related to the second. Further investigations of effectiveness are not facilitated by relative ratings. The computing procedures are not routinely available and the data which emerge are not student-level data. In a regression situation, in contrast, staff can use the regression equations to investigate the residuals for each student and use this information for investigations of their own practices. In other words, regression approaches provide the schools with tools for further enquiry whereas relative ratings present a figure which is a department-level aggregate whose provenance may remain a mystery.

With regard to the competition between departments, it could be argued that it is a valid reflection of reality: if students do well in one subject it is at the expense of another subject. They are spending time on one subject which could have been spent on the other. The argument could be that such trade-offs are real. But is there any evidence for this? Do students respond to some departments very positively, and do more homework and therefore achieve more highly, at the expense of their work in other departments? If there were evidence for this trade-off effect then relative ratings might be seen as reflecting a reality of academic work: a zero sum game attributable possibly to the scarce resource of time. Time devoted to one subject means less time devoted to another subject. Less time means lower achievements and we have a trade-off situation.

However, despite a superficial plausibility there is little evidence for such effects. Certainly at A-level time spent on homework does not turn out to be a powerful predictor at all (Fitz-Gibbon, 1984a; Tymms and Fitz-Gibbon, 1992a) and large amounts of time can even be associated with poorer results. Furthermore, if there were this trade-off effect, it should show in the student-level residuals: positive residuals in one subject should be associated with negative residuals in a neglected subject. However, student-level residuals generally correlate positively: students doing better than expected in one subject were doing better than expected in their other subjects (Fitz-Gibbon, 1991a, Table A7). This is not to say that there is not any validity in the concept of trade-offs. The positive residuals could come from errors in the measure of their prior achievement. Nevertheless, there is not strong enough evidence for trade-offs to make the concept of relative ratings summing to zero an entirely comfortable one.

Using the value added approach, it is possible for all departments in a school to have positive indicators, whereas this would never be the case for relative ratings. On the other hand, a school could not get all negative indicators on relative ratings and this is perhaps only fair. A whole school effect in which all departments were negative would suggest that some important factors had not been taken into account. Considerations such as this suggest that running the value added and relative rating systems in tandem is probably desirable, as long as possible negative impacts are avoided.

A procedure which would bring the advantages of regression analysis into the relative ratings procedure is to obtain the Kelly–Lawley correction factors and apply them to students' grades. These grades will then have been adjusted for subject difficulties and can be compared directly. To produce departmental indicators, regression lines can be developed which use each student's average adjusted grade as the input and the subject grade as the output. This will produce student-by-student residuals which can be used in further investigations. However, this procedure (Lawley adjustments followed by ordinary least squares regression) cannot circumvent the fact that a student's performance will be judged against his or her performance in other subjects.

COMPARING EXAMINATION DIFFICULTIES USING REGRESSION AND RELATIVE RATINGS

The difficulties of examinations can be looked at using regression equations and noting where the regression line intersects with the vertical axis – a figure often produced by statistical packages and called 'the intercept'. Since relative rating also produces measures of difficulty, it is of interest to compare the two.

Table 15.2 *The relative difficulty of the 1989 A-level examinations*

Subject	Intercept from OLS regression[a]	Difficulty rank OLS	Difficulty rank Lawley[b]	Lawley correction factors	N
Physics	–9.8	1	1	0.58	867
French	–8.5	2	5	0.12	371
Chemistry	–8.0	3	4	0.28	853
Mathematics	–7.4	4	3	0.31	1,357
Gen. Studies	–7.4	5	2	0.36	1,087
Biology	–6.7	6	9	–0.54	667
Geography	–6.0	7	8	–0.66	630
Economics	–5.7	8	7	–0.18	606
English	–4.6	9	10	–0.75	831
History	–4.1	10	6	–0.15	674

Table reproduced from Fitz-Gibbon (1991a). OLS = Ordinary Least Squares
[a] Based on 1989 ALIS data.
[b] Based on the subset of candidates taking two or more subjects.

Applying both regression and relative ratings to A-level results yielded the data shown in Table 15.2 for a set of A-level results. The two methods yielded very similar rank orders of difficulty. Physics showed up as the most difficult, with a correction factor of 0.58 in relative ratings, indicating the need to *add* something to the grade to make physics of equivalent difficulty to the other subjects. At the other end of the scale, for the Lawley correction factors for 1989 A-level examinations, English appeared easiest; there would be a need to *subtract* a correction factor to make English of equivalent difficulty to other subjects.

It is quite reasonable that these two measures of difficulty should not be in total agreement, since they used different kinds of information: the regression equations used prior achievement as an indicator of general ability from which A-level grades could be predicted, and the Lawley correction factors used concurrent achievement as the information which indicated the general level of aptitude of the student.

A report prepared for the School Curriculum and Assessment Authority using 1993 data showed difficulties of subjects very similar to those based on the 1989 A-levels (Fitz-Gibbon and Vincent, 1994). The sciences, foreign languages and

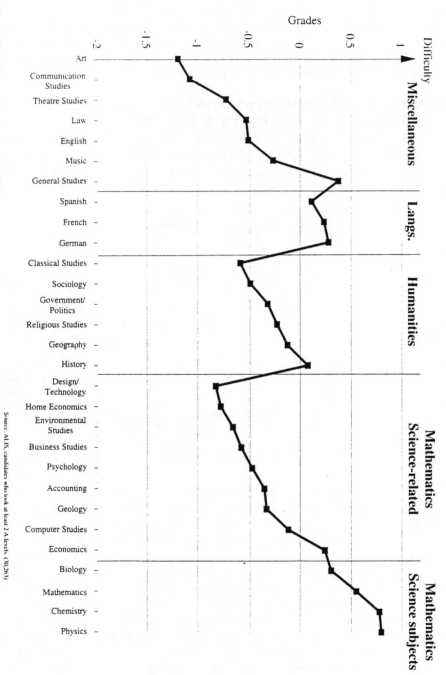

Figure 15.1 *Correction factors for 1993*

Source: ALIS, candidates who took at least 2 A levels. (10,261)

138

general studies were difficult subjects, and the easiest subjects were art, communication studies, theatre studies, and design and technology.

There may be objections raised to saying that a subject is difficult or easy. Can we compare, say, English with mathematics at A-level? We can in terms of the grades achieved, because grades are to some extent regarded as common currency. University places are often offered initially on the basis of points achieved at A-level. Employers may look at grades, considering each A-level subject to be of equivalent difficulty. The accountancy firm Robson Rhodes is selling schools pseudo value added analyses on the assumption that all subjects at A-level are expected to yield the same grades for the same student. Teachers of the difficult subjects are sometimes criticized for their 'poor' examination results. League tables are based on grades without any distinction being drawn between one subject and another. Whether or not it makes sense to compare grades across subjects, it is common practice to do so.

Clearly we can talk about subjects being 'difficult' or, what is equivalent, 'severely graded' without attempting to evaluate their intrinsic difficulty in some absolute fashion. Whether you look at

- the grades achieved by the same student taking pairs of subjects;
- the value added as measured against prior achievement;
- the value added as measured against an aptitude test;
- relative ratings;

the answers are much the same: mathematics, science and foreign languages are 'difficult' or 'severely graded'.

Why should this happen? The explanation needs to be a very general one, for these differences are seen in almost every examining system. The simplest explanation would seem to be that this difficulty level has crept into the system because more able students opt for mathematics, science and foreign languages in greater numbers than less able students. The students opting for these 'difficult' subjects are more able not only mathematically but also on verbal tests (Fitz-Gibbon, 1992; Fitz-Gibbon and Vincent, 1994). With a higher-ability intake, the examiners' reference points are set higher. In the UK, indeed, there was the expectation for A-levels that certain percentages would achieve each grade. For example, 30 per cent were to fail A-levels (it is extraordinary that two years on an optional course of exceptionally high levels of achievement internationally, by the most able students, was rewarded with 30 per cent failure). Failing 30 per cent of a highly able group results in a more difficult grading standard than failing 30 per cent of a less able group.

This use of value added and relative ratings to identify subject difficulties illustrates nicely the value of a monitoring system: the data arising from the monitoring help everyone to understand more accurately how the system is working. Without this understanding, teachers are appraised incorrectly, students get false feedback and employers and admissions officers may come to less effective and less fair decisions. False information hurts people.

COMPARISON OF INDICATORS PRODUCED BY RELATIVE RATINGS AND REGRESSION

Relative ratings generally correlate strongly with value added measures for departments. For example, in the work referred to in Table 15.2, the correlations in art, biology, chemistry, English, French, geography, history, mathematics, physics and secretarial studies were not less than 0.64 and seven correlations were above 0.70. These kinds of strong positive correlations have also been found in the YELLIS project. They indicate that departments doing well relative to others in the school (i.e. on relative ratings) tended to be the ones doing well relative to departments in other schools containing similar students (regression residuals).

SUMMARY

If there is no baseline, such as prior achievement or an ability measure, then comparisons between departments' examination results can be made by the procedure developed in Scotland and called relative ratings. These relative ratings represent a more sophisticated approach to the widely used procedure of comparing examination results with those in other departments.

The question answered by value added approaches is different from that answered by relative ratings. For examination results in a subject, the question answered by value added is: *How do the results in my department compare with the results in other schools with similar students enrolled for the subject?* or briefly *how does my department compare with similar departments?*

The question answered by relative ratings is: *Taking into account the difficulty of the subject as seen in the entire sample, and the students who entered for the subject in my school, how good were the results compared with those of other departments in the school?*

Chapter 16

Aggregation and Segregation: What Does 'Means on Means' Mean?

What is the relationship between home background and achievement? Many people believe it to be very strong indeed. In the UK at the present this belief has been bolstered by graphs showing strong relationships between the percentage of pupils receiving free school meals (a proxy for measures of poverty or disadvantage) and each school's average performance at GCSE.

This kind of 'contextualization' has been widely promoted for two reasons: it seems only fair and the analysis can be easily done because the data are often available.

This chapter will show the dangers in this approach to providing fair performance indicators for schools. The problem is not confined to the UK, as can be seen in the following quotation from the US. The suggestion that home background is not strongly related to achievement is likely to produce angry responses but, despite deep-seated and idealistic beliefs, we must look at the data, get the statistics correct and then think carefully about the interpretation.

> Despite evidence to the contrary, the belief that socio-economic status is a major factor in determining educational and occupational outcomes remains a widely held misperception. What is the source of the misperceptions? In exploring this issue White (1982) found that correlation between SES and academic achievement typically ranged from .10 to .80. The higher correlations were usually found when data were aggregated. When school or school district was used as the unit of analysis, correlations averaged .73. The average correlation dropped to .22 when the individual student was considered as the unit of analysis. The higher correlations found with aggregated data resulted from the mathematical properties of the statistical formulas. As the homogeneity of the unit of analysis decreased, the resulting correlation increased, leading researchers to draw inappropriate conclusions on the relationship of interest.
>
> (Barrett and Depinet, 1991, p. 1012)

The 'mathematical properties of the statistical formulas' makes this concept sound less accessible than it really is. The situation is easily understood with diagrams. The point is that, even though there is only a very weak correlation between home background and achievement, the correlation between the two can look very strong *if there is a tendency for segregation by home background*, i.e. if there are schools in wealthy areas and other schools in poorer areas – as is usually the case in most cities. This is shown first in Figure 16.1,

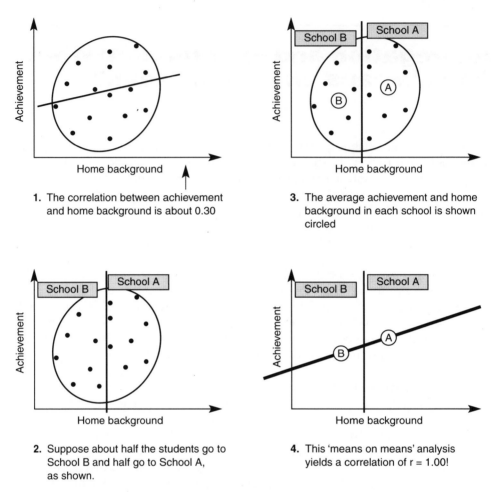

1. The correlation between achievement and home background is about 0.30

3. The average achievement and home background in each school is shown circled

2. Suppose about half the students go to School B and half go to School A, as shown.

4. This 'means on means' analysis yields a correlation of r = 1.00!

Figure 16.1 *The effect of segregation on aggregated statistics*

taking the most extreme situation of complete segregation by socio-economic status (SES) and then by the use of real data.

In summary, if there is clustering of high SES homes and low SES homes in different areas, then when the aggregated data for home background and examination results for each school are analysed (the 'means on means' graph shown in Figure 16.1), the correlation looks very strong even though the true, underlying correlation is very weak. This is an example of a problem which has long been recognized and is called the 'ecological fallacy'. Indeed, the relationship within aggregation units could even contradict the relationship between units using aggregated data (Figure 16.2). The correlation within each school is negative but between schools it is positive.

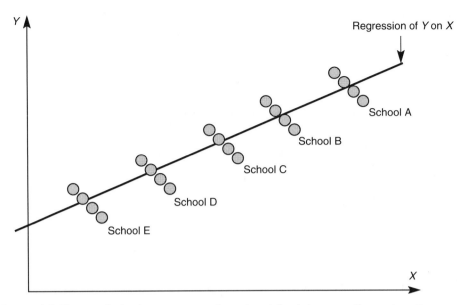

Figure 16.2 *The correlation between means (aggregated data) does not tell you about the correlation between the variables*

AN EXAMPLE USING REAL DATA

The way in which the amount of segregation influences the correlations found in aggregate data can be easily illustrated with real data.

Any measures of achievement and home background could be used. For achievement we use GCSE grades in mathematics, a subject taken by many students and one that correlates strongly with many other subjects. For a measure of home background which should correlate as highly as possible with achievement, we use a 'cultural capital' scale. Cultural capital is based on the support in the home for education as measured by responses students make to a series of questions concerning such matters as the number of books in the home, the use of dictionaries, visits to museums, and parents asking about homework.

First there are data for an entire sample of 695 students, and then for the same students in their individual schools. After showing that the student-level data for the whole sample and within each school give correlations of only about 0.30 between achievement and the home-background measure, the means on means analysis is presented to show that it tells you more about segregation than about the underlying correlation.

The influence of segregation on the correlation found in aggregate data

Figure 16.3 shows the relationship between students' GCSE mathematics scores and the home-background measures called cultural capital. The graph is based on data from 695 pupils, as indicated in the accompanying table. You cannot see the 695 dots in the scatter graph because many of the dots are 'on top of each other', particularly in the central areas of the graph and along the regression line. The

143

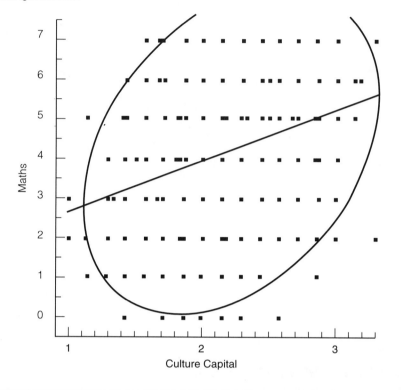

Variable	Mean	SD	Correlation	Prob.	Number
Cult. cap.	2.21	0.449	0.34	0.0000	695
Maths	4.21	1.680			

Figure 16.3 *Data on achievement related to home background (specifically mathematics at GCSE and 'cultural capital' in the home)*

ellipse is drawn to indicate the region where most of the scores fall. (It is a 95 per cent confidence ellipse, for those who are concerned.)

The correlation between these measures of home background and achieve-.ment, was 0.34, i.e. moderate to weak, and typical of the relationships generally found, here and in other countries. You can see that if you were trying to predict a student's GCSE score in mathematics, knowing a student's cultural capital score would be of little use. The (95 per cent confidence) ellipse is fat.

How does the relationship look within each school? Notice from Figure 16.3 that there were 695 cases. In Figure 16.4 is a scatter plot from one school with just 123 cases. As you would expect, the same relationship is there, with a similar correlation, this time 0.39. Looking *within* four other schools, the other correlations were 0.37, 0.38, 0.34 and 0.32 as shown by the tables in Figure 16.4.

When the 695 students were randomly assigned into five groups (representing 'schools'), the correlation found from a means on means analysis was essentially zero.

When the same students were clustered in five completely segregated

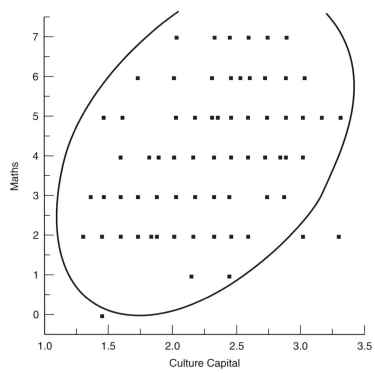

Variable	Mean	SD	Correlation	*p* value	Number
Cult. cap.	2.22	0.47	0.39	0.0000	123
Maths	4.13	1.68			

Variable	Mean	SD	Correlation	*p* value	Number
Cult. cap.	2.21	0.46	0.37	0.0000	144
Maths	4.08	1.55			

Variable	Mean	SD	Correlation	*p* value	Number
Cult. cap.	2.22	0.43	0.38	0.0000	146
Maths	4.08	1.71			

Variable	Mean	SD	Correlation	*p* value	Number
Cult. cap.	2.18	0.43	0.34	0.0000	154
Maths	4.26	1.63			

Variable	Mean	SD	Correlation	*p* value	Number
Cult. cap.	2.21	0.45	0.22	0.0112	128
Maths	4.04	1.79			

Figure 16.4 *Data on achievement related to home background within each of five schools*

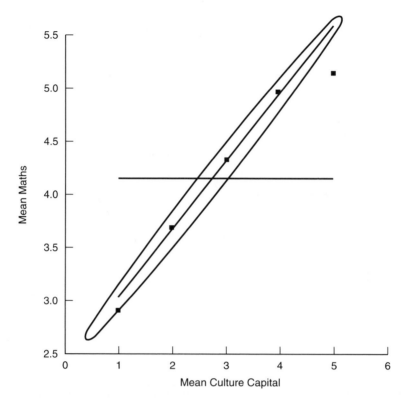

Figure 16.5 *Means on means in totally segregated conditions (r=0.99)*

'schools' the correlation for means on means analysis was almost perfect (0.99) (Figure 16.5).

When students were grouped into their actual schools the means on means correlation was 0.83 (Figure 16.6).

To summarize, aggregated statistics do not tell you what you think they tell you. If the grades of individual students are summarized in some way (e.g. 'average number of passes per student') making a single statistic for the school, then the school is being used as the unit of aggregation. It is now widely recognized that student-level data, rather than aggregate data, must be collected and the analysis must link pupil-at-time-1 to the same student at time 2. The most frequently cited article on this topic is by Aitkin and Longford (1986). They advocated the more sophisticated modelling of levels using 'multilevel modelling'. Woodhouse and Goldstein (1988) and Woodhouse (1990) show the unfortunate effects of using LEA-level data in regression: different analyses, each based on equally plausible assumptions, give very different results. Here the effect of the amount of segregation on the extent of the correlation has been shown.

The use of data aggregated to the school level has produced a misleading impression that SES is as strong a predictor of achievement as prior achievement. *The predictive validity of variables should only be compared when they are each measured at the student level.* At this level the correlation of SES measures with performance is generally about 0.3, whereas correlations with

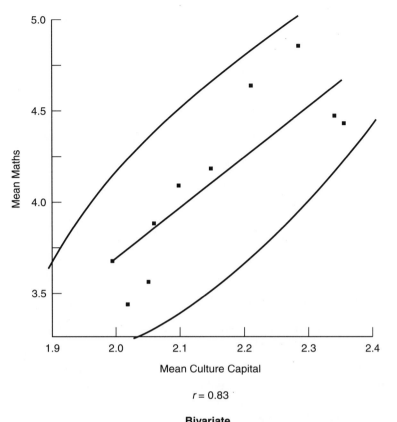

$r = 0.83$

	Mean	**SD**	**Bivariate**		
Variable	**Mean**	**SD**	**Correlation**	**_p_ value**	**Number**
Mean (Cult.cap)	2.17	0.125	0.83	0.0000	939
Mean (Maths)	4.15	0.427			

Figure 16.6 *Means on means when grouping was in actual schools: shows a fair amount of segregation*

prior achievement are often about 0.6 or higher. In terms of variance 'accounted for', these figures mean that only 9 per cent is related to SES, as opposed to 36 per cent for measures of prior achievement.

The scatterplot shown in Figure 16.3 can be contrasted with data in Figure 16.8 from the same sample showing the correlation with a prior aptitude measure (the YELLIS assessment tests for which the correlation was 0.75).

CONCLUSIONS

In this chapter, so far, a statistical concept which is not widely appreciated has been illustrated. Now, in summarizing and drawing conclusions, further considerations are brought into the argument, making, I believe, an overwhelmingly strong case for not using aggregated data or home-background data in monitoring school performance.

147

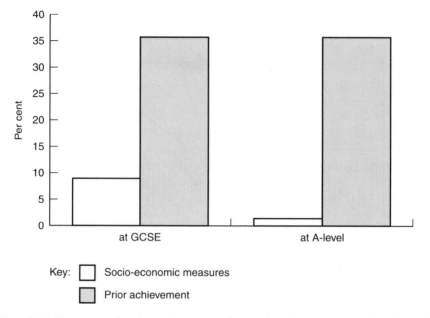

Figure 16.7 *Percentage of variance in examination results which can be predicted from SES measures and from prior achievement measures*

- Aggregate data are not adequate, and cannot be used in a fair system because the extent to which data will be adjusted will be dependent on the level of segregation. In an area where schools have a social mix in intake, there will be no adjustments made if SES data is all that is being taken into account. Prior achievement measures are essential. No value added measure without prior achievement is fair to teachers and schools.

- Adjusting for SES can be seen as a denigration and excuse. Teachers do not wish to be told to expect less because a student is from a low-SES family. Teachers take students as they find them and the expectations for student achievement can only be based on past achievement, not home circumstances.

- Promoting the idea of vast differences in the achievement of different SES groups is very much a two edged sword for schools. Seeing a graph showing an apparently strong association will result in parents feeling they have to struggle to get their children into high-SES schools. This panic is simply not consistent with the data and could ultimately lead further towards 'sink' schools and two-tier systems. It might give the school an excuse regarding raw examination grades, but it also makes people believe that good results cannot come out of inner-city schools, which is not true.

Nevertheless, when all is said and done, many still feel that the home-background issue is critical. It could be that the effects are to be seen in a few dramatic instances which do not affect general figures. Averages are not everything.

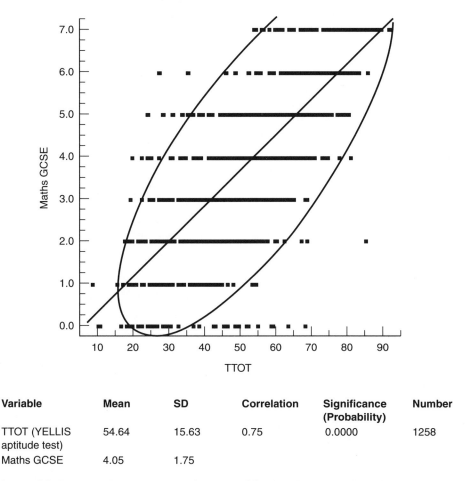

Figure 16.8 *Data on achievement related to a test of developed aptitudes (specifically mathematics at GCSE and the YELLIS test.)*

Variable	Mean	SD	Correlation	Significance (Probability)	Number
TTOT (YELLIS aptitude test)	54.64	15.63	0.75	0.0000	1258
Maths GCSE	4.05	1.75			

Furthermore, we need to continue to monitor for possible SES effects. Some methods of assessment, for example, may emphasize the influence of the home – e.g. project work, in which the high cultural capital home will assist the student more. Correlations with home background and participation rates may increase if there are financial incentives or penalties associated with continuing in education.

It is also argued that the effects of home background are already present in the measures of prior achievement or developed abilities. This must certainly be true, and we might expect that the effect of the home would be considerable if we went back to primary schools. This will become more apparent as value added measures are collected and analysed in primary schools. However, the evidence so far is that, in predicting who will learn to read, home-background measures do not come close to simple measures of skills. The nature–nurture debate will doubtless continue, but in the meantime, to be as fair as possible to everyone, we need value added measures based on cognitive measures and student-level data, not on home-background measures and not on aggregated data.

PART SIX

The Design of Performance Indicator Systems

The world is too complicated for words.

(Tymms, in press)

In this section the design of performance indicator systems is considered. A performance indicator can be defined as 'an item of information collected at regular intervals to track the performance of a system', (Fitz-Gibbon, 1990, p. 1). If you are setting out to create a system of performance indicators, or are evaluating systems that have been proposed or tried, then these design chapters could be helpful. The monitoring of schools and colleges will involve *more than* the creation of indicator systems – but anyone seriously trying to keep track of their own work, let alone that of others, will not want *less than* a good system of quantitative performance indicators.

A very simple rationale is presented in Chapter 17. It can be applied to any system (a business, industry, school, etc.) for which indicators are needed. It simply serves to draw attention to the main types of indicators and to the need to conceive of indicators as elements in a model of the system.

It should come as no surprise that indicator systems are difficult to set up. The universities and funding councils are struggling, as are the police and the health service. *Basically, a good deal has to be known about how the system works before adequate performance indicators can be designed.* Then ensue issues of how to use the indicators, their likely impact, and their acceptability. *Indicators need researching.*

In Chapter 18 criteria are offered against which performance indicators can be evaluated.

In Chapter 19 the debate widens to consider the broader features of the educational system and some of the developments that must follow as second- and third-generation indicator systems get off the ground.

Chapter 17

A General Rationale for the Design of Performance Indicator Systems

> Problems don't have solutions, they only have outcomes.
>
> (Connor Cruise O'Brian)

It is outcomes that we must track. There is a great danger of regarding any piece of information that drops off a computer as a potential performance indicator. Such an approach leads to drowning in data and an unproductive accumulation of uninterpreted information. The Coopers & Lybrand report on local management of schools (Coopers & Lybrand, 1988), for example, presented a list of indicators in the Appendix. Some were rather odd, such as 'staff demeanour'.

Not every whimsical or even non-whimsical idea can be included in a monitoring system. There needs to be a rationale behind the selection of variables to include. Before data are collected, tentative models of how the system is working must be adopted and the variables selected should be elements of that model and meet the criteria of quality indicated in Figure 13.1.

One approach to creating a monitoring system is described below.

For visualizers,[1] there is a diagram (Figure 17.1), emphasizing that we should start with the outputs, then consider the relevant inputs, and then add on the processes as an optional extra which is probably important.

For verbalizers, here is the same ground covered in words. First, consider 'What are the outcomes that we care about enough to bother measuring them?' Having identified those, the next step is to consider what features of the situation are out of the control of the school and yet will affect those outcomes. These are 'contextual' factors and should be taken into account. In other words, this is the search for 'covariates', i.e. things which co-vary with the outcome. The influence

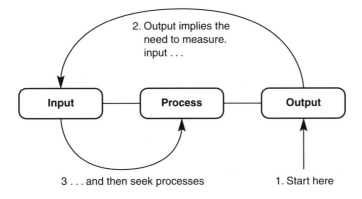

Figure 17.1 *First discussions for any indicator system*

Outcomes: Things we care about enough to measure
- ?
- ?
- ?

Covariates: may be needed to make fair comparisons
- ?
- ?
- ?

Process variables: to search for improvements
- ?
- ?
- ?

Figure 17.2 *A rationale for any indicator system*

of these must be measured in order that the outcome can be fairly interpreted in a comparative fashion across schools. For example, if achievement is an outcome, prior achievements will have to be taken into account if comparisons between schools are to be fair.

The rationale could stop there, with measurement of outcomes adjusted for important intakes to give fair comparisons across schools. This would provide a framework for quality assurance and constitute an information system.

The obvious question that would then arise, however, is what is going on in those schools in which students' attitudes are very positive and/or their achievements are exceptional? Mere curiosity would urge the collection of process indicators, but there are other reasons, to be discussed shortly.

In summary, a rationale can be approached by stepping through Figure 17.1, which can be used for initial planning of what to measure – the choice of variables to study.

There are likely to be problems at every turn. One of the first problems relates to the units which are to be monitored: every department or the whole school? The decision needs to be informed by data. If schools were uniformly effective, then there might be no need to monitor departments. The choice of outcomes involves consideration of values, of legal requirements, of control and accountability. What goals *are* or *should be* adopted? Who decides? Covariates cannot be chosen until it is known what variables *do* co-vary with outcomes. And the selection of processes to be considered has to be seen as an ongoing quest to be based on yearly revisions to the monitoring system. *In short, monitoring systems need to be researched.* They cannot emerge fully fledged to everyone's satisfaction. In education, years of research in school effectiveness are available. The health service, police and universities may not have such an adequate basis and may also face more complicated problems regarding goal definition and acceptance.

OUTCOMES AND OUTPUTS

These words are sometimes given different meanings. It may be worth mentioning that the term 'output' has been used to represent the immediate fruit of endeavours (e.g. examination results as an output from a course) and the term 'outcome' has been used for the longer-term consequences, such as subsequent employment. Which meanings of words will catch on is unpredictable, but the concept of short-term and long-term outcomes is important. The long-term outcomes are often the more important but in the absence of good evidence about influences across the long term, it is difficult to use long-term outcomes as goals or performance indicators. The best evidence of causal relationships over long periods of time would come from controlled experiments.

THE IMPORTANCE OF INCLUDING PROCESS INDICATORS

It is important that some process indicators are provided in a quality assurance/performance indicator system for several reasons:

- *Since a major purpose is to seek ways to improve, process indicators can sometimes provide clues, and serve as the basis for grounded hypotheses, i.e. hypotheses grounded in data.*
  Process indicators can be correlated with the residuals, to see which processes appear to predict good progress. The findings from these investigations will not be definitive, since *correlation is not causation*, and we are dealing with a highly complex system, full of self-adjusting mechanisms which hide cause and effect. For example, the processes might present teachers' responses to the students rather than chosen inputs. 'Setting essays frequently' may be an indicator of a hard-working teacher rather than a cause of achievement. Or it may be an indicator of an able class of students who produce essays which are easy to mark – hence more essays are set. Or just setting essays may not be enough – it may be the type of teaching which led to essays and which cannot easily be copied by others even if it were discovered. In short, processes might not be causes, and even if some were, they might not be exportable. Nevertheless, as a source of hypotheses grounded in data they might be valuable.

  Even if no valuable relationships are found between achievement and classroom processes, the indicators will have been useful in showing how complex is the teaching–learning situation, and how difficult it is to predict from observation of the process what the outcome will be. If processes do not correlate with achievement, this suggests that teaching and learning activities can be chosen for reasons of enjoyment or their supposed long-term impact. Indeed, in the context of an established curriculum, it may be that all teachers cover the content and learning is robust, but attitudes may differ according to the teaching. Much research remains to be undertaken on these issues.

- Ethos: *the inclusion of process indicators focuses attention on what can be done, what we can learn, rather than on who can be blamed.* The presence of process indicators makes the system

155

interesting for development – such indicators promote the spirit of investigation. They provide a good basis for discussion and the sharing of expertise and ideas – if old-fashioned sharing still occurs among schools pushed into competition with each other.

- *Process indicators can deflect the winds of fashion and thus defend teachers.* Winds of fashion do indeed sweep across advisors, inspectors, consultants and researchers. Thus the teaching profession might be subjected first to a decade of 'work in groups' advocacy followed by a contradictory decade of 'direct whole class instruction' advocacy: project work for a decade and then the three 'R's. As we gain experience from monitoring systems of exactly how difficult it is to relate process to outcome, we can at least use this information to moderate those who see a panacea in some particular item in teachers' diverse repertoires of skills.

AVOIDING PROCESS INDICATORS WHEN OUTCOMES WOULD BE MORE VALID

In working with sixth form colleges the following issue arose. It had been suggested, largely as a result of working with BTEC, that a question about course induction procedures should be asked. How satisfactory did students find the induction for the course? But some courses did not have a defined period or activity called 'induction'. It was felt that an outcome indicator was more relevant than a response about the process. Consequently, students were asked about the major desired outcome of 'induction' or its equivalent: did they know what to expect on the course?

In short, *how* a college ensured that students knew what to expect might be left to the college. *That* students knew could be monitored.

This represents a small example of the general strategy: 'by their fruits shall ye know them' – *go for the outcomes*.

COMPLIANCE INDICATORS AS OPPOSED TO PERFORMANCE INDICATORS

One exception to the general admonition to 'go for the outcomes' arises in a situation in which there are processes that are universally acknowledged to be desirable. When such is the case, these processes should be designated compliance indicators (Richards, 1988). For example, health and safety rules are a matter for compliance. Freedom from being subjected to prejudiced comments could be a recognized right, and compliance with this might be required. Freedom from physical punishment is now a matter of compliance on the part of schools, not of their own judgement. These kinds of compliance indicators should represent the justified application of democratic decisions informed by research. Some such indicators may be properly assessed by inspection.

RATIONALE REVISITED

For performance indicators in schooling, the question marks in Figure 17.2 are often completed with variables which fall into the categories indicated in Figure 17.3.

Outcomes: things we care about enough to measure
- Achievement
- Attitudes to the school
- Attitudes to school subjects
- Aspirations
- Quality of life indicators

Covariates: may be needed to make fair comparisons
- Prior achievement
- Prior attitudes
- Gender
- Ethnicity
- ESL status
- SES

Process variables: to search for improvement
- Alterable classroom variables
- Alterable school management variables

Notes: ESL = English as a second language
SES = socio-economic status. Please see Chapter 16 for a discussion of the role of
socio-economic status as a covariate for educational achievement.

Figure 17.3 *Outcomes: things we care enough about to measure*

The term 'alterable' was adopted by Bloom in an important article on 'alterable variables' (Bloom, 1979). The point is to study things which can be changed, like setting essays, and not things which probably cannot, like charisma. By measuring teaching and learning processes for each department (such as the amount of homework given, the extent to which past examination papers are practised, the amount of individual help given and the use of computers in the course) we can at least demonstrate the complexity of the system.

COVARIATES

One of the more difficult parts of designing a performance indicator system is the choice of covariates – what inputs are 'relevant' to the outputs, and what must be taken into account? – not to mention how these should be measured. We have seen examples in Figure 17.3 and in Chapter 7, and more will be considered in Chapter 19.

NOTES

1 One of the most consistently found differences in learning styles is between visualizers (imagers) and verbalizers.

Chapter 18

The Development and Use of Indicator Systems[1]

When Lord Keynes was an adviser to the Chancellor of the Exchequer a colleague came up to him, waved a piece of paper under his nose.

'Keynes', he said 'this year you gave the Chancellor completely different advice on this issue to that which you gave him last year. How do you explain this?'

Keynes said 'When I am wrong I change my mind. What do you do?'

(Heiser, 1993, p. 20)

The systems we set up must be regarded as drafts, current versions, to be developed in the framework of dialogues with, in particular, those running the system and those receiving the services – staff, students, parents, school governing boards, councillors etc. Additionally, links need to develop with other influential parts of the web of interlocking systems: funding agencies, examining bodies, political parties, the press, professional organizations like the Institute of Physics, and technical parts of the systems like computer infrastructures, such as management information systems and the people developing these. In the UK there is a system which ensures the rapid spread of news in the educational world in the form of a newspaper which is very widely read indeed: the *Times Educational Supplement*.

Contacts with these networks of information – keeping an ear to the ground – can be expected to be a source of effectiveness, since complex organizations constantly need to adapt to their environment and that means having good information to guide the adaptation in a world of increasing complexity.

In work with ALIS and YELLIS, for example, steering groups with the Association of Principals of Sixth Form Colleges (APVIC), the National Association of Head Teachers (NAHT), the Secondary Heads Association (SHA) and representatives of numerous LEAs have been vital and highly valued by those of us developing the indicator systems.

SETTING CRITERIA FOR INDICATORS

As the constant interchange of information leads to the development of possible performance indicators, these will need to be evaluated. Some of this evaluation cannot be pre-specified – it will be specific to the situation. It is possible, however, to suggest some widely applicable criteria, derived from a logical analysis of the features that a performance indicator must have *if it is to be valuable as feedback*.

Logical analysis

If performance indicators are going to provide feedback which can be used to assure and develop quality, then the indicators must provide *valid information* relevant to accepted goals – things people care about enough to bother measuring. If the performance indicators are to be *relevant to* actions that can be taken or avoided, it follows that the indicators must contain information about units of the system which are managed, i.e. the units within which changes can be made if necessary, the units for which some defined persons feel responsible. Then, if change is to occur, those persons must accept the indicators and not reject them. (Of course, indicators can be externally imposed, but then a variety of distortions occur in the system; Smith (1995).) To make acceptance likely, the indicators need to be *clearly fair* as well as informative, and to be *worth the time and money* involved in acquiring them (though this assessment is a very difficult one to make). And then if improvements occur, the indicators must be able to reflect the improvements – without this property there is no reinforcing feedback. In short, indicators must reflect the performance of the system's management units, sensitively and validly. This analysis is summarized by adopting the following criteria.

Criterion 1. Indicators refer to valued outcomes of managed units Values are often taken for granted, and rightly so. Long discussions of theoretical value systems can be unproductive. However, it cannot be denied that the goals for which people work reflect their values, consciously or unconsciously. If organizations have 'values', then it will not be difficult to agree on goals – the outcomes cared about enough to bother measuring them.

But outcomes cannot be defined without consideration as to what part of each organization is responsible for particular outcomes. A start has to be made by choosing a unit for which indicators will be prepared. In schools the department is a clear choice. In universities the choice is not so clear – for research purposes research groups are the managed units. Depending upon the structure of the organization and the extent of consensus, this first criterion may be profoundly difficult (e.g. if monitoring the police or the health service) or fairly straightforward.

Criterion 2. Indicators relate to outcomes over which staff can reasonably be expected to have an influence In other words, there is no accountability without causality. Indicators about aspects which schools feel unable to alter are not fair, though they may be of interest. Whether or not an item of information is regarded as a performance indicator or simply as information will depend upon the climate and the reporting requirements in the system. Delinquency rates, for example, fall into the 'are schools responsible?' category. Until it is demonstrable that schools can influence delinquency rates it hardly seems fair to judge schools on their delinquency rates. Showing causal relationships is no trivial matter and requires, ideally, gold standard, experimental data (Chapter 2).

These first two criteria relate to the first actions which must be taken in designing an indicator system: establishing agreement on goals for units which are managed. The next three criteria concern the extent to which indicators will be informative.

Criterion 3. The major outcome indicators are contextualized Outcome indicators must be contextualized, as otherwise they are neither fair nor interpretable.

This criterion almost always requires that indicators are part of a larger system to provide the variables which enable fair comparisons to be made. For example, a single institution cannot evaluate most indicators – evaluation usually has to be relative. In the simple case of examination results, the difficulties of each subject must be known, not just the relationship within one school between prior achievement and examination outcome.

Continuing the logical analysis that indicators should provide information about units which are managed, it is also obvious that the management units must receive the information if they are to be affected by it. Hence:

Criterion 4. Indicators are fed back to the units of management – and they get back There may be some differentiation in the amount of information fed back to various levels of the system, but in general the smallest unit of management should receive all the data relevant to that unit. Indicators which simply remain 'on file' are failing to have their informative value used.

On the other hand, at the level of an LEA, some extract of the available indicators may be all that is needed on a routine basis. The director of Strathclyde referred to 'scanning indicators', a senior adviser in Fife referred to 'warning lights' and Goldstein *et al.* (1992) refer to a 'screening device', all echoing the view of 'fire-fighting' expressed by Gene Glass (Chapter 5). There is a growing consensus that whilst not everything is captured by indicators, there must be indicators available to be scanned regularly.

Feeding indicators back to the smallest units of management not only informs those who need to know but also promotes the spirit of open information systems and collaborative enquiry, the kind of climate in which information is used most constructively. Systems which appear secretive and beyond scrutiny could produce subverting activities.

Indicators might be produced and reported but if they are rejected there will not be any chance to see if they have any beneficial impact. How can it be made most likely that indicators will be initially accepted by the management units? This is a complex question about various levels of openness to new practices and information but there are a few important features.

Criterion 5. Indicators are, and are perceived to be, fair In the first instance the indicators themselves need face validity – they should relate to goals on which there is widespread agreement. Examination results are generally accepted, as is some measure of client satisfaction.

Fairness is not always easy to design and the solution often has to be the use of multiple indicators. For example, it would not be fair to expect lower achievement from students from poor as opposed to rich homes. Given the same aptitudes, the students should be expected to achieve the same levels of learning. Fairness to students and all SES groups (i.e. what is sometimes called 'equity' in the literature) demands that home factors are ignored in the production of indicators. Yet if home-background factors cannot be overcome by schooling, then it is only fair to schools to take this into account. We can only know the extent to which home factors have an influence beyond the reach of the school by monitoring. Research may help a little but it is always going out of date. New situations may make it irrelevant. Monitoring with indicators which take account of home factors, and other indicators which do not, will allow us to check each unit on its 'equity', year by year. For example, increasing reliance on project work could increase the influence of home background on achievement.

Indicators need to be understood and/or taken on trust, or taken on trial. In the long term, understanding would seem to be best and this leads to the next two criteria.

Criterion 6. Indicators are accessible If not understood, indicators may be rejected or ignored. It must be recognized that many staff will have had little to do with anything remotely mathematical for many years. Their feelings of being competent and on top of their subject – feelings engendered by teaching – may be threatened when they have to confront tables of numbers and explanations in terms of graphs for which they have no 'feel'.

Because it is important that indicators are understood, it may sometimes be better to live with slightly larger errors of estimation than to use complex procedures which present barriers to understanding.

Criterion 7. Indicators are explained Indicators do not need to be instantly understood. Explanations delivered in the course of in-service work lead to a higher level of professionalization, more sophisticated use of indicators and greater interest in them. Face-to-face presentations from those who create the indicators can be very helpful. The chance to ask questions and the provision of help within the institution seem to be particularly important, in addition to explanatory written materials.

Having the profession take on an understanding of performance indicators as part of their professional skills can only raise the status of the profession. With a sound understanding of residuals, they can deal with auditors and inspectors with some aplomb.

Criterion 8. Indicators are incorruptible Justice must be seen to be done. There have been instances of data being altered in a variety of ways in order to alter indicators. The greater the extent to which the indicators are used publicly to pressure institutions, the greater the need for incorruptible indicators. Truancy rates, for example, were manipulable simply by interpretations as to what did and did not constitute truancy. Once truancy rates had to be published, the data became of lower credibility.

Criterion 9. Indicators are checkable Nothing so secures acceptance as the chance to check up on the indicator. There are plenty of errors which can creep into the processing of indicators, so a chance to check your own from original data is desirable.

The criteria listed so far would be expected to lead to an initial acceptance of indicators. How long will the acceptance last? Will it lead on to actions which improve education? Longer-term acceptance will depend upon the indicators behaving in a way which is reasonably consonant with direct experience and upon a continuing ethos of rational response to information. The rational response is more likely if the indicators behave as can be reasonably expected, leading to the next pair of criteria.

Criterion 10. Indicators perceptibly improve if the unit improves its performance over time Once schools have received indicators department by department, one of their major interests becomes watching how the indicator changes from year to year, to see whether they are getting better or getting worse or just varying around an acceptable level. However, variability must be *expected*. It is the rule, not the exception. (See Figure 14.8.)

In short, indicators are required which retain their interpretation from year to year and which make sensitive, longitudinal comparisons possible. Regression-based indicators generally meet this criterion. At least some of the indicators for each management unit should be able to improve if the unit improves its performance.

Criterion 11. Behavioural implications of the indicators are beneficial The crucial question is whether or not the actions taken in response to the indicators will, in fact, be educationally beneficial.

Several examples of corrupting indicators were given in Chapter 4, including percentage pass rates.

Given the dearth of research on the impact of indicator systems, we may need to turn to evidence from other fields of social science to generate hypotheses, and hope the analogies are indicative.

There is an extensive literature on the effect of feedback on performance. Indeed, the Hawthorne studies, which led to the well-known term 'the Hawthorne effect', were reinterpreted as a demonstration not of the effect of *attention* but of the effect of *feedback*. In an article published in the prestigious journal *Science*, using a fine integration of qualitative and quantitative records from the original study, Parsons (1974) formulated and provided support for the hypothesis that the steadily increasing production was a result of feedback to the operators. Where feedback operated, people observed their own level of performance and found ways to improve it.

The effects of feedback of different kinds and varying intensities needs to be investigated empirically. Ideally, we need experiments varying the costs, styles and content of information systems in the framework of an experimental design. Important variables would be:

- The balance between fair comparisons (residuals) and raw data (simple information).

- The amount of process information.

- Other aspects which have been shown to be related to the effectiveness of evaluation reports (Cousins and Leithwood, 1986): sophistication, decision-relevance, consistency with users' beliefs, user involvement, relevance to problems.

- The context of use. The most important source of influence will probably be the context: punitive–public or investigative–confidential would be two extremes. Or one could contrast old-style macho management with the approach of a statistician/scientist.

In summary, such evidence as there is suggests that monitoring might turn out to be beneficial and motivating, or destructive and demotivating. More research is needed.

The next, final criterion will be difficult to achieve in the absence of such research.

Criterion 12. Indicators are cost-effective The only way to assess adequately whether or not the costs are reasonable is to have some assessment of the cost–benefits or cost-effectiveness of the system. However, the impact of indicators cannot be assessed empirically until an indicator system is up and running. The strategy would seem to be to run economically and look for ways to establish indicators about the effects of the indicator system.

A model of foresight and economy was the introduction by the Scottish Office Education Department of the relative rating system, with three years' data upon its first publication. By embedding the indicator system in the work of the Scottish Examinations Board (SEB), the Scottish Office Education Department created an impressively cost-efficient system. Furthermore, not only were the indicators produced economically as part of the SEB's routine computing system, but they were produced very promptly. This timeliness is a major concern in schools; old news is not useful. Interest in last summer's examinations wanes as a new year gets under way. As always, criteria overlap and *timeliness* is part of overall effectiveness of indicators.

Summary
Twelve criteria have been suggested and discussed. These criteria can be grouped into five main concerns: that indicators shall be relevant, informative, acceptable, beneficial and cost-effective as shown below.

1. **Relevant**:
   - Valued goals for identified units of management.
   - Indicators refer to outcomes over which staff have influence.
2. **Informative**:
   - Indicators are contextualized.
   - Indicators are fed back to the units of management.

3. **Acceptable**:
- Indicators are perceived to be fair.
- Indicators are accessible.
- Indicators are explained.
- Indicators are incorruptible.
- Indicators are checkable.
- Indicators change if the unit changes its performance over time.

4. **Beneficial**: Behavioural implications of the indicators are beneficial.

5. **Cost-effective**: Indicators are of reasonable cost.

Each set of criteria leads to the need to undertake certain actions:

1. **Relevant**:
- Create consensus on goals.
- Locate units of management.

2. **Informative**:
- Take account of context.
- Design good feedback procedures.
- Include alterable process variables.

3. **Acceptable**:
- Keep checking validity and equity.
- Provide statistics with a human face.

4. **Beneficial**: Check on impact use.

5. **Cost-effective**: Check costs and benefits.

USES OF INDICATORS

The single strongest influence on the kind of indicators that can be adopted, and on the impact they will have, is the use to which they are to be put. In this book indicators are seen primarily as feedback to self-organizing systems. Perhaps this is a naive view. Certainly the major issues will surround the use to which indicators will be put. Chapter 21 considers the use of indicators for performance-related pay, and Chapter 20 considers the impact of indicators on management. The reader will have gathered that the imposition of targets or the development of ossified plans is not the approach which seems to fit best with the ideas of complex systems thriving in a region of complexity on the edge of chaos.

This chapter concludes with a brief look at one of the most fraught issues surrounding indicators.

The issue of the publication of indicators

There is a real problem surrounding the publication of data. On the one hand, a commitment to freedom of information in a democratic society would seem to dictate publication. On the other hand, given that the large variations are between departments, and that work in a particular subject such as music or geography might be due to one teacher, the publication of data department by department would come close to doing personnel work in public – which is

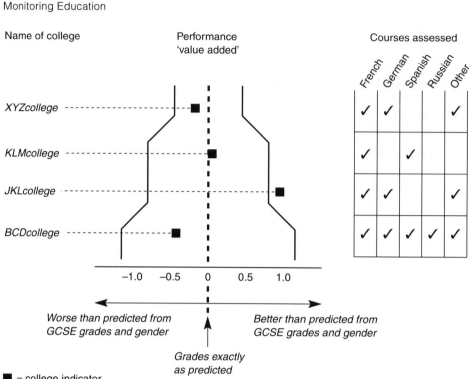

Name of college

Performance
'value added'

Courses assessed

French *German* *Spanish* *Russian* *Other*

-1.0   -0.5   0   0.5   1.0

Worse than predicted from
GCSE grades and gender

Better than predicted from
GCSE grades and gender

Grades exactly
as predicted

■ = college indicator

Figure 18.1 *Presenting college indicators in public: a possible format*

entirely unacceptable. Even inspectors are not to name individual teachers. A system which had teachers evaluated in public could well be counterproductive as well as inhumane.

Faced with the possibility that colleges might be required to publish their indicators, a solution was sought which:

- met the reasonable information needs of parents and students;
- did not mislead the public into thinking whole institutions were either good or bad;
- did not amount to doing personnel work in public;
- avoided the misleading use of rank orders in which the middle range of indicators hardly changes at all and yet people look at the position in the league table.

The solution suggested was to publish residuals by *subject areas*, so that they represent the work of several departments, and rank order only by size. The rank ordering by size allows the range of acceptable limits to be shown for each indicator as a smooth line, and it has the added benefit of indicating to parents and others the size of the departments. Some students may prefer small departments over large ones or vice versa. In Figure 18.1 the Shewhart idea has been turned into a vertical presentation with colleges rank-ordered by size.

A good deal of information is presented in the graphs. Suppose you are interested in several colleges at which to study languages. You find the colleges in the languages graph. Then:

- From the position of each one in the 'expected variation funnel' you can see whether the language faculty is large (those in the narrow part of the funnel) or small (those in the wide part of the funnel). You may have some preferences for size of faculty.

- From the table to the right of the graph you can see which subjects have been included in the data for the graph. If a subject is missing, perhaps the college does not offer it.

- From the location of the dark square you can see the average 'value added', i.e. the extent to which students that year in that subject area achieved higher or lower grades than predicted from their GCSE results. You would not take this information as decisive – there are many more factors to be considered – but it would generally assure you that you are not about to enrol in a faculty in real trouble.

The fact that there will be different tables for each subject area (foreign languages, mathematics & sciences, expressive arts, humanities etc.) would mean that the public can see that colleges generally show variation within themselves and do not simply have either good or poor indicators on everything.

Acceptable variation from year to year

It must be noted that the choice of where to draw the acceptable limits – the upper and lower confidence limits or the 'funnel' – may seem arbitrary. That is because it is arbitrary. There has been a tradition of treating findings as significant if they reach a certain level (the 0.05 level, which suggests use of 95 per cent confidence limits which implies placing the lines at about two standardized residuals from zero). However, the only way to decide what is and is not *educationally important* as opposed to the arbitrary criterion of *statistically significant* is to watch the indicators from year to year and know what else is happening.

The best way to use indicators is thus light monitoring by those closest to the data.

NOTES

1 The first part of this chapter is adapted from Fitz-Gibbon (1991), a report for the Scottish Office Education Department.

Chapter 19

Further Generations of Indicators: Monitoring Systems Evolve

This chapter contains speculations about the ways in which monitoring systems may evolve – the data that might be collected and the sources of such data. This is an essentially dangerous thing to do, since the future is unpredictable, but trying to make predictions or see the way forward is important. Before considering what might go into the monitoring systems for schools, we need to acknowledge the use of monitoring systems at other levels and their important role in informing policy.

DIFFERENT STRATEGIES FOR DIFFERENT LEVELS OF MONITORING

At a *national* level there is the entire educational system to be monitored. In-depth, single-focus surveys, such as the Audit Commission's study of post-16 education and the Elton committee's report on discipline, can tackle particular issues. Regular light sampling of representative data enable an eye to be kept on national trends, as in the 10 per cent samples of the Scottish School Leaver's Survey conducted over many years since 1971 by the Centre for Educational Sociology (Directors Andrew McPherson and David Raffe) at the University of Edinburgh, and the various sweeps of the Youth Cohort Study (e.g. Courtenay, 1988; Gray, *et al.*, 1993).

In order to make *international* comparisons there have been several studies organized through the International Association for Educational Assessment (IAEA) (e.g. Husèn, 1987; Comber and Keeves, 1973; Cresswell and Gubb, 1987). Samples which are intended to be representative are measured with similar tests translated into all the necessary languages, and results are compared country by country. All these activities represent kinds of monitoring and all have an important impact. The international studies seem to impact particularly on politicians and spark off demands for 'world class standards' – target setting for nations which is as fraught an activity as any other target setting.

Here we shall stay with a focus on monitoring with feedback for the education system within a country or part of a country. Further, the position is adopted in this chapter that eventually there will be extensive, regular, 100 per cent sampling systems for many variables. *Computers make it possible and the need for local information seems implied by (a) the current thinking on complex systems and (b) the intrinsic motivations of teachers who take an interest in individuals.* Furthermore, once student-by-student sampling systems are in place, it is a trivial matter to summarize or sample from this database for the purpose of national monitoring. Aggregation is easy; dis-aggregation is often impossible if only light samples or summary statistics have been collected. The

	Inputs		Processes	Immediate outputs			Long-term outcomes
Age	Inputs	(OECD-3) Resources – human and material	Process variables for generating hypotheses	(OECD-1) Achievement	(OECD-4) Attitudes and expectations	(OECD-2) Flow indicators	Employment Satisfaction Socialisation
16 to 18 years (ALIS)	• LSE • Prior qualifications • Gender • Ethnicity • Parental occupation	• Material resources, e.g. IT • Extent of help from private tutors, parents, peers • Class size • Timetabled time	• Teaching and learning processes • Homework • Out-of-school responsibilities (e.g. jobs, children)	• A-level examinations • Teacher assessments • Artefacts • Qualifications	• Attitude to the subjects studied • Attitudes to the school • Aspirations controlling for ability	• Numbers of students qualifying in various academic and vocational areas • Numbers likely to go on to HE • Curriculum balance	Follow-up studies assessing quality of life, salary and expected salary, careers and life events (A special ESRC-funded project)
14 to 16 years (YELLIS)	• LSE • Developed ability • Gender • Ethnicity • Cultural capital • Academic expectations • Traumas experienced at home	• Use of supply teachers (substitutes for absent teachers)	• Target setting • Work experience • Match in academic subjects • Homework • Sources of careers help	• GCSE examinations	• Attitudes to english, mathematics and science • Attitudes to the school • Aspirations • Truanting and skipping lessons • Feeling safe • Freedom from insults	• Staying-on rates • Number of students qualifying in various subject areas • Curriculum balance	• Destinations as logged by the careers' service

Note: LSE = Likelihood of staying in education, a measure of aspirations; OECD = Organisation for Economic Cooperation and Development. A working party for OECD reported on groups of indicators shown here.

Figure 19.1 *Examples of variables included in two up-and-running monitoring systems (ALIS and YELLIS)*

difficulty of interpreting summary statistics (such as means on means analyses) were the topic of Chapter 16.

A FRAMEWORK FOR DATA COLLECTION

In order to describe the education provided in a classroom, in a school, or in a country, we need to state *who is taught what, for how long,* and *how effectively.* School effectiveness research has generally concentrated on the last item of information: how effectively are students taught? Thus measures of student progress have been important and have come to be called 'value added'.

It can be cogently argued, however, that what is taught may be of more consequence than how effectively it is taught. The subjects studied may have greater impact on the long-term, retained knowledge of students and may have more consequences for their subsequent life chances – such as employment opportunities and quality of life. The choices made of subjects to study will also, as they accumulate, have national consequences, such as was seen in the development of shortages in the supply of mathematics, science and foreign language teachers in the UK in the 1980s (Straker, 1988).

An assessment transcript was outlined in Chapter 9 and could form the basic data source for tracking who is taught what and for how long. For issues of effectiveness (value added) and students' attitudes, a framework is needed. Figure 19.1 illustrates one choice of components of time periods (stages of education) and persons. The stages follow the current divisions proposed in the UK, as they seem to be a good compromise between too frequent and too infrequent monitoring.

The stages used should be those at which there are well-designed, externally set and marked assessments, and checks on children's motivation and well-being, so that every phase of education has an accountability check. How the data are used, particularly in primary years, is a difficult issue. Certainly the data on student progress will need to be provided to the appropriate teachers and administrators. Perhaps the data should also be available to those responsible for overall oversight of the system – LEAs or their successors. Dangers of labelling pupils need careful and sensitive consideration by teachers.

The part of these stages that most worries teachers is the breaking up of the five years of secondary schooling. There is often a desire to have an indicator system which looks at the intake to secondary school and then the examination results five years later. Whilst this can certainly be done, there is a possible problem. No one would feel completely responsible for the results across all those five years. There might well have been different teachers in the early part of secondary school from the later years and there could also have been substantial mobility (losses and gains) of students, meaning that the group present at intake *and* then for the examinations could, in some schools, be a small and unrepresentative sample. In the Year 11 Information System (YELLIS) we have therefore instituted an aptitude test on intake to Year 10, as a baseline. We then have a feedback module for the last two years in which the same teachers will often have taught a fairly stable group of students for the two years leading up to the examinations.

Figure 19.1 is not filled in. It is a framework into which we might gradually

		Data collected from				
Stage	up to age	Students	Staff	Parents	Governors	Local bodies
Advanced	18 years					
Standard	16 years					
KS3	14 years					
KS2	11 years					
KS1	7 years					
Pre-school	5 years					

Figure 19.2 *A data collection framework for school monitoring*

add items. Although the key stages are listed (KS1 etc.), at the time of writing (1994) there is not a great deal of confidence in the proposed tests for these stages if they are still internally marked.

There are, of course, complications when there are 'middle schools' and other unusual breaks in the stages.

DATA ACQUISITION

The costs associated with generating data from any of the groups indicated in Figure 19.2 have to be weighed against the benefits of more information.

If the costs of data acquisition need to be very low, then this can be achieved by collecting data from only one group. In this case the group must almost certainly be the students, because they represent the focus of the influence efforts which constitute education – they embody the outcomes. The second most important group may be the school staff. They deliver education. If staff are demoralized by policies, for example, this is like throwing grit into the engine; there will be trouble.

The costs of data acquisition are considerably reduced if the data are already available and do not need to be specially generated. They will still need to be collected and processed, since data analysis cannot profitably be done within a single school but must be done with a large pooled set of data at some central location in order to generate the necessary fair comparisons, compute the regression lines etc. School self-evaluation is not really possible, since most data must be considered relative to other data in order to be interpreted. For examination results, the regression lines could be provided by simple sampling on a national basis or within examination boards, and it is amazing that the examination results at 16 were not matched years ago, student by student, with examinations at 18.

There may be data available which are relevant to the school but not immediately available within the school, for example, housing records, and accidents and health statistics may be held as administrative data by the local authority. Such data may only be made available with elaborate anonymization techniques such as those pioneered by the late Cathie Marsh.

As information systems develop, some data will become available automatically, on a yearly basis if not more often. Thus students' timetables are already automatically available in schools which are using computer packages for timetabling. Once pooled with data from other schools, these can provide comparative curriculum balance information and measures of 'flow' and 'yield', i.e. how students are flowing through the system and what kinds of qualifications and in what quantity will be yielded.

Examination entries are another kind of data which are often automatically available. Thus data acquisition can be, in some instances, simply the collection of existing data – through electronic mail when all schools are on a network, through a modem or on disks at present. This all saves on the considerable costs of getting data typed into the computer – 'data entry'.

However, client response data, such as students' attitudes, are generally not available automatically – they have to be specially collected, generated data, subsequently typed into computer files, preferably with data-checking routines to ensure accuracy. An alternative to paper and pencil data collection may be machines programmed to collect student responses. Students, therefore, input their own data. Programs could be developed to collect student responses over an electronic network. Optical mark readers may help to automate data entry but they impose demands on the formatting of questionnaires.

Once data are collected, the question of data management becomes paramount. We have shifted to a relational database management system and have seen a new level of efficiency reached, due to the system or to the person in charge of it (Martin Wright) or both.

THE QUESTION OF WHAT TO MONITOR

How do we decide what to measure? How do we choose performance indicators? In response to tradition? On the basis of a theory, a model or a philosophy? On the recommendation of experts?

This issue was approached in Chapter 17 by suggesting a democratic approach. But what of theory and experts?

Theory-based approaches to the issue of what to measure

Ideally, performance indicators should be based on models of how the system 'works'. The performance indicators should measure the components which seem to produce outcomes (Fitz-Gibbon and Morris, 1975).

So we need to hypothesize about how schooling works, to have a working model, a tentative theory. In Figure 19.3 two broad-brush models are suggested, one for the major outcome of achievement and the other for what may eventually come to be seen as just as important for civilized society: the social outcomes of education. The concern with social outcomes can be seen as a tender-minded concern with people's happiness and adjustment or as a tough-minded businessman's concern with a willing and cohesive labour force. Take your pick, but no

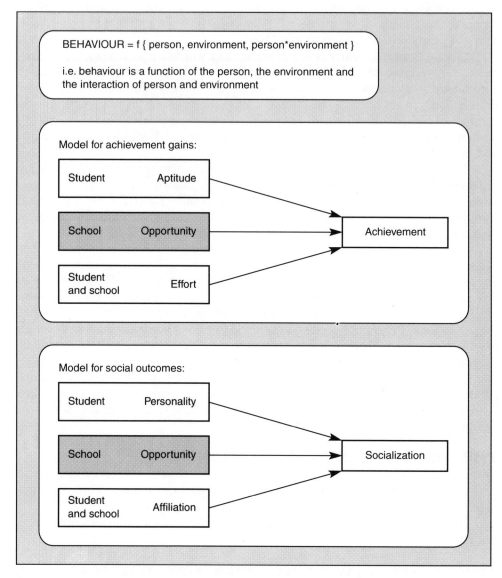

BEHAVIOUR = f { person, environment, person*environment }

i.e. behaviour is a function of the person, the environment and the interaction of person and environment

Model for achievement gains:

Student	Aptitude
School	Opportunity
Student and school	Effort

Achievement

Model for social outcomes:

Student	Personality
School	Opportunity
Student and school	Affiliation

Socialization

Figure 19.3 *Outline models for cognitive and social outcomes*

one is much in favour of poor social outcomes: a disaffected underclass is bad for human happiness and for business.

Figure 19.3 starts from a fundamental proposition: that what people do ('behaviour', whether in the classroom, on a test, or in adopting certain attitudes) is the result of factors in the person, of factors in the environment in which the person is living and of the ways in which these factors interact. This could be called nature, nurture and their interaction, but in the models both nature and nurture from home are incorporated in the student who arrives at the school. The 'nurture' for which the school is responsible lies in the experiences provided by the school. For the achievement model we can think of how lessons are taught as certainly being part of the school's possible effect on the student. There may be other influences on achievement – such as the peer group.

All outcomes are important and this is often recognized. Thus the UK government wanted truancy – one of the *social* outcomes – included in league tables. The problem was that publication was very threatening to schools and truancy was very difficult to define. The demand, predictably, had to be modified. As Deming said, 'Whenever there is fear, we get the wrong figures.' The requirement of publication would actually have made less likely the careful monitoring of truancy by schools, rather than have promoted it.

The problem which confronts us on social outcomes is that they are often difficult to measure and long-term. The short-term nature of most performance indicators may need to be counteracted by use of indicators of long-term outcomes. Again we encounter the hope that research will guide us; research on a representative sample might be sufficient to give us clues as to what to measure, but only experiments will sort out cause from correlation. The development of *indicators* which represent some *outcomes* that are *causally linked to actions* will be difficult, but essential if long-term outcomes are to feed back and inform current practices. Such feedback will be needed to engender the feelings of responsibility that self-organizing units need if they are to be responsive to long-term goals.

Schooling regimes may have some long-term outcomes which have not as yet been demonstrated. Consider, for example, these conclusions drawn by Reynolds from observations of how schools dealt with issues such as dress codes and smoking:

> . . . the evidence from these schools suggests that the more a school
> seeks high control over its more senior pupils by increasing
> organisational compulsion and decreasing pupil autonomy, the more
> these pupils may regard their schools as maladjusted to their needs . . .
> The attempt by the school to exercise control . . . is likely to set in
> motion a circular process of deviancy amplification: the pupils will
> regard the teachers as using illegitimate authority and will be less likely
> to defer to their authority in other areas of school life.
>
> (Reynolds, 1976, p. 226 and 228)

The hypothesis needs following up with experiments but it has the ring of truth, annoying though it might be to think that a school may not be able simply to 'enforce rules' with impunity. Just as the world would be a good deal simpler to deal with if only flogging worked, so it would also be easier to deal with if tough discipline improved matters for everyone. The point is that the experiments need to be done and the monitoring systems need to be put in place. *Unanticipated* outcomes arise from many social actions, both of the tough-minded and of the tender-hearted kind, as we saw in Chapter 3.

For the social outcomes, what are the important variables? One way in which students fail to affiliate to school and become, quite early, identifiable as 'at risk' of becoming delinquent, is probably if they find themselves under threat. Perhaps they feel stupid or are at the mercy of bullies. Development in a tense, unhappy situation is unlikely to be effective. As for the 'opportunities' which the school provides relating to social outcomes, maybe it is largely a matter of staff – student relationships, ethos or whatever, but it is possible that there are more concrete strategies. We can consider the existence of helping facilities, careers guidance, peer tutoring opportunities and all the many strategies teachers have for helping 'the whole child'.

Advice from research

A major article, consuming, with comments from leading US researchers, an entire issue of the *American Educational Research Journal*, attempted to identify variables associated with effective learning. The conclusion was that 'Distal variables, like state, district, and school level policy and demographics, have little influence on school learning' (Wang *et al.*, 1993, p. 276). The authors commented that this finding was 'inconsistent with current conventional wisdom which argues for policy-driven solutions, like school re-structuring, school-site management, and tougher teacher credential requirements and evaluation' (Wang, *et al.*, 1993, p.276). However, we can see here the potential for interactions. School site management without good outcome measures and feedback may be ineffective. (The USA lacks good outcome measures and feedback, so re-structuring may not have worked for that reason.) Equally, feedback can hardly be effective if given in a situation in which there are few options for action, e.g. without the conjunction of site management.

The proximal variables identified by the meta-analysis were classified as psychological, instructional or related to the home environment. The *psychological* consisted mainly of aptitudes and motivational characteristics of students, but metacognitive strategies were specially mentioned and included comprehension monitoring, generalization, self-regulatory and self-control strategies and reciprocal teaching. (Note that all these activities at the student level are ones which provide the student with feedback. Students, too, are complex adaptive systems which need feedback. Although they are listed as single 'variables', it would seem that these could all be operationalized in many and complex ways. We are no closer to simplicity for having decided upon proximal rather than distal variables.

The *instructional* variables included many of the features identified by Kounin (1970) relating to smooth transitions and 'with-it-ness' in classroom management. Questioning behaviour, teacher-student social interactions and peer and cross-age tutoring were also mentioned – none constituting a simple variable.

The *home environment* variables were much like the cultural capital variables developed by Bordieu and Passeron (1977) and now used in several monitoring systems: measures of parents' expression of interest in students' school work, participation in meetings, ensuring homework and attendance – i.e. various ways in which the parent assists the child in meeting the daily goals of the school. Once again, although a variable such as attendance might be measured, it is complex in definition and even more complex in the interpretation of causes.

Turning to an academic expert in monitoring, we can consult Willms (1992). When he looked at past research he came up with the following list of topics which a school effectiveness indicator system might include:

- ecology and milieu constructs;
- segregation;
- disciplinary climate;
- academic press;
- intended *versus* enacted curriculum;
- student attitudes – feelings of efficacy, attitudes toward school, quality of school life;
- teacher attitudes – feelings of efficacy, commitment and morale, working conditions;
- instructional leadership of principals.

He says, with mild understatement, 'To measure all of these constructs well, on an annual basis, would be costly.' However, as he goes on to say, costs could be reduced by sampling from items or time periods (Willms, 1992, pp. 148–9). The interesting list was based on his reading of the educational research literature but there is no guarantee that educational researchers have been studying important factors. Academia can simply feed on itself and there are few mechanisms for holding academics responsible for being useful to schools and colleges. (Indeed, they have done damage, as described in Chapter 3.) Grants are largely won from government or academic bodies, but less often from the professions themselves.

A set of questions could be established covering the Willms list and then relating each item to the framework given in Figure 19.2. The enacted curriculum is the heading under which would fall the proximal variables referred to above, and the difficulties of obtaining information on what actually happens are recognized.

> The enacted curriculum depends on the content of each lesson, the method of instruction, and the relative emphasis placed on each topic... One strategy to measure the enacted curriculum is to ask pupils whether they have covered particular topics, but pupils may tend to recall being taught only the material they have learned well... Another strategy is to ask teachers directly what topics they have covered, but this too has problems in that their responses do not necessarily capture the depth of coverage and the method of instruction.
>
> (Willms, 1992, p. 75)

Willms' discussion of the intended curriculum shows the need the US has for examination boards and externally set and marked examinations.

For the views of another set of experts we could turn to the panels set up by the Organisation for Economic Co-operation and Development (OECD). The OECD set up working parties to look at:

1. achievement;
2. flow indicators;
3. resources;
4. attitudes and expectations.

These areas of attention may well point the way forward for the subsequent development of indicator systems. They have been incorporated into Figure 19.3 in which variables currently measured for two of the stages of education are outlined. The variables are just some of those measured in the ALIS project and in the extended version of YELLIS, the Year 11 Information System.

The inclusion of 'resources' in the OECD list was made despite a body of writing that suggested that resources and outcomes were not linked (e.g. Hanushek, 1989). However, a meta-analysis has now suggested that resources do matter (Hedges, *et al.*, 1994). The earlier findings were based on the notoriously wrong but widely used method of 'vote counting' (Hedges and Olkin, 1980) as a method of research synthesis. (Vote counting consists of counting the proportion of studies which yielded statistically significant findings and believing that to be a guide to the significance of the findings.) However, detailed monitoring will be needed to identify ways in which resources are deployed, which may be complex and idiosyncratic. The complexity may account for the confusing findings currently in the literature. This illustrates once again the need for local information, monitoring in detail, if the complexities are to be adequately represented.

Going beyond value added: curriculum balance and the 'pulling power' of departments

There is currently, around the world, concern with the 'quality' of schooling and this is translated into a concern about student achievement – how good are the grades? But a grade 'A' or a grade 'C' might not be as important for subsequent usefulness as the nature of the subject which has been studied. Does the curriculum matter? How should it be measured?

It was national alarm in the USA following the launch of the Russian Sputnik in 1957, which led to the creation of the National Science Foundation and a proliferation of new curricula in science and mathematics. Experiments comparing the various new curricula with traditional courses were reviewed by Walker and Schaffarzick (1974), in an attempt to find the curriculum which was best and produced most learning amongst the students. They came to the conclusion, somewhat reluctantly, that students learnt what they were taught and did not learn what they were not taught. Comparisons between different curricula could not, therefore, be made on the basis of global measures of student achievement.

Earlier studies had also cast doubt on the notion that ways of teaching had important effects. Wallen and Travers (1963) had concluded 'Teaching methods do not seem to make a difference' with regard to classroom teaching. These studies must have contributed to the credibility of the Coleman *et al.*, (1966) report, which came to the conclusion that schools make little difference. Stephens (1967) undertook a massive study of school processes such as individual tutoring, counselling, time spent in study, students' jobs, size of school and many more variables and came to the conclusion that he had failed to find significant and consistent influences associated with student achievement and any of the variables studied. Many of these studies were cited by Walker and Schaffarzick when they urged that their survey of experiments in science curricula demonstrated that *content inclusion and emphasis* counted for far more variation in the outcomes than did the quality of teaching.

However, all the studies cited above originated in the US, where there have been few agreed standards with regard to who was taught what. With no examination boards of the kind known in the UK, 'delivery standards' are a major source of concern – what are teachers teaching? Without knowledge of the content taught, attempts to measure achievement are beset with difficulties. Because of these problems that confront efforts to measure school effectiveness in the US, negative findings need to be viewed tentatively.

It is not surprising that the first challenges to the Coleman report came from countries with examination systems and made use of the curriculum-embedded, authentic testing provided by examination boards as outcome measures (Kellaghan and Madaus, 1979; Rutter *et al.*, 1979). Thereafter, 'school effectiveness' research increased in volume considerably, as though the field had taken heart. 'School Matters' was the title that Mortimore *et al.*, (1988) chose for their study of primary schools.

The curriculum issue of content was raised in the UK by Preece (1983), studying achievement in science. He suggested that the curriculum offered has far more impact than variations in the effectiveness of the instruction and referred to this as the qualitative hypothesis: 'Learning is largely unaffected by differences in teaching style and approach.'

At present there do not appear to be any league tables showing the balance of the curriculum; there is no attempt to assess which schools and colleges are making moves to ameliorate the national problem of a shortage of skills in technology, maths, science and foreign languages. Such curriculum balance might be more important than whether or not the grades achieved show an extra point or two of 'value added'.

The 'pulling power' of departments In the early days of the ALIS project it was noted that the relative proportions of students in mathematics and English varied considerably from school to school. One year, for example, they ranged from 0.6 as the ratio of mathematics to English candidates (indicating more students taking English than taking mathematics) to 4.5, indicating four and a half students in mathematics for every student in English.

The school which has the 0.6 ratio (more in English) was the school whose anxieties about mathematics had led to the start of the ALIS project. A thriving and very attractive English department was, in a sense, recruiting students who might in some other school have ended up in the mathematics department. This situation clearly emphasized the need to look at each department in terms of the students it had attracted into it and, indeed, to regard this attraction of the department as one of its features.

The school with the 4.5 ratio, a ratio which might have solved the shortage of mathematics teachers and other needs for numeracy had it been repeated in all the schools, was a school which was in fear of being closed because of its small sixth form. It was located in a lower middle class housing estate and had gained neither recognition nor notoriety. The mathematics results at the time were good and it even had a further mathematics class. Yet the school was not noted; there was no discussion. One of the pleasantest events in running indicator systems is to locate highly effective departments which are quite unrecognized and give recognition.

FURTHER DEVELOPMENTS: MULTI-SITE FIELD TRIALS VIA NETWORKING

Once monitoring systems are in place there is a constant flow of type 3 data: fair comparisons. With further effort we will be able to set up situations in which type 4 data, the gold standard of controlled trials or 'experiments' can be set up. By forming networks and planning experiments, schools and colleges will be able to investigate new methods of teaching, and new methods of running the institution. If truancy, for example, is a concern, various sites can agree to implement various strategies with similar students (as identified by the monitoring system's intake measures). The outcomes on all measures will become available as the monitoring system reports, and evaluations can be conducted within the network.

PRESENTATION OF INFORMATION: HOW TO GET IT ALL ACROSS

The technical infrastructure for information systems is improving constantly and monitoring systems will soon be giving information back in videos, interactive or ordinary, embedded in computer programs and enriched by colour and graphics. These developments will make data more acceptable to more people and may help to create the rationality and wish to look at evidence that might just save us much of the misery that stems from the incapacity of social science to make progress.

As the technical infrastructure develops, receiving feedback from your local monitoring system may become more like playing an arcade game. This, it is hoped, will increase people's interest in evidence and locate the power of information in the hands of those closest to the action and with most responsibility. Social scientists have not been noticeably successful in ameliorating social problems but those who run social services, including education, may be dramatically more successful as they become the action researchers of the future.

These may be merely wishes but they do seem more promising than hoping for dream solutions to be discovered by academic research.

PART SEVEN

The Impact of Monitoring on Other Systems

This Part explores the impacts which the creation of monitoring systems might have on various systems which interact with, or are part of, education.

Chapter 20 considers management in general, and there is particular reference to performance related pay in Chapter 21. The endangered structure, the LEA, is the topic of Chapter 22. That invalidated and costly activity called inspection, represented by the newly constituted OFSTED, is looked at in Chapter 23, and politics is the topic of Chapter 24. Finally, the university needs to be considered as the place to which more and more educational products (students) are being channelled. Chapter 25 takes up two issues: is education properly a university subject, and will universities survive with their capacity to 'speak without fear or favour' intact?

Chapter 20

Wanted: Better Management

THE PERUTZ HYPOTHESIS REGARDING MANAGEMENT STYLES

Max Perutz is a Nobel Prize-winning scientist and the former Director of the Medical Research Council's Unit for Molecular Biology in Cambridge. He was so horrified in 1989 at some proposals from the Advisory Board for the Research Councils that he wrote an article for the *New Scientist* drawing analogies with Stalinist centralization. The proposals, from a Conservative government, were for the setting up of councils staffed by scientists and engineers with training and experience in management who would be able to oversee accounting, marketing and policy roles and produce five-year plans. Perutz recalled the time when, fifty years earlier, physicist Bernal had advocated a Marxist approach to research management: the establishment of a monolithic, centralized organization for planning every aspect of science from physics to medicine and economics.

> I reflected at the time that in the period between the Wars, British scientists had been the first to split the atom, that they had discovered atomic isotopes, the neutron and the need for anti-matter; they had isolated new vitamins and found how nerve impulses are triggered . . . by contrast, despite the much larger numbers of scientists employed there, few significant advances had been made in the Soviet Union, where their science was organised on Bernal's Marxist principles.
>
> (Perutz, 1989)

It is salutary to recognize that both the left and the right politically often take ideological positions which include highly centralized planning, and a 'macho' approach to management, an approach which presumes to knowledge and is driven by ideology, principles and beliefs rather than evidence.

Max Perutz went on to recall his experience with working with the Medical Research Council (MRC), which he saw as having an international reputation for excellence.

> The MRC's enlightened scientific policies have been matched by an understanding of the human relations needed to motivate scientists to do creative work. Many years ago, I held a grant from the Department of Scientific and Industrial Research, now the Science and Engineering Research Council. I dutifully submitted annual reports, they vanished into a file and elicited no echoes. At the time, I also had an Imperial Chemical Industry's fellowship, but ICI ignored my existence. After I was appointed to the staff of the MRC, my first report drew a letter from

> Arthur Lonsborough . . . expressing interest and satisfaction at my
> progress in tackling a hard problem. That was long before I had any
> tangible results and it gave me enormous encouragement.
>
> (Perutz, 1989)

He goes on to describe how, even though now much larger, the MRC still operates a system in which individual researchers are in contact with individual administrators who become familiar with their work and 'do everything possible to help them do their research'.

> The only other research organisation I know that has pursued such a
> policy of personal contact between administrators and scientists is the
> Rockefeller Foundation. Perhaps it was no accident that genes were first
> found to be made of DNA at the Rockefeller Institute, and the structure
> of DNA was solved in an MRC unit. (Perutz, 1989)

Perhaps it was no accident, or perhaps it was an accident. Let us call it the Perutz Hypothesis: *the opinion that personal contact by an expert, a supportive oversight, a facilitating approach is the effective way to manage a research organization.* The hypothesis is highly persuasive but it does still remain an opinion.

The Science Policy Research Unit (SPRU) at the University of Sussex undertakes historical and survey work trying to resolve these kinds of questions about ways to run scientific organizations. Their careful work may well produce type 3 data with some fair comparisons and some reasonably compelling arguments, but they are unlikely to be able to obtain the gold standard, type 4 data. Will there ever be a time when large organizations recognize that they too can set up experiments? Research councils could operate in two different modes under two different styles of administration, one following the Perutz hypothesis and the other setting five-year targets etc. The extent to which over ten or twenty years these different modes of operation produced good science could be evaluated. A third possibility would be some random assignment of research money to proposals which had merely survived an initial vetting – or to all top-rated proposals. Randomization has probably served evolution well – we could mimic it in society.

Whether this particular experiment is actually worth pursuing or not is an issue I am not in a position to judge – people at the SPRU may be better able to weigh the feasibility – but the *possibility* should be entertained because the greatest enemy of learning is the presumption that we already know the answers. Nowhere does such presumption seem so unquestioned as in management. If we could admit to not knowing, we could become an experimenting society and find out.

If education is a complex system, then trying to manage it as though it were a production line – a predictable, closed, linear system shielded from influences, with clearly defined and accurately measurable inputs and outputs – may not make sense. Can development plans and targets feature if efficiency lies on the edge of chaos, if the future is essentially unpredictable?

The Perutz hypothesis is here as a marker for the human values and insights which guide any human activity. Indicators do not overrule this – they are informative, not decisive. But Perutz was writing about the management of scientific research. Do his ideas apply to the management of organizations? I believe so. The two are made equivalent by their common feature: problem-solving.

CAN COMPLEX ORGANIZATIONS BE MANAGED?

Deming saw problem location and problem-solving as the main task of management: 'When there is a problem, management must analyse.' Popper's approach to life, let alone management, rests on problem-solving. Simon sees problem-solving and evolution as similar processes and notes that:

> . . . human problem solving, from the most blundering to the most insightful, involves nothing more than varying mixture of trial and error and selectivity . . . various paths are tried out, the consequences of following them are noted, and this information is used to guide further search.
>
> (Simon, 1988, p. 201)

The 'noting' of consequences is exactly what participation in an ongoing monitoring system makes possible. The management of organizations looks very much like the management of a scientific enterprise.

THE MANAGER AS SCIENTIST

The concept of the manager as scientist is a powerful one, for it implies not only a methodology – open empirical investigation, the collection and interpretation of evidence – but also an ethos. The ethos of science is

- *democratic* – information and evidence are the decisive factors, not authority;
- *open* – information should be widely available, open to debate;
- *tentative* – interpretations of data are simply the best we know so far, not eternal truths, and it is important to state what is *not* known as well as what is known, and to report the errors that accompany any measurement.

Deming's philosophy certainly fits in with this notion of the manager as scientist and with Simon's view of a need, in designing a system, to understand and take account of 'the knowledge base'.

> The Scientific Approach requires deep understanding of the nature of variation, particularly its division into controlled and uncontrolled components due respectively to common and special causes. This is a very crucial aspect of what Deming now refers to as 'Profound Knowledge' . . . The Scientific Approach calls for decision-making and policy making on the basis of good information, both numerical and non-numerical – not just by 'gut feel' or mere short-term considerations. It will often include the analysis of data by statistical techniques and SPC (Statistical Process Control) but it also includes knowledge and understanding of the limitations of such techniques, and awareness of the crucial impertinence of phenomena which cannot be quantified.
>
> (Neave, 1990, p. 34)

This last quotation makes an important point – about that which cannot be quantified. Processes in particular are difficult to define, let alone quantify, as is the atmosphere created by the way people relate to each other, the way the management relates to those whose work they are there to enhance and facilitate.

It was emphasized in early chapters that monitoring carries messages – about what we care about enough to measure. Not only what is measured, but also the way this information is used by managers, may be critical to these messages and to the reception of a monitoring system. Monitoring does not provide managers with decisions; it provides information and it carries messages which may be one of the most influential parts of the system.

HEADTEACHERS (AND OTHER MANAGERS) CONSIDERING THE USE OF MONITORING

Headteachers are usually the persons who make the decision to have a school or college join an information system. Some of the consequent decisions are listed below. They illustrate the kinds of decisions which will face managers as data from monitoring systems become available:

- *Entry*: Whether to obtain such data for their own schools. If yes, then which system (if there is a choice)? Criteria for performance indicators (Chapter 7) may help here.

- *Presentation*: How should the system be introduced to the staff? Most systems cannot be hidden: either students are completing information or large amounts of staff time are devoted to supplying information. How is the activity to be presented to students? Generally, the information system should offer support and advice on these issues, especially since the actions adopted may affect the quality of the data obtained.

- *Distribution*: Who is to receive the various parts of the data? Governors? Heads of department? Everyone? In what format? Are departments to see the data from other departments?

- *Interpretation*: Can the school interpret the data itself? Is there help available? Who in the school can best support staff in interpreting their data? Who would be fair, non-biased, non-gossipy and competent in such a role?

- *Action*: When should actions be taken on the basis of the data? Should this be left to the units (e.g. departments)? How can we sort out routine variations from problems or strengths? (Common cause from special cause – Demming.) How can we avoid taking actions which make things worse?

- *Authority*: Will the existence of data undermine your authority, which previously rested in part on the fact that, in the absence of any 'objective' evidence, your evaluation was what counted? Statisticians who have consulted for industry, on quality systems for example, have sometimes felt that opposition from some levels of management was due precisely to this potential loss of a role which gave them enormous power over others. Are you ready to be a scientist rather than an authority?

- *Empowerment*: The other side of the authority coin is empowerment. The profession as a whole, as well as individual school departments, can feel a new sense of power because they have data on their own performance which is as good or better than anyone else's. (See Chapter 23.)

Chapter 21

Performance-Related Pay or 'Merit Pay': A Dead Alley?

Clearly, the monitoring systems which are the subject of this book produce a glint in the eye of those eager to introduce performance-related pay, for suddenly there seems to be hard data on the effectiveness of departments and could not this be used as the basis for performance-related pay?

It should be pointed out right away that the fairest residuals that can be produced, that is the fairest measures of value added or the effectiveness of a department, are nevertheless only 'residuals', what is left over after some important factors have been taken into account. A large proportion of the variation in outcomes remains unexplained in a system as complex as education. Whereas the residual is the best available indicator, not all the variation from year to year in the residuals can be attributed to those teaching the subject. There are further complications in that teams teach many subjects, and the work in a mathematics department may be heavily influenced by work in a physics department and by colleagues who taught the students previously. The notion that teachers are in some sense individually responsible for students' achievements would be a difficult one to sustain were there to be challenges to the adequacy of a system which was rewarding teachers as individuals.

Nevertheless, if we believed it to be true that 'the only way to turn around an organization is to introduce performance-related pay' (a statement made to a professional body by a Sir who will be left nameless since the statement he made is so clearly false), we should indeed look towards using a monitoring system to introduce performance-related pay. However, the statement made is insupportable. In the first place, there are very few examples of performance-related pay systems at work in any strict sense of the term. With regard to the US, Jacobsen wrote

> . . . in practice the notion of rewarding teachers for exceptional
> performance, as promoted by 'first wave' merit pay advocates, appears
> not to have gained much of a foothold in the USA. On the other hand,
> findings from the same survey indicate that the 'second wave' reforms
> of the Holmes Group (1986) and the Carnegie Forum on Education and
> Economy (1986) have been implemented more broadly. Specifically,
> these reports recommend the use of career ladders to expand teachers'
> responsibilities to include mentor and master teacher roles.
>
> (Jacobsen, 1992, p. 48)

Jacobsen concluded that 'Examining Performance Related Pay in practice revealed that it has been more a subject of debate than a reality in the USA' (Jacobsen, 1992, p. 50).

Citing Murnane and Cohen (1985), Jacobsen stated that over 99 per cent of US teachers were employed in school districts that utilized uniform salary scales rather than performance-related pay. The few exceptions appeared to be wealthy districts giving discreet, inconspicuous awards to almost all their teachers, and it was commented that these plans did not appear to have an effect on the way teachers teach.

The Assistant Masters and Mistresses Association (now the Association of Teachers and Lecturers) commissioned David Mayston (Professor of Public Sector Economics, Finance and Accountancy, University of York) to survey the literature and draw conclusions relating school performance indicators and performance-related pay. He cited several studies showing little uptake of performance-related pay.

> Incomes Data Services (1988) found that out of 50 companies that had actually expressed strong interest in Performance Related Pay, only two had actually proceeded to register their companies as using that method, *despite tax incentives*. (Emphasis added) (Mayston, 1992)

In the *Handbook of Personnel Management Practice* we find

> . . . what recent research has taught us is that badly designed and poorly implemented PRP schemes probably de-motivate staff more effectively than well designed and implemented schemes motivate them.
>
> (Armstrong, 1991, cited by Mayston, 1992)

A consultative document on performance-related pay (School Teacher's Review Body, July 1994) discussed the views of seven primary, seven secondary and one special school participating in a pilot.

> Among the many objections, it was suggested that PRP could be divisive and demotivate those that missed out; that it could undermine teamwork and collective endeavour; that the performance of heads and deputies could not be measured; that there would be too great a focus on simplistic, quantitative measures; that any scheme was bound to become complicated and too time-consuming to manage properly; and that any payments to individuals would be at the expense of other priorities. (School Teachers Review Body, p. 2)

Undeterred (or was it externally constrained perhaps?), the Review Body went on to recommend a scheme by which governors (who may frequently be neighbours of headteachers, if not friends) would fill out an application, agree goals peculiar to the school, and fill out a second form to say if the goals had been met. Headteachers and deputies might then get bonuses of 2 or 3 per cent of pay. The pay would not come out of the school's budget but from some other pocket of educational expenditure (a convenient way to make local whistle-blowing in the school less of a potential problem). OFSTED could check up when inspecting, but since performance was deemed not measurable ('only observable') it might have trouble with the verification. Who can adequately verify attendance records, for example? Attendance was one of the more measurable indicators suggested.

All in all, the proposed scheme seemed as leaky a mechanism as the original proposals for internally marked SATs. It is strange that there is a *negative* view of people as being motivated only by pay, along with total *positive* faith in their willingness to turn in poor indicators of their own performance, when they could easily distort the indicator and gain the financial reward which is considered to be so essential for motivation.

The authors of the consultative document offered no evidence in favour of performance-related pay, nor did they propose properly controlled trials. However, they did comment: 'General experience is that such schemes may quickly need to be adapted to changing circumstances and can have a relatively short life.' This, of course, could lead to a waste of public funds.

Nevertheless, in the following paragraphs we will consider carefully the possible costs of performance-related pay systems, the possible benefits (which will be largely hypothetical, since there is little in the way of hard evidence), the opinions of experts and the question of alternative ways of recognizing valued performance on the job.

COSTS

Setting aside briefly the question of the indicators which would trigger performance-related pay, let us consider the amount that would be required. Is £500 for a one-off bonus adequate to reflect a year's work or to reflect three years' consistently good performance, or might it be regarded as an insulting level of recognition? Tomlinson (1992) reports typical values of 10 per cent of the pay packet for 'junior managers' and 25 per cent for 'chief executives'. Twenty-five per cent of a chief executive's salary could be a substantial sum of money. Perhaps we need to discount the opinions of people with a vested interest, such as remuneration consultants, headteachers and chief executives, who stand to gain the most from performance-related pay. The next question is where this money would come from. If it was skimmed off the limited devolved budget, for every winner, somebody would essentially, even though not obviously, be a loser. If, on the other hand, extra funds are available, where are they to come from?

Is there any justification for greater bonuses for headteachers? If we look at the school effectiveness literature, the proportion of variance accounted for by departments is as much as twice that accounted for by a general school effect which might, if one were being very generous, be attributed to the effect of the headteacher. Does this mean that department heads should be awarded performance-related pay at twice the rate of headteachers, or should the effect be multiplied by the number of students upon whom there is an effect? In the latter case, headteachers would win out substantially every time, by being able to claim an effect on all students in the school, even though in reality they might have little effect. Many are certainly not missed when not in the school. The effects just cited are effects on examination results; effects on attitudes may be more substantial but are rarely available, although with the advent of comprehensive quality assurance systems such measures may become more widely developed.

Could, then, performance-related pay be tied to examination residuals? This would certainly be better than tying pay to other indicators which might produce perverse behaviour and bad incentives. Percentage pass rates, for example, would

191

encourage teaching to the borderline, neglecting the most able and excluding candidates likely to fail, a set of behaviours which, on a national basis, would be deleterious to quality and, in a norm-referenced system, doomed to failure.

There are many problems with tying performance assessment to residuals. Often residuals are unstable and only partly, if that, attributable to the efforts made by teachers as opposed to random variation in the system.

Of possibly greatest concern is the negative impact on relationships between teachers: strife in the staffroom, de-motivation or suspicion of currying favour.

A relationship which the literature seems not to have mentioned is that between the teachers and their students. One can imagine there being some taunting of teachers who are trying to cajole students into working hard and fore-going pleasures in order to achieve: 'you only want us to work so that you get paid more because we get better results – it's not for our benefit.'

Finally, the costs in time and effort of implementation must be taken into account. The effort required to implement a performance-related pay system has been described as 'hard, sometimes unremitting toil' (Murlis, 1987). It has to be decided who will collect all the data required to operate the scheme and who will make the decisions; perhaps headteacher, teachers or governors. The situation of governors whose friends are on the staff of the school also has to be considered.

BENEFITS

Rewarding effective performance is expected to encourage teachers to try harder. It is seen as only fair to set salaries appropriate to performance; it is seen as a way to encourage less effective teachers to leave the profession; and it is seen as a way to reward teachers for staying in the classroom and being effective in the classroom. The fact that increases in salary too often are available only by leaving the classroom and taking on managerial responsibilities has certainly long been recognized as a problem in the structure of education. Each of these hoped-for benefits is discussed below.

With regard to the 'try harder' argument, it is important to question the implied assumption that teachers are not already working hard at their jobs. There is no evidence presented for such a diagnosis. It is also important to note that we have no evidence that 'trying harder' produces better examination results or more satisfied students and parents. In 'trying harder' some teachers could become over-demanding and cause conflicts; others might try to be entertaining or friendly to extreme degrees. No-one should imagine that there is a body of knowledge about how to teach which can be adopted with confidence that outcomes (examination results or students' attitudes) will certainly improve. Given the complexity of teaching, pressures to try harder could be counterpro-ductive, in much the way identified by Deming (1986) as 'tampering'.

The need to reward teachers who remain in the classroom is an interesting problem. The use of indicators such as examination residuals and students' atti-tudes might help, over several years, to identify exceptionally effective teachers and make possible the 'promotion' of such teachers, perhaps providing them with time to serve as mentors to others. This is quite different from suggesting that their pay fluctuate year by year with indicators. Interestingly, the problem of keeping people in their area of expertise was recognized in IBM with a system referred to as the 'dual ladder concept'. This 'allows careers for suitably qualified individuals to progress to the most senior level in the company structure, *without managerial responsibility*' (Sapsed, 1992, p. 76, emphasis·added).

All in all, such benefits as are claimed are based only on the fairly subjective interpretation of very limited case studies (or perhaps just opinion – the notion that opinions are based on case studies is offered here generously). The widespread unwillingness to accept performance-related pay schemes may signal that there are grave doubts as to the long-term benefits of the introduction of this kind of numerically based reward system.

TESTIMONY OF 'EXPERTS'

Sapsed described an appraisal and counselling process applicable to all IBM employees, and an associated merit pay system which had been operating in the UK for more than 25 years. The general level of salaries was set with reference to the outside market for similar responsibilities as determined by IBM's participation in surveys covering such professions as accountancy, personnel, legal and occupational health. These surveys allowed the setting of the general level of remuneration within which a merit pay scheme could operate.

The description of the IBM merit pay scheme is a rigid description of a process which Sapsed not once describes as problematic. For example:

- 'IBM uses a system of job evaluation to assess the relative worth of each job to the company.' (Sapsed, 1992, p. 77)

- 'The manager and the employee ... develop job objectives, usually five to ten in number, based on an annual cycle.' (Sapsed, 1992, p. 78)

- 'Each objective is accompanied by performance criteria defining how the objective will be measured.' (Sapsed, 1992, p. 79)

- 'Current pilot testing within IBM of on-line objective setting maintained within the internal computer network, encourages ... updates.' (Sapsed, 1992, p. 79)

In fairness it must be said that he did state that the system was still undergoing revision. Sapsed reported an innovation for 1991, which was to survey IBM's customers and set targets for improvement in customer satisfaction ratings, targets which, if achieved, would then result in merit pay as a percentage of salary to all employees. In addition to this planned customer satisfaction share, there were incentive payments and awards. The entire structure seems to have been meticulously thought out and implemented.

How effective was it? Sapsed reports that surveys of employee satisfaction with their pay give the same answers now as 20 years ago, about 35 per cent expressing satisfaction and a further 30 per cent neither satisfied nor dissatisfied. Presumably, that means 35 per cent are dissatisfied. He goes on to say, however, that 'the ultimate test of IBM's personnel practices . . . might be the attrition rate. It is exceptionally low at around 3% per annum; fewer than 2% of professionals leave in any year.' However, those figures were written in the present tense in, presumably, 1991 or 1992, when there was a decline in opportunity for employment due to considerable recession in the economy.

It must also be mentioned that, at about the time when the article appeared, IBM turned in the largest deficit in business history. It has had to be completely re-structured.

Single case studies are informative and interesting but cannot establish widely general principles. It might be noted, however, that the apparently highly formal structures and target setting and procedures of IBM must have absorbed a great deal of employee effort and, certainly, did not look like a system living 'on the edge of chaos'. Widespread knowledge of the functioning of an organization, as provided by performance indicators, is quite a different proposition from over-loading these indicators with incentives.

AN ALTERNATIVE TO PERFORMANCE-RELATED PAY

What is the approach of Deming to performance appraisal and the setting of salaries? Heywood (1992) reported a summary from the British Deming Association's Appraisal Research Group, emphasizing that performance contains a large random element, that setting individual or department targets and objectives can divert people from the team work needed to produce the best results, and that reliance on pay as a motivator can be counter-productive. Deming's advice is to base salaries, wages and bonuses on:

- market rate;
- accumulation of skills;
- accumulation of responsibility;
- seniority ('greatness takes time');
- prosperity (sharing in the general welfare of the institution).

To add to this list and relate it particularly to teaching, I would suggest a category called 'relevant rewards'. If a teacher is perceived to be excellent and demonstrably getting good value added results and positive student attitudes, the teacher may be given the opportunity to earn more by training others, teaching extra sessions in the summer, or serving on policy committees. Such teachers might also be allowed to teach larger classes. For example, if a teacher is attracting students to his or her classes in the post-16 phase of schooling, where students have a choice of where to study and what to study, then the teacher may be willing to take on a larger workload and work longer hours. The salary paid for teaching a large class should be higher than that for teaching a small class, with safeguards for some baseline so that the minority subjects are not underpaid. Other relevant rewards would be representing the school or college at conferences and having an influence on policy in the school, in particular on hiring teachers – although we have no way of knowing whether good teachers are good at spotting other good teachers.

There is so much about management and the running of organizations that is still conjectural, and on which there have not been good studies, that what passes for evidence is anecdotal, with unknown biases in both the observer and in the selection of the sample that is observed. Gold standard data on management practices are desperately needed.

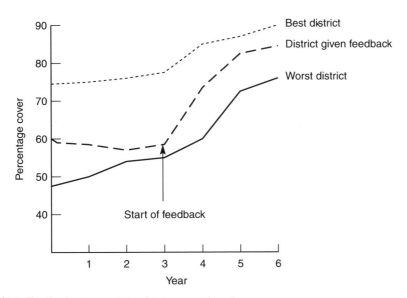

Figure 21.1 *Feedback appears to lead to improved performance*

FINAL COMMENT

It is just possible that performance-related pay is a waste of public money. The argument is as follows. Before you can establish performance-related pay, you need to measure performance. If you are measuring outcomes and feeding the information back, you have a monitoring-with-feedback system already in place. Before tying any bonuses or performance-related pay to this system, the effects of the system itself should be assessed. If feedback alone produces improvements, why add performance-related pay? If both are introduced simultaneously, we lose the chance to see the effects of each independently. I am indebted to Dr Alan Colver for the following illustration of this idea. He was concerned about rates of immunization in various health clinics. He started monitoring these at the time shown in Figure 21.1 and fed the results back to the clinics. As can be seen from Figure 21.1, over the next few years those clinics moved from being among the worst to among the best in the data set. This was as a result not of any payment, incentive, training, or target setting, but simply of feeding information back to the management unit responsible for the action. Ironically the government then, in about 1992, introduced payment for immunization, spending money when it is likely that information alone would have had the same effect.

Before we rush into tying money to performance, with all the dubious links of causality and all the potential de-motivating effects of trying to isolate the effect of individuals in the system, we should at the very least collect evidence on the effect of monitoring with feedback. It might be all we need.

Chapter 22

LEAs: Is Resuscitation Overdue?

There has been a very strong move towards centralization of control in education. Schools have been encouraged to opt out of local control and put themselves under the control of a central government agency. Thus 'grant maintained' schools wishing to get funds for staff development must apply directly to the government, whereas local authority schools apply to their local authorities. Does it make sense for such management to be centralized? If we accept the Perutz hypothesis that close interest and personal support are important in leading to the creative and effective use of funds (see Chapter 20), then what kind of system would be likely to be effective?

One answer might be the existing structures, including local education authorities (LEAs), but with some further accountability built into the system. For example, there could be some strengthening of the role of the Audit Commission, which checks on the use of public funds by LEAs (Figure 22.1). Some strengthening has already taken place and yet, simultaneously, the LEAs have been almost destroyed and in their place have developed un-elected Training and

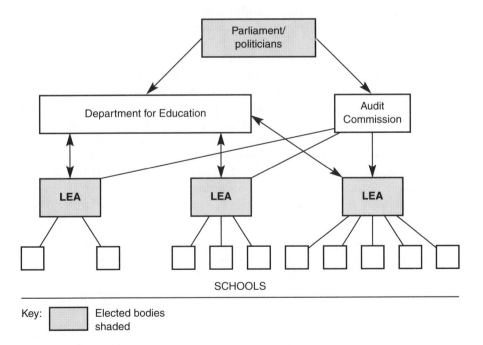

Figure 22.1 *A structure of accountability*

Enterprise Councils. Perhaps these new bodies, held accountable largely by short-term contracts with central government, will become effective agencies. Their evaluation will no doubt be undertaken eventually. Meanwhile, though, there is the danger of losing a reasonably effective, and economical, structure: the LEA.

The particular reasons for valuing the LEAs are that they are representatives of local democratic processes and they have a brief to take an overview of the region. People develop commitments according to their work roles. Headteachers and their staff are committed to their own students and their own school or college. Yet someone needs a broader commitment to the whole local system, an overview regarding the data, so that it can be interpreted with reference to the whole region, and an overview of the fairness and effectiveness of not just one institution but of the entire provision of education in the region. The provision must take into account the educational needs of diverse groups, e.g. the very bright, the special needs children, non-English-speaking children, the musically talented, the emotionally disturbed and the poor. Someone needs to organize for the good of all. The LEAs had this role in the past.

But there seem to have been problems. The LEAs were left largely unaccountable except for the election process. Schools more or less had to take whatever the LEA said. There have even been cases of appointments being made by LEA personnel over and against the wishes of headteachers and teaching staff, and on what looked suspiciously like political and personal friendship grounds. Of course, poor criteria could also be used by headteachers in making appointments. The only solution would be to have procedures with checks and balances – no power should be exercised without accountability and scrutiny. The LEAs should have been subject to closer scrutiny and monitoring and, if this were now introduced, the LEAs could surely evolve to be vital components of the complex system of education.

Although local authorities were supposed to monitor, there is little evidence that they took the need for good information seriously. If they had done, they would surely have started relating O-levels to A-levels many decades ago, and would have employed statisticians and people familiar with research to assist them in assessing the effectiveness of schools. Yet until quite recently few LEAs had adequate in-house computing systems. They paid large amounts simply to have data cross-tabulated. Few had research or statistical units of any size.

Given the lack of expertise in research methods, it is not surprising that the LEAs in general did not take up the monitoring role with alacrity when it was assigned to them by the Coopers & Lybrand report (Coopers & Lybrand, 1988) and circular 7/88 from the DES:

> The Secretary of State will expect schemes submitted to him for
> approval to include the following elements: . . . the monitoring and
> evaluation procedures to be applied under the scheme, including the
> measures the LEA propose to use to evaluate the performance of
> schools. (Department of Education and Science, 1988, p. 31)

Indeed, most seemed to make no new effort to monitor schools. Perhaps this was because they already thought they were monitoring by having their staff visit schools. Some re-named advisors as 'inspectors' and almost all subscribed to the National Consortium for Examination Results (NCER). But NCER only reformatted data. It did this in ways which would help LEAs meet reporting requirements and gave, for example, gender breakdowns by schools, but there was no attempt at providing anything which modelled the system, such as value added scores.

The fact that many, indeed probably most, LEAs were content with raw or comparative data and made little attempt to develop fair comparisons must surely be due to the lack of expertise in LEAs in research methods appropriate to education. By this I mean expertise to actually collect and analyse data, not just read the literature and write essays. Any LEA, for example, could have started the ALIS project years before I was asked to comment on some A-level results and so started the project. LEA advisors must have been asked many times to comment on results.

This is not to say there was no one with expertise – there were certainly a few individuals. But perhaps it takes a critical mass to have funds allocated to such an activity, with people at every level interested in the data.

This lack of expertise is a national problem now recognized in the training requirements for doctorates in the social sciences. It may take a long time to remedy and may require changes in the way social science is taught throughout the system.

The analysis just presented may be wrong. It should be treated entirely as a set of hypotheses based largely on what 'experts' have commented on. The important questions are who should operate as LEAs, who should be an intermediate layer between the schools and the government, and how the outcomes of LEAs should be evaluated. Work by Willms in Scotland has suggested that the proportion of variance in examination outcomes attributable to LEAs is very small indeed, about 1 per cent. This implies that in the current mode of performance of LEAs there is little to choose between them. As monitoring systems develop, however, it may emerge that some LEAs can be more effective than others. We could even have some adopt the Perutz hypothesis, which involves having administrators/inspectors/advisers who are themselves highly skilled, providing them with good information, and having them discuss and facilitate the work in schools on a person-to-person basis. Others, meanwhile, might adopt the management model of five-year plans written out at length, target setting and the philosophy expressed by the new head of OFSTED: 'a little fear is not a bad thing'. We could also experiment with having LEAs staffed by people elected by teachers.

Once a monitoring system is up and running, the capacity of the system to experiment and evaluate is greatly enhanced. In the UK we are near to having good monitoring systems, and the experimentation will surely follow.

Chapter 23

Inspection: The Accounts are Overdue

> It's not what a man doesn't know that makes him a fool but what he
> does know that ain't so.

Being threatened for advising people to behave scientifically is quite extraordinary. Having now received both written and verbal threats, I feel compelled to record these strange events. When this advice/threat comes from persons high in the power ladder and with some influence on inspection, you begin to wonder what it is they have to worry about and how safe schools are in the face of such an organization.

When OFSTED (the Office of Standards in Education) was set up, I wrote to the then part-time chief, pointing out that schools participating in a monitoring system now had their own measurements of their own effectiveness and they would be able to check on the accuracy of inspectors' judgements. I offered to explain these systems to inspectors and I was hoping to open a dialogue about what inspection might and might not accomplish. I suggested that by having schools keep their data to themselves until *after* an inspection, they could provide a valuable validity check on inspectors' judgements. This idea should not disturb inspectors who are confident that they can identify effective teaching by sitting in classrooms – a belief they share with many people and which simply needs putting to the test. The chief's reply drew my attention to the threat of a 'Level 2' fine should schools not give their data to inspectors. I was amazed, and discovered that it is even written into the Act of Parliament that if data are on a computer the school must help the inspectors to get them off!

Later, a very senior person told me that if I advised schools to run a validity check by only showing inspectors the data *after* an inspection, I too would be liable to a fine. Thus, sound scientific advice would be punished. I would have thought the person who threatened me was a very nice person, yet there he was, threatening me. Nor did he seem overly concerned when I suggested that, for some sensitive people, being told that they had been running a 'failing school' could cause enormous pain, if not lead to suicide. I put his strangely out-of-character behaviour down to the corrupting effect of power. He had too long occupied the role of inspector, been the recipient of acquiescent if not fawning behaviour, and had lost his sense of proper humility and humanity. Let would-be inspectors beware: the job could damage your character.

One problem is that, since teachers are not used to being treated like criminals, no one has a clue what a 'Level 2' fine is.

HER MAJESTY'S INSPECTORS AND THEIR SUCCESSORS: OFSTED

There is a long history of 'inspection' in the UK, thoroughly documented in Dunford (1992). Starting in 1839, Her Majesty's Inspectors (HMIs) were employed as masters in their fields to inspect schools 'without fear or favour'. They reported to the education minister, and the Chief HMI therefore had some influence. However, inspections were few and far between, and in 1993 HMI were either disbanded or re-employed in OFSTED – the Office of Standards in Education. For a while there was a proposal that inspection should be a service which schools themselves purchased. Exactly why the House of Lords threw this out and the government gave up on this market approach would make an interesting study. OFSTED, headed by a part-time chief, a professor of religious studies, was told to inspect one school in four each year, with teams headed by trained 'registered inspectors' and including lay members.

Inspection – the process of having visitors in a school for about a week who then write a report – requires the use of subjective judgements. There is nothing wrong with this. Subjective judgements are what often matter to us, and there are established procedures for checking their reliability and validity (Chapter 13).

TESTING THE COST-EFFECTIVENESS OF INSPECTION – A SCIENTIFIC APPROACH

The system of using subjective judgements is in principle unexceptional. Given the existence of established ways of checking on the reliability and validity of judgements, OFSTED inspectors simply need, as a minimum, to have some credible research into their methodology. *After more than a century of inspection, surely some studies of its reliability, validity, costs and benefits are overdue.*

An OFSTED inspection is a measurement – e.g. 'failing' or 'not failing' – which rests on a series of other measurements, e.g. '70 per cent of lessons were satisfactory'. Since an inspection is a measurement resting on a series of measurements, it needs to be subjected to the kind of tests to which measurements are subjected. These were summarized in Figure 13.1.

To assist esteemed colleagues in OFSTED in designing the kind of tests of their system which they will wish to implement, I spell out below the tests to the system which arise from absolutely standard practices of measurement.

Working from Figure 13.1 we have the following numerous tests which could properly be made.

Reliability

Can different inspectors *independently* arrive at the same set of judgements? If this information is available (e.g. because inspectors rate lessons numerically) can we know the inter-rater reliability?

The critical point is to maintain the independence of the measurements. Second marking is not a check on the first marking if you know the mark awarded. Similarly, we are not asking if inspectors can agree a rating. We are asking if, without any intercommunication, they can come up with the same or similar ratings:

- of the same lesson, looking at the same 'item' of behaviour (the easiest test to pass).

- across different lessons in the same department, since that is the unit on which a judgement is passed. What is the internal consistency of the measures made about a single department? Does it depend upon which inspectors are observing? If so, how do we check out individual inspectors? Are these reliability checks built into the system as a quality system would require.?

These questions can be repeated for the whole school. Does the item–total correlation for various judgements show that some observations are out of line with the summary judgement? I would hope so, since in the experience of most of us there is a great deal of variation within a school.

What if different teams of inspectors visited on different occasions? Would the judgements agree? Judgements should be independently made and written down and any evaluator should have access to these and be able to report on their reliability.

Any study of reliability reveals that, other things being equal, longer tests (more or longer measurements) are more reliable than shorter ones. Calculations can be made as to the sample size needed for any given level of reliability, e.g. for observing mathematics classes and estimating the percentage of students 'on task' (Fitz-Gibbon and Clark, 1982) found that counts made every 2 minutes over 20 minutes in the middle of a lesson would yield reliable measures in urban secondary school mathematics classes once the researcher had been in the class for several lessons in order to become less of a disturbing influence.

Validity

A check on *concurrent validity* requires checking that two quite different ways of measuring the same thing yield the same answer. OFSTED inspectors comment on the effectiveness of teachers, as in this comment from an OFSTED report on a primary school: 'Most teachers work hard to serve the interests of the children but are not given the guidance and structure *which would allow them to be fully effective.*' The report offered, however, no evidence on effectiveness of the teachers.

Those schools that are in a system like ALIS or YELLIS have data which come as close as possible to measuring teacher effectiveness so this could be checked against the inspectors' opinions. But if the inspectors demand to see the data first, before going off to sit in classes, then they would be likely to see whatever the data had suggested that they would see. If there was a conflict, it is not clear what people would trust most. But if inspectors are saying teachers are not 'fully effective', they should be interested in all sources of evidence and keep these sources independent of each other. It needs to be determined to what extent inspectors' ratings correlate with independent quantitative indicators.

Predictive validity asks the question of a measurement: 'Does it predict in the way it should?' If inspectors judge lessons to be 'satisfactory' or not, then does this judgement accurately predict the examination performance of students receiving those lessons? For example, if a department was rated as unsatisfactory, would that department be found to have negative residuals – students achieving less than might reasonably be expected? There could be many reasons why not, one being that the lessons observed are unlikely to be typical, as the inspectors announce their visits in advance, and the school can prepare for weeks or months.

'An inspection isn't a research project', one apologist said, 'the canons of reliability and validity don't apply in the same way.' But, on the contrary, they should be applied with maximum severity, because an inspection involves passing judgements on other people's lives; it involves the possibility of great harm.

And justice must be seen to be done, which brings us to item 6 in Figure 13.1, *face validity* – does the instrument look as though it will produce valid measurements? Inspectors are not always experts, and when they come to the judgement that 'students are not being stretched' (a common comment, since it must always be true of some students and is very difficult to gainsay) does their method for arriving at this judgement command your complete confidence? Have they accurately measured (judged) your students in a way you have not? Could others stretch everyone in the class at once without losing students? Have these judgements received any independent validation of a kind which at least has face validity?

Construct validity – are we measuring what is meant to be measured? Whilst much of what has already been said would be easy and inexpensive to implement, the question of construct validity is critical, and a research programme is required to begin to establish this fundamental kind of validity, because a broad range of evidence is needed.

However, we can apply Popper's scientific method – if it can withstand attempts at falsification, then we have more confidence in the hypothesis. Can we challenge the construct validity of inspection and will it withstand the challenge? For example, inspectors are supposed to judge on what they see, but perhaps they are influenced by rumours, complaints etc.

One experiment which might already be underway is for headteachers around the country to participate in the what we might call the 'plant test'. The headteacher plants an idea with inspectors at their first meeting. The Head might grimace when, say, history is mentioned, and then say, fair-mindedly, 'Well *you* see what *you* think of history.' Do the inspectors turn in a good report on the history department? If they do, then your confidence in their ability to see without prejudice is enhanced.

Another approach to construct validity is to look at relevant bodies of research. Gray and Hannon (1986) found that inspectors could rarely find an inner-city school which was 'good' and rarely find a wealthy school that was 'bad'. HMI did not seem to be adequately contextualizing. However, it *is* very difficult to make fair comparisons – in fact, it might be impossible without extensive data.

A key problem for construct validity is the pre-announced visit. Unannounced visits would surely be more valid. Biased samples are not a source of valid conclusions about general patterns. Random, representative samples are generally the norm. How does this fundamental methodology impact on the design of an inspection in a school?

How are the inspectors going to disentangle the impact of out-of-school factors on school performance, whether these be private tutors in wealthy areas or the need for baby-sitting in poor areas? Do they know the proportion of variance which is generally attributable to a contextual effect?

Is the judgement passed on a school a measure of the headteacher's skills in public relations or skills in writing documentation, such as the school development plan? In other words, is it peripheral appearances which are influential? Should the headteacher concentrate strongly on public relations, even to the detriment of his or her attention to students?

System failures are always a good source of understanding the validity of a system. What had happened at the school which forced the inspectors to withdraw and rewrite their non-negotiable report?

Another problem with construct validity is the concentration on judging a whole school. The whole school is not the best unit of analysis, as has been argued elsewhere in this book. There is great variation possible within schools and to judge the whole is to give the wrong messages.

For an example of the problems of measuring students' attitudes using the kinds of methods adopted by inspectors, see Chapter 11.

Costs

Does OFSTED provide value for money? An inspection apparently costs about £30 000 per school. Other costs are the time and effort spent on producing the documentation to give to the inspectors. Where is the evidence that schools with large amounts of documentation are doing any better than schools with less or none? The notions of efficiency on the edge of chaos and ever-increasing complexity would seem to caution against large amounts of written plans.

Perhaps inspections have good effects, encouraging a new collegiality in the face of an external threat or encouraging people to look at data. Perhaps they raise morale among staff when the school survives the ordeal. Perhaps evidence for these beneficial effects will become available. To date there has only been what has represented to the public as an 'independent' evaluation by Coopers & Lybrand (OFSTED/Coopers & Lybrand, 1994). This was a disgraceful misrepresentation. Coopers & Lybrand merely 'reviewed the evidence' and 'contributed substantially to the report' provided by questionnaires which OFSTED had mailed out to its first 100 schools. There was no mention of anonymity being guaranteed, so we must recognize that schools were replying to the organization which had the capacity to close them down or damage their reputation and which was due to return in three years. Given this situation, it is surprising that the majority did not agree that the much vaunted 'Framework' 'had an impact on school management and organisation'. The percentages agreeing from three groups were: headteachers 33 per cent; teachers 18 per cent and governors 14 per cent (OFSTED/Coopers & Lybrand, 1994, Annex B). Considering that the 'evaluation' stated that 'The proof of inspection will be in its effects on school improvement' (paragraph 92), why were not the various groups asked if the inspection had improved their schools? Had they learned anything? Was it value for money?

EXTRACTS FROM AN INSPECTION REPORT

The reader may be interested in seeing the kind of report for which the public purse is paying many times more than it is spending on research. The school inspected was an inner-city primary school with 56 per cent of pupils in receipt of free school meals. Attendance was logged at about 92 per cent. Here are some of the comments from inspectors:

> The organisation and administration of the school are satisfactory and daily routines are well-established. (p. 18)

> The pupils' attendance record is satisfactory overall although a minority of pupils arrive late. The attendance registers are well kept and are in accordance with the requirements of Circular 11/91.

> The school is a caring community: teachers are concerned about the pupils' welfare and standards of behaviour are generally satisfactory. (p. 6)

> The co-ordinator has written a scheme of work but this requires elaboration and refinement *and is not in use.*

> The school development plan has been drawn up by groups of staff but it lacks detail and does not identify correctly the major issues currently facing the school.

> The school promotes satisfactorily the *social* and *moral* development of the pupils, but not their *spiritual* and *cultural* development.

> Overall, the school provides poor value for money. (p. 7)

Such a report does not seem to provide indicators which meet the standards discussed in Chapter 19:

- relevant;
- informative;
- acceptable;
- beneficial;
- cost-effective.

WHAT SHOULD AN INSPECTION LOOK LIKE?

The concentration on second-guessing educational effectiveness is, I would guess, a mistake. Effectiveness can be well measured with open-to-inspection instruments (examinations) and fair procedures. Many other outcomes can be assessed by locally developed quality assurance procedures, such as questionnaires to students. Inspection in industry often consists more of a study of systems for creating and maintaining quality rather than a presumption that a stranger can assess quality for you.

The distinction must be made between the need for compliance inspection – for health, safety, humanity and legality (e.g. with the National Curriculum), which are suitable topics for inspectors to address – and other topics, like effectiveness, which could be better and more economically addressed by other means. Health and safety inspectors are needed – they are experts and deal with processes which are required. They are there to check on compliance with standards which should have been rationally developed on the basis of known hazards.

FEFC inspection plans

FEFC Circular 93/28 (Further Education Funding Council, 1993) was about an open professional dialogue, developing a system, and an on-going relationship between an inspector and a college. Most welcome were the openness, the recognition of diversity and ongoing change, the broad set of goals which colleges could adopt and the need for a wide variety of evidence, including quantitative indicators, direct observation and the college's own investigations.

The document contained much that was welcome. For example, achievement was not to be assessed on a single global indicator but by major curriculum areas. In addition to performance in examinations, the FEFC framework proposed further areas for assessment which were broad and yet specific enough to be measurable. This was a welcome move towards quantitative monitoring of the diverse outcomes of education, not just examinations, important as they are. Inspection was seen as a 'dialogue' between the assessors and those assessed. The inspection process itself was to be evaluated not only by the inspection team but also by the college being inspected. The openness was to be promoted by having a member of the college participate in the entire inspection process, including meetings of the inspectors. There was a recognition that there is probably no single way to be a good teacher, but possibly many ways to be effective: 'it is unrealistic to expect there to be a single method of delivering further education curricula to ensure a high quality of experience' (Further Education Funding Council, 1993).

However, there are still some problems. Dr Haydn, a college principal, pointed out problems of definition ('standards', 'quality') and the major issue with regard to assessing achievement, which can be expressed as: *why do it? of what? whose achievement? who assesses? how? and what happens then?*

In his response to the consultation on the document, Dr Haydn pointed out that all of the following have some responsibility for outcomes:

- government;
- FEFC;
- students;
- college staff;
- college 'managers';
- college boards;
- individual colleges as entities;
- all colleges across the sector;
- external contractors such as the Training and Enterprise Councils;
- employers;

- parents;
- examining bodies;
- whoever monitors examining bodies.

The complexity of the situation is evident, and therefore it is as well that FEFC gave explicit recognition of the dynamic nature of the educational scene, so that the need constantly to review arrangements is recognized. Systems evolve and no one gets a complicated system right the first time. But clearly some get inspection more right than others. (Appendix 4 contains a response made for colleges in ALIS to the FEFC inspection plans.)

IS THERE ANY ALTERNATIVE TO INSPECTION?

Cannot schools inspect each other? Independent schools seem to favour mutual evaluation. Evaluation by those actually doing the job is an attractive idea, but there are problems with such arrangements. Here is what one participant in a mutual inspection/accreditation visit in the US had to say:

> Experience over six years of serving on (an accreditation scheme) has demonstrated that the process lacks the rigour necessary to provide schools with constructive criticism. There are no objective criteria in the . . . process, and its value is vitiated by the reluctance of peers to expose themselves to reprisal. (Mitchell, 1990)

The accreditation visitors suffer both from fear of reprisals and from the fact that they are pulled away from a demanding job and to fail a school would be to create masses of work for themselves on appeals and recommendation.

> Perhaps the most damning feature of peer teams is that they visit each others schools. Horse-trading is a constant hidden agenda. You find, after the fact, that punches were pulled at this or that school because the principal is to visit the team chair's school next year. At a particularly poor school, a superintendent refused to go along with my desire to withdraw accreditation because she said: 'I'm not here to deal with the problems of this district'. (Mitchell, 1990, p. 78)

CONCLUSION

Inspection is just another part of the design of complex systems. It needs its own outcome measures and fair comparisons. It needs checks and balances, a hierarchical structure and a knowledge base. It needs to adopt the scientific stance advocated throughout this book – scientific humanism with a concern for overall positive impacts.

Schools and colleges should undoubtedly be subject to inspection in the same way that units within any organization are open to inspection *by those responsible*. This qualification is important. Each organization needs to be accountable for achieving something. How, then, can the inspectorates – the bodies which conduct inspections – be held accountable? They should be held accountable for *genuine outcomes*. A national inspectorate should be held responsible for national outcomes. This will require that national outcomes are measured. There could, for example, be five-yearly studies of the teaching profession, on recruitment, retention and morale. There could be national surveys of levels of achievement of the education system in absolute terms, using tests designed to provide comparisons of changes over time – to measure improvements or otherwise in the system as a whole. Such national monitoring was undertaken with distinction by the Assessment of Performance Unit. It is time to restore it. *Only when the inspectorate is subject to outcome accountability can we enable it to receive feedback and take responsibility for the impact of its inspections.*

Until its methods are validated and it is held accountable for outcomes, money is misspent on OFSTED. How large is its budget? It appears to be at least as large, if not larger, than the entire budget of the Economic and Social Research Council which deals with *research* in *all* the social sciences: economics, education, psychology, sociology and management. We need a VFM (value for money) study of OFSTED.

Chapter 24

Politics Could Be So Much Better

> British voters are unimpressed by the way MPs conduct themselves in
> the House of Commons; they would prefer fewer animal noises and
> some sign, now and then, of intelligent debate.
>
> <div align="right"><i>The Economist</i> (1994)</div>

RATIONAL POLITICS

It is often considered naive to think that politics could change and become something better, but the world is facing grim problems. If those with power do not
tackle the problems as intelligently as possible, the chances for our grandchildren
are reduced. Fortunately, this naive hope is increasingly being expressed.

In the following paragraph which was quoted by Sykes (1990, p. 193) Schon
expresses the need for a self-learning system such as monitoring with feedback
can provide:

> For government to become a learning system both the social system of
> agencies and the theory of policy implementation must change.
> Government cannot play the role of 'experimenter for the nation'
> seeking first to identify the correct solution, then to train society at
> large in its adaptation. The opportunity for learning is primarily in
> discovered systems at the periphery, not in the nexus of official policies
> at the centre. Central's role is to detect significant shifts at the
> periphery, to pay explicit attention to the emergence of ideas in good
> currency, and to derive themes of policy by induction.
>
> (Schon, 1983, p. 177)

Politicians should not pretend to know the answers so much as be alert to well-
evaluated improvements, using systems set up so that we can all learn from them,
i.e. using monitoring with feedback.

One of the major responsibilities of politicians, then, is setting up systems
that can learn. If you are looking for significant improvements to the system for
which you are responsible, quantitative indicators are highly valuable but you
also need to be able to get behind the data, to evaluate the richness of what is
happening. This you cannot do when there are too many data. The amount of
information which can be efficiently and effectively used needs to be considered,
when it is, we might find that LEAs or something like them are needed – the
system must be modularized.

THE ROLE OF POLITICIANS

What is the role of the politicians? They need to set goals and set up systems.

One of the goals will be equity, in a fair society. Another will be economy, since time and resources are limited. Another will be effectiveness in reaching the goals. Cheap systems which do not deliver are not efficient (Thomas, 1990).

This is how Sykes spelled out the role which the central government in the USA is supposed to play (and generally tries to play):

> In the US, injustice and inequity are woven deeply into the fabric of society. Schools, for better or worse, are widely viewed as front-line agencies in the struggle to create a more equitable, just and democratic society. Consequently, judicial and legislative actions frequently bring the coercive power of the state to bear on local education.
>
> This perspective provides a counter-image to Big Brother, for what frequently drives authority upward is the aim of protecting the weak, the disenfranchised and those in the minority. (Sykes, 1990, p. 188)

He goes on to cite federal interventions in racial segregation, gender bias in athletics provision, appropriate instruction for non-English-speaking pupils and handicapped pupils and redressing gross imbalances in financial resources to school districts (LEAs). The list reminds us that none of the problems is simple. The need is to keep monitoring and build in the checks and balances.

The steady increase in the amount and openness of information systems will have a substantial impact on politics. As more and more indicators are collected, it will become more difficult to present false information, such as the idea that most parents are dissatisfied with their children's schooling. Perhaps as people have local, live data, referring to their own schools and their own work, and the validity of which they can check, they will be less likely to accept mere opinions.

Indicators in education will have the same effect as economic indicators. Without the numerical measures of the economy we could be sold all sorts of accounts about the ending of the recession, the rates of unemployment etc., the validity of which we could not have checked except against limited local experience. Indicators keep politicians – and all of us – humbled by the necessity for evidence.

If politicians accepted the role of explicating values, and funding science to find out how to implement systems which deliver on those values, then there would be less temptation to advise, at election time: 'Don't vote, it only encourages them'.

Chapter 25

Universities: Just Another Kind of Business or Something Else?

This chapter is concerned with the role of universities, the difference between research and design, the endemic stereotyping in social science, and the way in which live data from monitoring systems can wean us from such inadequate practice.

IS THE DEVELOPMENT OF PERFORMANCE INDICATORS 'RESEARCH'?

This question was put to a colleague at a job interview. He indicated he did not care whether or not it was called research – it was very useful. Is there a problem here? Should work done in universities be 'useful' or should applied work be left to others while university staff busy themselves on the edge of basic knowledge?

Questions that are asked are whether education belongs in a university or whether it should be studied only in teacher training colleges, and whether educational researchers are 'real' psychologists and sociologists. (Clifford and Guthrie, 1988; Thomas, 1990). There has been much concern over these kinds of questions and the tension between practice and theory. The issues seem to have been best resolved by H. A. Simon, who wrote at length about the difference between *science* – seeking fundamental laws – and *design* – using scientific knowledge and methods to achieve goals.

As already briefly discussed in Part 2, H. A. Simon, Nobel Laureate, economist, psychologist and a creator of the discipline of artificial intelligence, argued that education, like engineering, medicine or law, is a 'design discipline' centrally concerned with the design of complex systems (Simon, 1981). The notion that education is about *the design of systems that achieve goals* comes from an academically impeccable, highly revered source, and it provides a rationale for the existence of education in universities.

EDUCATION AS A DESIGN DISCIPLINE

Applied researchers, in education departments, have a responsibility to improve education, just as engineers have some responsibility to contribute something useful. A primary task, then, is to develop systems which work. Just as engineers need to build engines, test them and tune them and experiment with them, until the engine can achieve its purposes, so educational researchers need to develop systems, try them out in real circumstances, research and develop them. A performance monitoring system is one example. Others would be the development of effective teaching strategies or systems for media-assisted instruction. Design demands a knowledge base, and extending that knowledge base is another kind of educational research.

Unfortunately, despite Simon, not everyone in universities will agree that design work is a proper use of time. Some researchers will see the creation of indicator systems only in terms of ways to get research data. Once there are sufficient numbers to create a credible sample, interest in expanding the system may wane. There may be the belief that broad findings can be derived from the data and can then be used to improve education through the normal channels of analysis, drawing conclusions and publishing.

In contrast, I think we need to entertain the hypothesis that *only local knowledge available to every school will improve education through 'research'*. I wish to emphasize a distinction between the data gathered in an indicator system and fed back promptly to every department in every school every year – live data – and the dead, one-off, cross-sectional data which are too often the poor fruit of the 'research project'. Examples will help.

'RESEARCH HAS SHOWN . . .' THE OVER-GENERALIZATION WHICH AMOUNTS TO STEREOTYPING BY STATISTICS

Suppose research showed no difference in effectiveness with age of teacher. What use is this generalization? The argument is then made (and was made) that schools might consider employing younger teachers since they cost less – although the possible detrimental effect of such policies on teacher morale was noted. It is certainly not the case that *all* older teachers get no more effective results than younger teachers. No headteacher would wish to be told to make judgements on individuals based on this 'pattern in the data' finding. What possible use is there for this potentially damaging statement? Yet this is the kind of statement which often arises from research: an exaggeration of a completely mixed picture, a computation of averages which can be more misleading than illuminating.

But if that trend is there in the data should it not be reported? This is a difficult question. The solution is to report such findings only in such a way that they will not be misused. Such findings should be reported with illustrations to show how little accuracy can be obtained from knowledge of this weak finding. To report the finding and then go on to suggest implications for individual actions on the basis of a weak relationship is irresponsible although it is entirely typical of research in social science.

We can look at this question in another way. It is entirely true that more men than women have contributed to the advancement of mathematics. But I doubt if the author of the above-mentioned age stereotyping would be happy suggesting that women be rejected for jobs on the basis of that trend. Yet such behaviour is exactly parallel to that suggested in his book: the use of group membership to infer other information. He would also be upset, I imagine, if he found that a headteacher had actually sent an older teacher into retirement simply on the basis of that statistical stereotyping.

These problems arise because we tend to think in terms of nomothetic research findings – general rules – especially based on simple correlations which grab people's attention, instead of in terms of setting up monitoring systems which measure the more difficult to measure but more relevant indicators.

Why have social scientists not learned to take their responsibilities seriously? The damage done by a US researcher reporting on the length of the school day was cited in Chapter 3. Perhaps social scientists are themselves not used to being taken seriously.

We all recognize how damaging stereotyping is when it occurs in words. People should be judged as individuals on the basis of their individual work, not on their group membership, their ethnicity, their gender or their age. Stereotyping is an over-generalization, the application of a general trend to a particular individual. The avoidance of stereotyping is such a fundamental aspect of equal opportunities and fairness in society that we must watch carefully that the people who most offend against it are not statisticians and educational researchers.

However, I now wish to back away from what is also an over-generalization: the idea that general trends should not be trusted for decisions about individuals. The decisions have to be seen in the context of the particular system. Every decision carries the possibility of costs and benefits, and the overall impact needs to be considered in terms of the costs and benefits *for that particular system*. This point will be argued in the context of another kind of decision about hiring teachers. Should there be efforts to get more males into nursery teaching? Here we have to take into account the finding that most child abuse is committed by men. Would that be a reason for excluding men from nursery teaching, or at least from supervision of very young and therefore very vulnerable children? Here it may be the case that the potential costs are so serious that the statistical trend should be influential. If it is the case that child abuse is almost always by men, i.e. if the security provided to young children would be very much improved by not hiring male nursery teachers, then a rule against hiring men should be acceptable.

The point is that each situation needs to be considered on the basis of carefully collected data and analysis of costs and benefits. We can only 'play the odds' in designing social systems, so for each particular situation we need to assess the odds and weigh up the probable costs and benefits.

It is arguable that we simply need to appreciate the meaning of overlapping distributions, the limited inferences that can fairly be drawn from cross-sectional as opposed to longitudinal data sets, and the fact that correlation is not causation, but I fear that these attainment targets are not widely achieved and in the meantime stereotyping in ways which can be hurtful should be avoided. The temptations to indulge in statistical stereotyping are a major source of discomfort to researchers who recognize the danger.

The relevance of this discussion of stereotyping by statistics to indicator systems is that the particularization, the live data, available in a thorough indicator system make it more likely that complexity is recognized than when a researcher works with dead data, a one-off sample of usually anonymous groups. With an indicator system in place, headteachers will be able to monitor the effectiveness of actual departments and resist the tendency to believe rumours, even when the rumours arise from the research literature.

Another point relevant to social science research in universities is that much statistical stereotyping is the result of going for easy pickings in the data. It is so easy to collect classification data – gender, social class, age, ethnicity – that much research looks at little else. Find some measurement such as achievement in mathematics, relate it to gender and you have a research paper. But of what use is it? If there are differences (and there usually are) there are nevertheless vast overlaps – many girls far exceed many boys in mathematics achievement, even though the differences in average achievement of the two groups is the other way round. If the students were divided by spatial ability rather than by gender, there would be less overlap, a greater difference between averages. Spatial ability is probably a better predictor than gender, but it is more difficult to measure, so social science continues to study group differences in performance. At a time when the world seems to contain far too many groups locked into hostilities on the basis of group membership, would it not be better that we emphasized the similarity of groups and the complexity of the world, using live data and avoiding statistical stereotypes?

One reason researchers go for the easy pickings of yet another article on group differences is the pressure to publish because, ironically, of performance indicators being applied to universities. Here we see a downside to indicator systems: short-termism. However, the publications are supposed to be read, not merely counted, so perhaps quality gets rated.

THE INDEPENDENCE OF UNIVERSITIES

It must be the case that social science is more easily distorted by opinion and selective reporting and sheer wishful thinking, than is 'hard' science. Yet the following letter exemplifies the concern seen from the vantage point of years of working close to a top-rated *computing* department:

> A . . . fundamental threat to the well-being of this country is the effect of changes in funding and status on the integrity of research in our universities.
>
> Most researchers are on short term contracts of two or three years. Much research is funded through contracts with industry for highly specific projects. The established staff, who are the grant holders for and leaders of the research, are only too aware that to maintain or enhance the research rating of the department, and hence the ability to attract students and funding, they must produce the requisite number of papers for publication each year.
>
> All these factors are forcing a short-term approach to research and an insidious, and largely unrecognised, bias towards getting the 'right' results, particularly where interpretation is required.
>
> We need people in the universities with an absolutely objective approach to research and provision of expert advice. They must not be constrained by either too many bureaucratic demands on their time or the need to provide quick results to ensure the next tranche of money.
>
> The danger is that if we don't keep a substantial core of academics in our universities who can uphold the objective approach and speak without fear or favour, we will lose the tradition and find it very difficult to retrieve.
>
> (E. Barraclough, Director Emeritus, Computing Service, University of Newcastle Upon Tyne. Letter to the *Guardian*)

STANDARDS IN UNIVERSITIES

Finally, a chapter on universities in a book on monitoring cannot avoid the 'quality systems' being suggested for universities. In the UK these involve something akin to inspection (Chapter 23) and such procedures deserve to be challenged. But there is also the question of standards. Universities do not subscribe to examination boards but conduct their own assessments. They too should use assessment transcripts as in Chapter 9 and the use of common examinations across universities is not impossible to imagine.

The notion that there should be common testing across universities, which is increasingly being suggested (Howarth, 1993; Coleman, 1994), is not popular. When it was suggested on the Internet (an electronic communication network used by many academics), it received comments like:

> . . . a national examine is even worse that dumb . . . it serves no real educational function. It's designed for politicians, legislators, business execs, funders . . . but not for students or teachers. It's set up to rank students (on bogus, irrelevant basis), districts, teachers, whatever. Though maybe Whittle and his bunch could charge higher advertising dollars if 'his' schools did better . . . maybe there is something to this after all. (D. Selwyn)

However, the philosopher Michael Scriven, originator of the terms 'formative' and 'summative' evaluation, commented thus:

> You were asking about rationales for national university exams. Three ones that seem non-trivial to me, and have been proposed are: (i) to give the consumers some idea of whether they are wasting their money on an expensive private institution, or large and famous state universities, when other places do as well with comparable entering classes; (ii) to give the institutions management and faculty the same information for them to use in the improvement of instruction; (iii) to see what the value-added contribution of the institution is on some general skills (this would require that exams be given at first and fourth year).

We see all the issues that face schools and the hostility to simplistic information passing into the public domain. League tables seem to get in the way of information gathering.

In universities, which should be teaching some courses at the cutting edge of the disciplines and in line with staff interests (since universities are there to create and disseminate knowledge), the notion of common tests is too easily dismissed. There are basic skills and information which can be assessed for some disciplines. The competence of students in a foreign language can apparently be cheaply and realistically assessed and there is growing voluntary use of such testing. Furthermore, many professional scientific bodies have examinations open to all, and performance on these could be a useful safeguard of some level of standards. If there are no safeguards, combined with the desperate need to get students in order to keep staff in post, then standards will be whimsical.

Some departments (mainly arts-based or education) have relied only on students' essays for assessment. The argument is made that when examinations are set the answers are depressing – poor quality – as though the students do not understand. But the essays are of good quality. Yet surely it is possible that the examinations were a more valid indicator of levels of comprehension? Perhaps the essays were carefully rephrased regurgitations of poorly understood ideas. There can also be problems with authorship and plagiarism which are almost impossible to eliminate. These problems must be confronted, and multiple assessment techniques used, if there are to be standards of some level of reliability in the increasing numbers of universities.

PART EIGHT

Signing Off

It is difficult to end this book. Even as it was being completed new events of relevance came to light. Two of them form the topic of the final chapter, which finishes with a list of questions.

Chapter 26

In Conclusion

Two events occurred as this book was almost typeset.

In February 1995 the CEM Centre was awarded the national contract to pilot a Value Added system. We are to conduct statistical tests and run two pilots, one in primary schools and another in secondary schools. We are very pleased, as, we hope, are all the schools, colleges, professional associations, LEAs and TECs who worked with us over the years simply because, in their judgement, we made sense. The CEM Centre's enthusiastic young research associates, who have been looking after and analysing all the data in recent years, rejoiced at this success. Most importantly, we will try to make the fairest and most cost-effective system possible, with feedback to every teacher. Many people have commented with pleasure that the scathing attacks on OFSTED (recorded in Chapter 23) had not resulted in any veto.

The award came as we were gearing up to differentiate our information systems to range from DIY (Do-It-Yourself) options to improvement-oriented systems incorporating networks conducting Randomized Controlled Trials RCTs – to collect type 4 data, the gold standard of evidence as advocated in Chapters 1 and 2. And RCTs were the topic of a second event to be noted with enthusiasm.

Also in February 1995, there was a burst of press publicity associated with the formation of the Centre for Evidence Based Medicine at Oxford University – dedicated to guiding medical practice on the basis of RCTs. David Sackett, who left McMaster Medical School in Ontario, Canada, to take up the Directorship of the Centre for Evidence Based Medicine in Oxford, is quoted as having said 'If you're scanning an article about therapy and it is not a randomized trial, why on earth are you wasting your time? And also:

> The most important development in health care in the past half century
> is the randomized controlled trial and the most important development
> in medicine in the next twenty years will be the systematic review of
> RCTs in health care.

It is good to record that the field of education contributed quite substantially to the methodologies and ideas of 'systematic review'. In 1982, Glass, McGaw and Smith published *Meta-analysis in social research* and this book was followed by numerous texts showing how to create quantitative syntheses of research results, particularly those arising from randomized controlled trials (e.g. Hedges and Olkin, 1985).

Importantly the books and articles on meta-analysis have shown up the flaw in the widespread practice of simply counting up whether results of various experiments were or were not statistically significant – another example of the significantly poor education in statistics that is all too often provided. Glass, McGaw and Smith also illustrated the bias which exists in publication and which has also been noted by the Evidence Based Medicine Group. There is a tendency for editors to accept strongly positive results more readily and to accept less readily studies which, while just as good methodologically, have not yielded dramatic results. One estimate presented by Glass, McGaw and Smith, (1982, p. 67) was that the publication bias appeared to be about one-third of a standard score. (The solution is surely to have a system in which reviewers and editors accept or reject articles on the basis of an account of the *methods*, with *results* being provided only after acceptance. Nothing else will remove publication bias.)

However, the first major problem for education is to persuade policy-makers and researchers of the need to conduct randomized controlled trials. There are plenty of such trials in small-scale research. For example, the positive effects on achievement of having older pupils tutor younger pupils are well established by numerous controlled experiments (Fitz-Gibbon, 1984 and 1992). But large-scale policies are rarely introduced in well controlled pilots. If randomized controlled trials are so good for medicine, would they not also be an appropriate way to evaluate a number of other areas, such as the effects of counselling, educational strategies, and management nostrums such as the introduction of highly expensive appraisal systems? Indeed, trials should have been conducted of indicator systems, as was argued in Chapter 7.

The hope now is that when monitoring systems are in place they will provide a stimulus to the development of an effective society – a society which can learn how to achieve important goals rather than lurching ineffectively from one fashion or nostrum to another. When information on valued outcomes is fed back to those responsible, adjustments can be made until the outcomes desired are, at least, approached, if not achieved. This requires that we measure all the outcomes of concern, not just one or two, such as profits or examination results (Sen, 1993).

In summary, some of the learning that society needs to achieve, in education and in medicine, can be by trial and error in the context of the continuing necessity to run schools and hospitals. But sorting cause and effect will always be difficult in such systems, although the longitudinal nature of monitoring will help. The other way in which we can acquire stronger evidence for effectiveness is by setting up randomized controlled trials – and the potential for these is greatly increased by the existence of regular systematic monitoring. A few dozen schools might agree to implement randomized trials, and the results will roll off the monitoring systems as a disturbance to the series of measurements being regularly made over time.

Give complex systems feedback and resources and they will learn to be effective. To use Popper's expressions: by 'piecemeal social engineering' we can 'minimise avoidable suffering'.

The questions, then, are:

- What are the outcomes of concern? What do we value enough to measure?

- What kind of feedback is required – which variables, how measured and how frequently measured? And what co-variates are needed to make fair comparisons (i.e. what predicts the outcomes of concern)?

- How should feedback be provided?

- What degree of confidentiality is desirable at each level of the system (i.e. who gets to know what)? How can the damage of publicity be balanced against the need for open information systems? What balance works most effectively?

- What kind of feedback is understood – with or without additional training?

- Are there process variables which relate to the outcomes of concern, i.e. are there 'alterable variables' – things people might choose to do which might make a difference, and should therefore be monitored? Can these be measured without raising false hopes of easy answers or risking widespread misinterpretation of correlation as causation?

- How can policy issues and improvement efforts be evaluated by multi-site randomized controlled trials?

- Can social science be scientific?

- Can politics become more intelligent?

Appendix 1

Chaotic Behaviour of a Very Simple Non-linear Equation

(This Appendix may not be of general interest.)

The behaviour of non-linear systems can be very simply demonstrated on a spreadsheet using the equation

$$X_{n+1} = p*X_{(n)}*[1-X_{(n)}]$$

This equation shows the behaviour described in Chapter 5, including sensitivity to initial conditions, for suitable parameter values (p). The 'initial condition', X_0, can be taken anywhere in the range 0 to 1. Here we use 0.2.

In case the reader is interested, the following description may assist him or her in creating the equations on a spreadsheet.

Put in the values $X_0 = 0.2$ and some value of p. In the following pages the values of p which have been used are 1, 2, 2.5, 3, 3.5, 3.57, 3.7, 4 and 5. Then you can produce the set of Xs (i.e. X_0 to X_{17}) by having a row for n with the values $n = 1,2,3,4 \ldots 17$ and using these for successive computations of X_{n+1}.

This was done on the EXCEL spreadsheet, which is produced in Figure A1.1. People enjoy trying other values.

References: Stewart (1989); Bartlett, 1990.

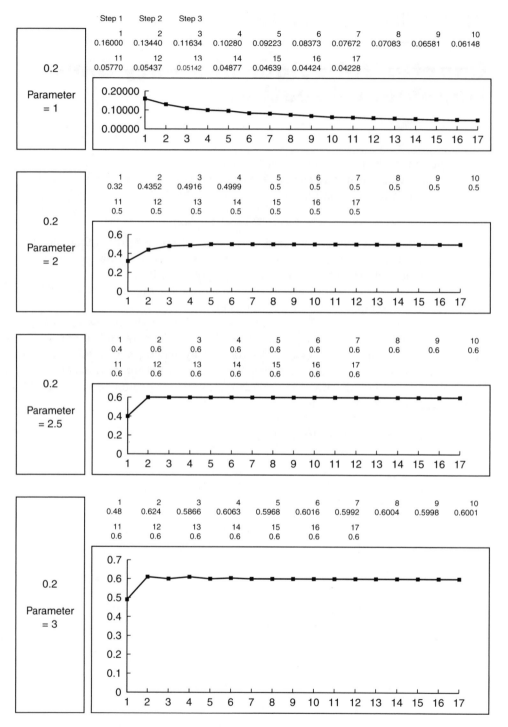

Step 1	Step 2	Step 3							
1	2	3	4	5	6	7	8	9	10
0.16000	0.13440	0.11634	0.10280	0.09223	0.08373	0.07672	0.07083	0.06581	0.06148
11	12	13	14	15	16	17			
0.05770	0.05437	0.05142	0.04877	0.04639	0.04424	0.04228			

0.2

Parameter
= 1

1	2	3	4	5	6	7	8	9	10
0.32	0.4352	0.4916	0.4999	0.5	0.5	0.5	0.5	0.5	0.5
11	12	13	14	15	16	17			
0.5	0.5	0.5	0.5	0.5	0.5	0.5			

0.2

Parameter
= 2

1	2	3	4	5	6	7	8	9	10
0.4	0.6	0.6	0.6	0.6	0.6	0.6	0.6	0.6	0.6
11	12	13	14	15	16	17			
0.6	0.6	0.6	0.6	0.6	0.6	0.6			

0.2

Parameter
= 2.5

1	2	3	4	5	6	7	8	9	10
0.48	0.624	0.5866	0.6063	0.5968	0.6016	0.5992	0.6004	0.5998	0.6001
11	12	13	14	15	16	17			
0.6	0.6	0.6	0.6	0.6	0.6	0.6			

0.2

Parameter
= 3

Figure A1.1(a) *The EXCEL spreadsheet*

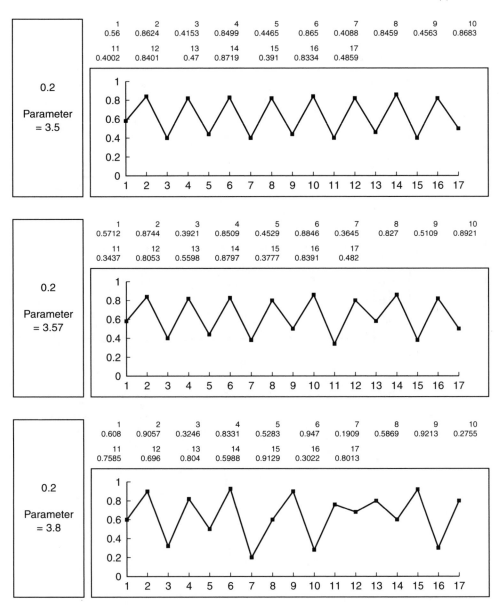

1	2	3	4	5	6	7	8	9	10
0.56	0.8624	0.4153	0.8499	0.4465	0.865	0.4088	0.8459	0.4563	0.8683

11	12	13	14	15	16	17
0.4002	0.8401	0.47	0.8719	0.391	0.8334	0.4859

0.2

Parameter = 3.5

1	2	3	4	5	6	7	8	9	10
0.5712	0.8744	0.3921	0.8509	0.4529	0.8846	0.3645	0.827	0.5109	0.8921

11	12	13	14	15	16	17
0.3437	0.8053	0.5598	0.8797	0.3777	0.8391	0.482

0.2

Parameter = 3.57

1	2	3	4	5	6	7	8	9	10
0.608	0.9057	0.3246	0.8331	0.5283	0.947	0.1909	0.5869	0.9213	0.2755

11	12	13	14	15	16	17
0.7585	0.696	0.804	0.5988	0.9129	0.3022	0.8013

0.2

Parameter = 3.8

Figure A1.1(b) *The EXCEL spreadsheet*

227

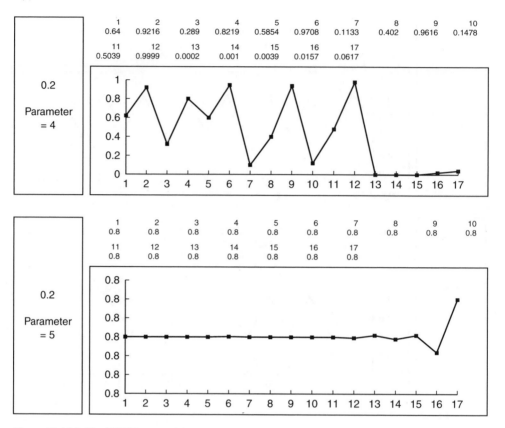

1	2	3	4	5	6	7	8	9	10
0.64	0.9216	0.289	0.8219	0.5854	0.9708	0.1133	0.402	0.9616	0.1478

11	12	13	14	15	16	17
0.5039	0.9999	0.0002	0.001	0.0039	0.0157	0.0617

0.2

Parameter = 4

1	2	3	4	5	6	7	8	9	10
0.8	0.8	0.8	0.8	0.8	0.8	0.8	0.8	0.8	0.8

11	12	13	14	15	16	17
0.8	0.8	0.8	0.8	0.8	0.8	0.8

0.2

Parameter = 5

Figure A1.1(c) *The EXCEL spreadsheet*

Appendix 2

Secondary Education in England and Wales: Comparisons with the USA

(Both US and UK* patterns may vary regionally but the ones illustrated give a general pattern.)

US name of year group	Name of the institution	UK* name of year group	Age on leaving	Exams	Name of the institution
Senior	University				
Junior		3rd year			University
Sophomore		2nd year			
Fresher		1st year			
12th grade	Senior high	Year 13	18	A-level (a)	Sixth form or FE college or school sixth form
11th grade		Year 12	17		
10th grade		Year 11	16 (b)	GCSE (KS4) (c)	Secondary school
9th grade	Junior high	Year 10	15		
8th		Year 9	14	Key Stage 3	
7th		Year 8	13		
6th	Elementary	Year 7	12	(d)	
5th		Year 6	11	Key Stage 2	Primary school
4th		Year 5	10		
3rd		Year 4	9		
2nd		Year 3	8		
1st grade		Year 2	7	Key Stage 1	
Kindergarten		Year 1	6		
			5		Reception class

* England and Wales

(a) Advanced level external examinations: Authentic, high stakes, externally set Examinations, based on syllabuses for each subject published by an examination board. Certificates are awarded to students showing the grade obtained (A, B etc.) in each subject and these certificates are widely used by employers and universities. See Appendix 3 for a description of the work of examination boards.

(b) Sixteen years of age is the leaving age, the last year in which schooling is compulsory. The post-16 phase of education is voluntary and is pursued in the same secondary school or in other schools or colleges, depending upon student choice and the availability of courses.

(c) KS = Key Stage. 'Key stage' tests were initially to be internally administered, criterion-referenced tests called SATs (Standard Assessment Tasks). Whilst KS4 linked into the existing examining system, earlier key stage tests were supposed to cover the National Curriculum and be criterion referenced – organizations were given a few months in which to create this edifice of criterion-referenced examining. Testing was to be undertaken by teachers working with their own students and it was planned to publish the results to evaluate schools.

(d) There used to be an 'Eleven plus' externally set and marked ability test which was used to select students age 11 and over for 'grammar schools': selective secondary schools enrolling the top 20–25 per cent. Grammar schools became rare after the Labour party introduced 'comprehensive schools' but there are attempts to reintroduce them by allowing selection of students by schools.

Appendix 3

UK Examination Boards: A Summary

WHAT ARE EXAMINATION BOARDS?

Essentially, examination boards are organizations which set and grade examinations. They thus provide independent outcome measures for the cognitive aims of schooling. In the UK they are non-profit organizations. If they make a surplus it must be ploughed back into the system. They are under the control of the Charity Commission in this regard. They also have to be approved by central government.

WHAT KIND OF EXAMINATIONS DO THEY SET?

The examinations are performance based, authentic, high stakes, sensitive to instructional effects, widely accepted and credible to employers, higher education, parents, students and teachers. Examination certificates are cherished documents and grades provide basic information for CVs.

HOW ARE THEY STAFFED?

They are staffed by groups of permanently employed educational professionals with a variety of skills: measurement and statistics, subject matter competencies, experience in teaching.

These permanent staff are augmented on an as-needed, *per diem* basis by practising teachers, representatives of higher education, representatives of business and industry, and representatives of professional organizations such as teacher unions.

In short, the permanent staff is consistently enhanced by representatives of important constituencies. Democracy, development and responsiveness are built into the procedures – with frequent revisions of syllabuses to reflect the advice of university staff, business, industry, teachers, etc.

HOW DO BOARDS FUNCTION?

The staff, permanent, full-time and part-time, form committees to devise and revise syllabuses, to set and scrutinize examination papers each year, and to supervise and keep under review the grading standards. An examination board undertakes to:

- provide examinations, usually defined by a subject (e.g. physics) at a given level (e.g. Ordinary Level at 16; Advanced Level at 18);
- publish syllabuses outlining the topics to be examined in each examination, and arrange for the administration of each examination at sites called centres;
- provide centres with instructions and materials so that the

231

examinations can be administered under standardized conditions at the same time of the same day throughout the country;

- arrange for the examinations to be assessed by competent professionals working to specified procedures;
- check the assessments by a variety of statistical measures and sampling, e.g. re-marking of borderline scripts, re-marking of scripts awarded a grade more than two grades discrepant from teachers' predictions, re-marking scripts from any marker who is out of line with other markers;
- inform students of the results of their examinations on a pre-specified date and provide them with certificates;
- inform institutions of higher education of the results when these are needed for admissions purposes;
- provide published analyses of the strengths and weaknesses exhibited by candidates in the examinations in each subject each year;
- keep in stock previously used examination papers so that these can be purchased and used for practice;
- conduct ongoing research into the fairness and adequacy of the examinations.

In the UK we have taken these fair and open systems for granted for so long that many educators and politicians have forgotten or failed to realize how good they are (Chapter 8).

Appendix 4

ALIS Indicators and FEFC Inspection Plans: A Booklet Written for Colleges

Colleagues who have attended ALIS INSET sessions will know how critical we are of OFSTED and its proposed inspections. It was a real pleasure to discover that FEFC, the body which will inspect colleges, has produced a much more promising approach. Although the following discussion will be of interest primarily to colleges, the school sector may like to note the positive points (and mention them pointedly to any OFSTED inspectors they encounter).

OVERVIEW

Sixth form colleges and FE colleges are now 'incorporated', operating independently of local education authorities and subject to inspection and funding decisions taken by the Further Education Funding Council (FEFC). Circular 93/28 from FEFC presents their framework for inspection and was produced after wide consultation. It is a document which contains much which is welcome. For example, achievement is not to be assessed on a single global indicator but grades will be assigned to major curriculum areas. We have argued for ten years in the ALIS project that schools and colleges vary within themselves and it is this departmental variation which must be monitored in order to assure quality across the college. Our vast body of data supports this view and it is good to see FEFC take the lead in recognizing this complexity (whilst others still look for league tables based on a single figure for an institution).

In addition to performance in examinations, the FEFC framework proposes further areas for assessment which are broad and yet specific enough to be measurable. Again this is a very welcome move towards monitoring the diverse outcomes of education, not just examinations, important as they are.

Another fine feature is the sense of openness in that assessment is seen as a 'dialogue' between the assessors and those assessed. The inspection process itself is to be evaluated not only by the inspection team but also by the college being inspected. The openness will be promoted by having a member of the college participate in the entire inspection process, including meetings of the inspectors. Each college will have a main full-time inspector who will get to know the college both before an inspection and during it, and who will then be monitoring the college's responses after the inspection. Long-term association seems to be envisaged between each college and the full-time inspector. This continuity of personnel and openness of procedures seems to bode well for a fully professional attempt to understand and interpret the evidence a college can present about its performance. There is also a most welcome recognition that there is probably no single way to be a good teacher, but possibly many ways to be effective. Thus we find in the circular the statement 'it is unrealistic to expect there to be a single method of delivering further education curricula to ensure a high quality of experience'.

There is explicit recognition of the dynamic nature of the educational scene, so the need to constantly review arrangements is recognized. Systems evolve and no one gets a complicated system right the first time.

In short, we welcome the openness, the recognition of diversity and ongoing change, the broad set of goals which colleges adopt and the need for a wide variety of evidence, including quantitative indicators, direct observation and the college's own investigations. FEFC is leading the way in quality assurance.

FEFC INSPECTION AND ALIS

In the following section I have tried to indicate ways in which the ALIS system can support colleges within this framework for inspection. Mostly the support is already there but it is worth pointing out the details, particularly for colleges newly joining the system. In some instances the FEFC circular has stimulated thinking about how to measure some important outcomes and this year will see considerable development of graphical methods of feedback for a wide variety of indicators, many of which will be relevant to the FEFC concerns. An APVIC/ALIS conference provided us with highly valued feedback about our procedures and we encourage all colleges to write to us, phone or fax whenever they have ideas for research topics or for improvement in the procedures or ideas for additions or subtractions to the list of the things we are measuring.

General notes about this document. In pointing out how the ALIS data fit in with features of the FEFC inspection framework, some technical terms will be used and, for simplicity, this document is written as if addressing colleges already in the ALIS project. Apologies if this sometimes makes for difficult reading. If terms are not understood, you have a litmus test indicating the need for INSET in the college. We are building a team of INSET providers throughout the country and a phone call to 0191 222 6397 will help you to get started in planning some relevant INSET.

In the following pages quotations from the FEFC circular 93/28 are followed by comments regarding how ALIS fits in with the inspection procedures.

> The inspection process will embrace . . . evaluation of the college's
> strategy for monitoring and enhancing the quality of its own provision
> (p. 8)

Clearly, the data provided by participation in the ALIS project make possible a reasonable strategy for monitoring and seeking to identify areas where quality can be improved or copied.

> . . . colleges will be invited to nominate a senior member of staff to act
> as the first point of contact with the inspectorate and to participate in
> the team inspection by joining team meetings, interpreting evidence
> and clarifying uncertainties (p. 8)

It would seem to be important that this senior member of staff is fully conversant with the ALIS data and how to interpret it. Whether an inspection team is given access to the ALIS data before or after the inspection is a matter that should be left to the discretion of colleges. At the CEM centre we do not disclose to anyone which colleges do and do not belong to the ALIS project.

> The main body of the report will set out the inspection team's judgements of the strengths and weaknesses of the following aspects of the college;
>
> - responsiveness and range of provision
> - governance and management
> - students recruitment, guidance and support
> - teaching and the promotion of learning
> - students' achievements
> - quality assurance
> - resources

(para 17, p. 9)

RESPONSIVENESS AND RANGE OF PROVISION

One of the areas of concern is provision for mature students. In the ALIS questionnaire revised for 1993/94 there are not only the usual questions about age which enable us to identify the percentage of mature students taking any particular subject but also questions about the extent to which mature students have heavy domestic responsibilities. Like several of the questions which have been added to the revised questionnaire, these particular questions arise from our work with BTEC and reflect our concern to evaluate fairly the Advanced GNVQ provisions which many colleges are now implementing.

Also under the explanation of 'responsiveness and range of provision', we find a 'positive feature' described as follows: 'there is access to, and participation in, post-compulsory education by groups traditionally under represented in further education' (p. 12).

> - The extent to which previously under-represented groups are represented in a college will presumably depend to a considerable extent on the location of the college. We will investigate being able to assess the percentage of students in the college from under-represented groups in comparison with the percentage in the area in which the college is located. This might necessitate a link with census data or a comparison with local schools in the area. We shall be investigating a way to provide fair comparisons which give some quantitative evidence for the extent to which the college is providing access for previously under-represented groups.

Another way in which the ALIS project can monitor the quality of opportunity is to examine the extent to which the residuals correlate with socio-economic status, ethnicity, gender, mature student status and English as a second language status. Clearly it will be necessary to compare the correlations within a college or within a department with the correlation found in similar departments elsewhere. We know, for example, that girls generally show less 'value added' (i.e. worse residuals) than boys, particularly in the science subjects at A-level. There would only be cause for concern if the correlation was much more strongly negative in a particular department than was normal for that department in similar colleges.

GOVERNANCE AND MANAGEMENT

> . . . responsibility for implementing and monitoring policies relating to matters such as equal opportunities (and) student support . . . are clearly allocated. (p. 12)

- The ALIS Co-ordinator will be in a position to assist in the monitoring of equal opportunities and student support. Student support is an area in which we have added several questions as a result of our work with BTEC. The new ALIS + 93/94 questionnaire asks students about induction procedures, counselling and other support services so there will be numerical indicators. You will be able to see your college in comparison with others on the student support dimension.

- Also under 'governance and management' the issue of 'unit costs' arises (p. 12). From its inception in 1993 the ALIS project has looked at the hours per week provided for instruction and the size of the teaching group. These two factors account for most of the costs in the provision of the course. We have been advised by many participants in the APVIC/ALIS conference that asking students the number of minutes per week of instruction is not such a good idea, as it slows down their response on the questionnaire and provides unreliable data. We shall therefore be acquiring the information on minutes per week and class sizes in an alternative manner through the sheets which will be sent to colleges for checking by staff.

- The process reports have always enabled you to look at the hours per week which you allocate to a course as compared with the general distribution allocations. Likewise, process reports have indicated the range of class sizes or size of teaching groups. However, a new method of presenting these data in a uniform graphical format is being developed which we think you will find useful and readily understood.

- Also under the heading 'governance and management' we find mention of 'retention rates' (p. 12). We have been moving towards the collection of data in November/December of the first year of a two-year course. This procedure is going ahead for everyone this year and will allow us to provide analyses of which kind of students are retained on courses and which tend to drop out. You will also receive comparative data on retention rates course by course so that you can see yourselves in the national picture. This kind of information is presumably one of the 'quantitative indicators' for which the FEFC calls.

- 'Student destinations' are also mentioned (p. 12). It would be possible for us to follow up students by mail a year or two after they have left college or to analyse data sent in by colleges. This would require some planning. Meanwhile Peter Tymms and Carol Fitz-Gibbon have an ESRC grant to find out what has happened to students who were in the ALIS project in 1988, and will be reporting on the findings of that research in due course.

- Closely related to student destinations is a concern about students' levels of aspiration for continued education and training. We have been measuring this for many years using what we call the Likelihood of Staying in Education (LSE) scale. The new method of graphical feedback will provide you with information on the constituent elements of the LSE scale and there is already a considerable amount of data in Tables F and G of the attitude report. Table G in particular shows whether your college for students in that particular subject have above or below average expectations taking account of the prior achievement levels of the students. If you have a negative residual in Table G, for example, it suggests that, in that particular course, the students were under-aspiring considering their GCSE grades. A positive residual suggests that they were somewhat over-aspiring considering their GCSE grades. Whether in absolute terms this is 'real' over-aspiration is very difficult to judge in the context of a rapidly changing university sector. In the table the comparison is with similar students in the ALIS sample.

STUDENTS' RECRUITMENT, GUIDANCE AND SUPPORT

Before entry students are provided with information and impartial guidance (p. 12)

The chance a student has of achieving various grades in various subjects might form part of the impartial guidance. The DOS disk available from the CEM Centre to colleges in the ALIS project (send us a disk and we send it back with a program on) enables you to type in the student's GCSE grades and give them a most likely predicted grade at A-level in each of 43 subjects, and also to throw up on the screen the Chances Graphs showing the likelihood of each possible grade predicted on the basis of the average GCSE of the student. The Chances Graphs are also available on paper that was sent out with Newsletter Number 3. A new version of the disk is being produced to run under Windows and this version will print out as well. Christopher Egdell will be sending out details when he has finished his programming.

Following entry there are effective induction programmes. (p. 13)

The new ALIS Plus questionnaire asks students to rate the adequacy of induction programmes and also tutorial support and guidance. Work experience is also assessed although this is not mentioned in the FEFC framework.

TEACHING AND THE PROMOTION OF LEARNING

It should be noted that there will be no whole college indicators under this heading. Teaching and the promotion of learning is clearly seen as the responsibility of each subject area, course or programme team. Under this heading on p. 13 of the document, we find listed a number of procedures which are thought to be 'good practice'. There is certainly research evidence to indicate that content inclusion and emphasis which could be called 'coverage' is quite decisive in its effect on students' learning. As for 'encouraging their personal development', the students' open-ended comments about their experience of taking A-levels and BTEC courses often indicated the sense of personal growth and development and general enjoyment of the experience of taking these courses.

In this section we find the statement 'devise teaching and learning schemes which . . . take account of the different abilities of students on the programme' (p. 13). We can best assess this in the ALIS project by seeing if the residuals are related to the ability level of the students. *Ability* is of course a difficult concept and may be considered to mean something different from prior *achievement* (GCSE grades, for example). For those colleges choosing to do the International Test of Developed Abilities we will have a measure which is as close to an ability measure as it is feasible to get, using a test devised specifically to compare abilities of students continuing in education beyond the age of 18.

You can see whether you are equally successful with more or less able students by grouping their residuals. Many of the other features that are recommended in the document on p. 13 are difficult to assess and do not necessarily relate to effectiveness. One is 'choose a variety of teaching and learning approaches which are appropriate for the subject being studied and encourage students to work on their own or in groups' (p. 13). We can provide indicators of the variety of approaches based on the questions that are answered and reported in the process report and we can provide information about the extent to which your students seem to work on their own or in groups compared with other similar students. This raises an issue which has been brought to our attention on several occasions. At present the Process Reports show how various teaching and learning processes relate to achievement and attitudinal outcomes. They do not, at present, contain any description of how teaching is done in any one department. It was felt in the early days of ALIS that this kind of information would be too much like a spy in the classroom and could be resented by staff. We have been asked again and again, however, to provide the data by teaching group for comparison with the general pattern of teaching and learning activities. We will work this year on a way to do this and to investigate these data tentatively in the full recognition of the principle mentioned earlier that there are many ways to be a good teacher and different people will find different ways to be effective. We do know that how people teach depends to a very large extent on what it is they teach. (Teaching and learning processes are being compared across vocational and academic courses of similar kinds in a research programme at the University of Newcastle-upon-Tyne being conducted by Tony Edwards, Carol Fitz-Gibbon, Roy Hayward and Nick Meagher. Colleges will hear the results of this two-year project as they become available and long before they see the light of day in publication format.)

Reinforce the learning through the use of teaching and learning aids. (p. 13)

The new questionnaire asks students about the use of computers and other aids in their learning.

STUDENTS' ACHIEVEMENTS

... bearing in mind their previous achievements and the objectives they have agreed with the institution, students ... enjoy their studies. (p. 13)

Clearly, the ALIS scales of attitude to the subject and attitude to the institution feature enjoyment as a major factor in these attitudes. The same paragraph on p. 13 of the inspection framework indicates that, when appropriate, students should 'speak and write about their work clearly and with enthusiasm'. The students' open-ended responses may help to provide evidence here. These open-ended responses have been extended to four items rather than the previous two items. The questions asked should provide answers which are clearly focused in praising some features of their programmes and suggesting areas for improvement. We expect the colleges to find this information very useful. It is important to have this information in confidence each year, to be used or not used as the college wishes.

Group work and practical work are mentioned in this section and with the new style feedback on processes – which will take some time to develop – you will be able to see whether the amount of group work and practical work reported by your students is higher or lower than generally reported in that subject in the rest of the ALIS sample.

The programme targets for success rates in the external examinations ... are achieved. (p. 14)

This is one of the very few negative points that we could possibly make about this otherwise excellent document. What is the point of setting targets to be judged against? Should one set low targets and exceed them or high targets and fail to meet them? This is just an unproductive game-playing exercise. This opinion is also put forward by W. Edwards Deming, notable for his introduction of total quality management. A constant striving for improvement is at the heart of 'quality'. However, this is a personal view and it is realized that there are national targets to meet which colleges take very seriously. These will only be achieved if the whole system constantly improves and such whole system improvement will not show up in residuals (measures of 'distance travelled', 'relative progress' or 'value added'). Absolute measures, rather than relative measures, will be needed on a national basis for such national targets. For a college the appropriate target would seem to be to keep up with or exceed national improvements and this would be indicated by attaining a zero or positive residual, within error, in each department. For example, if a department's residuals averaged over three years were equivalent to zero, this would indicate that the department was achieving appropriate results for its students.

QUALITY ASSURANCE

> At the institutional level there is an overall policy on quality and its assurance and control which is understood and supported by the staff and, where appropriate, the academic board. (p. 14)

We have always worked on the principle that the entire staff should understand the functioning of the ALIS information system. This is why we try to provide INSET in every college for all members of staff. Please contact us if you need more INSET. The INSET sessions also provide us with feedback about the working of the project and the tremendously positive reception that we generally encounter keeps us working overtime and in good cheer.

> The Strategy for Quality Monitoring and Enhancement includes the collection and systematic use of Performance Indicators. (p. 14)

The A-level Information System could as well have been called the quality indicator system. (In fact QUIS was the name suggested when we asked the DES to help us to provide ALIS nationally.) From the start we have recognized that a wide range of indicators is needed if the work of the college is to be fairly assessed.

> The strategy for quality monitoring and enhancement meets the needs of the institution and also takes account of the needs of the examining, validating and accrediting body and the Council's inspectorate.

One might ask if the needs of the council for the inspectorate are to be met, then would the council's inspectorate like to contribute to the cost?

> The strategy for quality monitoring and enhancement includes linked programmes of staff appraisal and staff development. (p. 14)

- Our view, and also W. Edwards Deming's view, is that staff appraisal should not be linked to indicators and should probably, therefore, be kept away from the quality strategies. Quality is about the working of the system and Deming has issued many warnings about the dangers of attributing deficiencies to individuals rather than investigating the system. There will be staff appraisal but the effort for quality should be kept apart from the appraisal system.

We are certainly seeing a very steep learning curve as staff all over the country become familiar with regression analysis, value added, residuals, statistical significance and, soon, effect sizes. Participation in ALIS enhances the professional skills of teachers and lecturers.

RESOURCES

> The size and layout of the accommodation are suitable for the courses and programmes of study adequate to meet the needs of students with physical disabilities. (p. 14)

Our 1994 questionnaire asks students about the adequacy of provisions such as study space, library facilities, computing access.

There is sufficient specialist equipment and information technology
equipment and adequate library facilities and other learning support
materials and resources are available and accessible to all students. (p. 14)

Of course the ALIS questionnaire picks up student's opinions about these
matters. The direct observations provided by inspectors are an invaluable alternative source of information, particularly as inspectors can bring their experience
from other schools and colleges and share it in some depth with staff. It is also
good to see it acknowledged in the framework that resources may be beyond the
control of the college.

All in all the FEFC document is admirable in content. Furthermore, it has been
presented very clearly and economically reproduced. Apart from the target
setting, we see it as a highly realistic and workable approach exceeding in quality
most other work on inspection and 'quality'.

REFERENCES

Aitkin, M. and Longford, N. (1986) 'Statistical modelling issues in school effectiveness studies', *Journal of the Royal Statistical Society, Series A,* 149 (1), 1–43.

Al Bayatti, M. F. and Green, J. R. (1986) *The Dependence of GCE Advanced Level Performance on Ordinary Level Performance and Other Variables.* Manchester: Roundthorn Publishing Ltd.

Alkin, M. C., Kosecoff, J. P. *et al.* (1974) *Evaluation and Decision-making: The Title VII Experience.* C.S.E. Monograph Series in Evaluation. Los Angeles: Center for the Study of Evaluation.

Audit Commission (1993) *Unfinished Business: Full-time Educational Courses for 16–19 Year Olds.* London: HMSO.

Barrett, G. V. and Depinet, R. L. (1991) 'A reconsideration of testing for competence rather than for intelligence', *American Psychologist,* **46** (1), 1012–24.

Bartlett, M. S. (1990) 'Chance or chaos?' *Journal of the Royal Statistical Society, Series A,* **153**(3), 321–47.

Black, P. (1988) *National Assessment and Testing: a Research Response.* London: British Educational Research Association.

Bloom, B. S. (1979) *Alterable Variables: the New Direction in Educational Research.* Edinburgh: Scottish Council for Research.

Bordieu, P. and Passeron, J. C. (1977) *Reproduction: in Education, Society and Culture.* London: Sage Publications.

Bowlby (1990) *Charles Darwin: A New Biography.* London: Pimlico.

Box, J. F. (1978) *R. A. Fisher. The Life of a Scientist.* New York: John Wiley & Sons.

Broadfoot, P. (1988) 'The national assessment framework and Records of Achievement', in H. Torrance (ed.) *National Assessment and Testing: a Research Response.* London: British Educational Research Association.

Bryk, A. and Raudenbush, S. (1992) *Hierarchical linear models.* Newbury, CA: Sage Publications.

Burnhill, P., Garner, C. and McPherson, A. (1988) 'Social change, school attainment and entry to Higher Education 1976–86, in D. Raffe (ed.) *Education and the Youth Labour Market.* Lewes: Falmer Press.

Burstein, L. (1980) 'Issues in the aggregation of data', in D. C. Berliner (ed.) *Review of Research in Education.* Washington, DC: American Educational Research Association.

Campbell, D. T. (1969) 'Reforms as experiments', *American Psychologist,* **24**, 409–29.

Campbell, D. T. and Fiske, D. W. (1959) 'Convergent and discriminant validation by the multitrait-multimethod matrix', *Psychological Bulletin*, **56**(2), 81–105.

Campbell, D. T. and Stanley, J. C. (1966) *Experimental and Quasi-experimental Designs for Research*. Chicago: Rand McNally.

Carroll, J. B. (1963) 'A model of school learning', *Teachers' College Record*, **64**, 723–33.

Clifford, G. J. and Guthrie, J. W. (1988) *Ed School: A Brief for Professional Education*. Chicago: University of Chicago Press.

Close, F. (1992) *Too Hot to Handle: the Story of the Race for Cold Fusion*. London: Penguin Books.

Cockcroft, W. H. (1982) *Mathematics Counts: Report of the Committee of Inquiry into the Teaching of Mathematics in Schools*. London: HMSO.

Cohen, G., Stanhope, N. and Conway, M. (1992) 'How long does education last? Very long term retention of cognitive psychology', *The Psychologist: Bulletin of the British Psychological Society*, **5**, 57–60.

Coleman, J. A. (1994) 'Profiling the advanced language learner: the C-test in British further and higher education', in R. Grotjahn (ed.) *Der C-test. Theoretische Grundlagen und Praktische Anwendungen*, Vol. 2. Bochum: Brockmeyer.

Coleman, J. *et al.* (1966) *Equality of Educational Opportunity*. Washington DC: US Government Printing Office.

Comber, L. C. and Keeves, J. (1973) 'Science education in nineteen countries: an empirical study', in J. Wiley (ed.) *International Studies in Evaluation*. New York.

Conger, J. J., Miller, W. C. and Rainy, R. V. (1966) 'Effects of driver education: the role of motivation, intelligence, social class and exposure', *Traffic Safety Research Review*, **10**, 213.

Cook, T. D. and Campbell, D. T. (1979) *Quasi-experimentation*. Chicago: Rand McNally.

Cooley, W. W. (1983) 'Improving the performance of an educational system', *Educational Researcher*, **12**(6), 4–12.

Cooley, W. W. and Lohnes, P. R. (1976) *Evaluation Research in Education*. New York: Halstead Press.

Coopers & Lybrand (1988) *Local Management of Schools*. A report to the Department of Education and Science. London: HMSO.

Courtenay, G. (1988) *England and Wales Youth Cohort: Report on Cohort 1, Sweep 1*. Sheffield: Department of Employment.

Cousins, J. B. and Leithwood, K. A. (1986) 'Current empirical research on evaluation utilization', *Review of Educational Research*, **56**(3), 331–64.

Cresswell, M. and Gubb, J. (1987) *The Second International Mathematics Study in England and Wales*. Windsor: NFER-Nelson.

Cronbach, L. J. and Meehl, P. E. (1965) 'Construct validation in psychological tests', *Psychological Bulletin*, **52**, 281–302.

Crowther Report (1959) *15–18: A Report of the Central Advisory Council for Education (England)*, 1. London: HMSO.

Daly, P. G. (1991) 'How large are secondary school effects in Northern Ireland?' Paper presented at the International Congress on School Effectiveness and School Improvement, Cardiff.

Davies, P. C. W. (1987) *The Cosmic Blueprint*. London: Heinemann.

Deming, W. E. (1982) *Out of the Crisis: Quality Productivity and Competitive Position*. Cambridge, MA: Cambridge University Press.

Department of Education and Science (1981) *Statistical Bulletin 8/81*. London: HMSO.

Department of Education and Science (1988). *Circular 7/88*. London: HMSO

Dunford, J. (1992) 'Her Majesty's Inspectorate of Schools in England and Wales 1944–1992'. Unpublished PhD thesis, University of Durham.

Engels, F. (1940) *Dialectics of Nature*. London: Lawrence and Wishart.

Epstein, J. L. and McPartland, J. M. (1976) 'The concept and measurement of the quality of school life', *American Educational Research Journal*, **13**(1) 15–30.

Feingold, A. (1988) 'Cognitive gender differences are disappearing', *American Psychologist*, **43**(2), 95–103.

Fitz-Gibbon, C. T. (1974) 'The identification of mentally gifted disadvantaged students at the Eighth Grade Level', *Journal of Negro Education*, **XL111**(1), 53–66.

Fitz-Gibbon, C. T. (1984a) *Combse 1984 A-level Results: Report to Participating Schools*. Newcastle Upon Tyne: School of Education, University of Newcastle.

Fitz-Gibbon, C. T. (1984b) 'Meta-analysis: an explication', *British Educational Research Journal*, **10**(2), 135–44.

Fitz-Gibbon, C. T. (1985) 'A-level results in comprehensive schools: the COMBSE project, Year 1', *Oxford Review of Education*, **11**(1), 43–58.

Fitz-Gibbon, C. T. (1990) *Performance Indicators: a BERA Dialogue*. Clevedon: Avon Multi-lingual Matters.

Fitz-Gibbon, C. T. (1991a) *Evaluation of School Performance in Public Examinations*. A report for the Scottish Office Education Department, Newcastle upon Tyne: Curriculum Evaluation and Management Centre.

Fitz-Gibbon, C. T. (1991b) 'Multi-level modelling in a indicator system', in S. W. Raudenbush and J. D. Willms (eds) *Schools, Classrooms, and Pupils*. San Diego: Academic Press.

Fitz-Gibbon, C. T. (1992a) 'The design of indicator systems, the role of education in universities, and the role of inspectors/advisers: a discussion and a case study', *Research Papers in Education*, **7**(3), 271–300.

Fitz-Gibbon, C. T. (1992b) 'Empower and monitor: the EM algorithm for the creation of effective schools', in J. Bashi and Z. Sass (ed.) *School Effectiveness and Improvement*. Proceedings of the Third International Congress for School Effectiveness. Jerusalem: Magnes Press.

Fitz-Gibbon, C. T. (1992c) *Performance Indicators and Examination Results*. Scottish Office Education Department, Interchange No. 11.

Fitz-Gibbon, C. T. (1992d) 'School effects at A-level: genesis of an information sustem', in D. Reynolds and P. Cuttance (eds) *School Effectiveness: Research, Policy and Practice*. London: Cassell.

Fitz-Gibbon, C. T. (1993a) *Intake Characteristics for the BTEC Added Value Project*. Report for Business and Technical Education Council (BTEC). Newcastle Upon Tyne: Curriculum, Evaluation and Management Centre, University of Newcastle.

Fitz-Gibbon, C. T. (1993b) 'Monitoring with feedback: the democratisation of data', in L. Paterson (ed.) *Measuring Schools: the Rights and Wrongs of Practices in Scotland*. Edinburgh: Centre for Educational Sociology, Edinburgh University.

Fitz-Gibbon, C. T. (1994) 'Long term consequences of curriculum choices'. Paper presented at the Annual Meeting of the British Educational Research Association, Oxford.

Fitz-Gibbon, C. T. and Clark, K. S. (1982) 'Time variables in classroom research: a study of eight urban secondary school mathematics classes', *British Journal of Educational Psychology*, **52**(3), 301–316.

Fitz-Gibbon, C. T. and Morris, L. (1975) 'Theory based evaluation', *Evaluation Comment*, **5**(1) 1–4.

Fitz-Gibbon, C. T. and Morris, L. (1987) *How to Analyze Data*. Beverley Hills: Sage Publications.

Fitz-Gibbon, C. T. and Vincent, L. (1994) *Candidates' Performance in Mathematics and Science. A Report for SCAA*. London: School Curriculum and Assessment Authority.

Further Education Funding Council (1993) *Assessing Achievement*, Circular 93/28.

Gipps, C. and Murphy, R. (1993) *A Fair Test? Assessment, Achievement and Equity*. Milton Keynes: Open University Press.

Glass, G. V. (1975) 'A paradox about excellence of schools and the people in them', *Educational Researcher*, **4**(3), 9–13.

Glass, G. V. (1979) 'Policy for the unpredictable' *Educational Researcher*, **8**(9), 12–14.

Glass, G. V. and Smith, M. L. (1979) 'Meta-analysis of research on class size and achievement', *Educational Evaluation and Policy Analysis*, 2–16.

Glass, G. V., McGaw, B. and Smith, M. L. (1981) *Meta-analysis in Social Research*. Beverley Hills: Sage Publications.

Gleick, J. (1988) *Chaos: Making a New Science*. London: Heinemann.

Goldstein, H. (1979) 'Consequences of using the Rasch model for educational assessment', *British Educational Research Journal*, **5**(2), 211–220.

Goldstein, H. (1984) 'The methodology of school comparisons', *Oxford Review of Education*, **10**(1), 69–74.

Goldstein, H. (1987) *Multilevel Models in Educational and Social Research*. London: Charles Griffin.

Goldstein, H., Rasbash, J., Yang, M., Woodhouse, G., Pan H., Nuttall D. and Thomas S. (1993) 'A multilevel analysis of school examination results', *Oxford Review of Education*, **19**(4), 425–33.

Gray, J. and Hannon, V. (1986) 'HMI interpretation of school's examination results', *Journal of Educational Policy*, **1**, 23–33.

Gray, J., Jesson, D. and Jones, B. (1986) 'The search for a fairer way of comparing schools' examination results', *Research Papers in Education*, **1**(2), 91–122.

Gray, J., Jesson, D. and Tranmer, M. (1993) *England and Wales Youth Cohort Study Boosting Post-16 Participation in Full-time Education: a Study of Some Key Factors*. Sheffield: Department of Employment.

Gray, J., McPherson, A. F. and Raffe, D. (1983) *Reconstructions of Secondary Education Theory, Myth and Practice Since the War*. London: Routledge & Kegan Paul.

Hanushek, E. A. (1989) 'The impact of differential expenditures on school performance', *Educational Researcher*, **18**(4), 45–51.

Hedges, L. V. and Olkin, I. (1980) 'Vote-counting methods in research synthesis', *Psychological Bulletin*, **88**, 359–69.

Hedges, L. V. and Olkin, I. (1985) *Statistical Methods for Meta-analysis*. New York: Academic Press.

Hedges, L. V., Laine, R. and Greenwald, R. (1994) 'Does money matter? A meta-analysis of studies of the effects of differential school inputs on student outcomes', *Educational Researcher*, **23**(3), 5–14.

Heim, A. H., Watts, K. P. and Simmonds, V. (1983) *Manual for the AH6 Group Tests of High-level Intelligence*. Windsor: NFER Publishing Company Ltd.

Heiser, T. (1993) 'Review of "The impact of population size on local authority costs and effectiveness" by Travers, Jones and Burnham', *SEARCH: Recent Work of the Joseph Rowntree Foundation*, **17**(Sept), 19–20.

Heywood, J. (1992) 'School teacher appraisal: for monetary reward, or professional development, or both?' in H. Tomlinson (ed.) (1992) *Performance-Related Pay in Education*, pp.131–50. London and New York: Routledge.

Higginson Report (1988) *Advancing A Levels: Report of a Committee Appointed by the Secretary of State for Education and Science and the Secretary of State for Wales*. London: HMSO.

Hodgson, W. (1994) 'Gender differences in mathematics and science: a study of GCE Advanced Level examinations in the United Kingdom.' A thesis submitted in partial fulfilment of the requirements for the degree of Doctor of Philosophy, University of Newcastle.

Holt, J. (1969) *The Underachieving School*. London: Pitman.

Howarth, C. (1993) 'Assuring the quality of teaching in universities', *Reflections on Higher Education*, **5**, 69–89.

Howson, G. (1987a) 'A Level mathematics: some thoughts', in T. Everton (ed.) *The Reform of A Level Mathematics*. A report of the conference held at the University of Leicester, SMP 16–19 project. Southampton: University of Southampton.

Howson, G. (1987b) 'Challenge and change.' Inaugural lecture given at the University of Southampton, January 1987. Faculty of Mathematical Studies.

Hunter, J. E. and Hunter, R. F. (1984) 'Validity and utility of alternative predictors of job performance', *Psychological Bulletin*, **96**(1) 72–98.

Husèn, T. (ed.) (1987) *International Study of Achievement in Mathematics: A Comparison of Twelve Countries*. New York: Wiley.

Husèn, T. and Tuijman, A. (1991) 'The contribution of formal schooling to the increase in intellectual capital', *Educational Researcher*, **20**(7), 17–25.

Ibrahim, A. bin (1992) 'The A-Level examination: qualitative and quantitative data in the context of a performance monitoring system.' PhD thesis, University of Newcastle.

Jacobsen, S. L. (1992) 'Performance-related pay for teachers: the American experience', in H. Tomlinson (ed.) (1992) *Performance-Related Pay in*

Education, pp. 53–4. London and New York: Routledge.

Karweit, N. (1976) 'Quantity of schooling a major educational factor?' *Educational Researcher*, **5**(2), 15–18.

Kellaghan, T. and Madaus, G. F. (1979) 'Within school variance in achievement: school effect or error?' *Studies in Educational Evaluation*, **5**, 101–7.

Kelly, A. (1976) 'A study of the comparability of external examinations in different subjects', *Research in Education*, **16**, 50–63.

Kerckhoff, A. C. (1990) *Getting Started: Transition to Adulthood in Great Britain*. Boulder, Co.: Westview.

Kingdon, M. (1991) *The Reform of Advanced Level*. London: Hodder & Stoughton.

Kounin, J. S. (1970) *Discipline and Group Management in Classrooms*. New York: Holt, Rinehart and Winston.

Kuhn, T. S. (1970) *The Structure of Scientific Revolutions*. Chicago: University of Chicago Press.

Lazar, I. (1977) (Chair) The Consortium on Developmental Continuity, Education Commission of the States. *The Persistence of Preschool Effects*. Washington, DC: US Department of Health, Education and Welfare.

Lazar, I. and Darlington, R. (1982) *Lasting Effects of Early Education.* Chicago: University of Chicago Press.

Lewin, R. (1993) *Complexity: Life at the Edge of Chaos*. London, J. M. Dent.

Linn, M. C. and Hyde, J. S. (1989) 'Gender, mathematics and science', *Educational Researcher* **18**(8), 17–19, 22–7.

Linn, R. L., Baker, E. L. and Dunbar, S. B. (1991) 'Complex performance-based assessment: expectations and validation criteria', *Educational Researcher*, November, 15–21.

McClelland, D. C. (1973) 'Testing for competence rather than for "intelligence"', *American Psychologist*, **28**, 1–14.

McCord, J. (1978) 'A thirty-year follow-up of treatment effects', *American Psychologist*, **33**, 284–9.

Macdonald, I., Bhavnani, R., Khan, L. and John, G. (1989) *Murder in the Playground: the Report of the Macdonald Inquiry into Racism and Racial Violence in Manchester Schools*. London: Longsight Press.

Magee, B. (1976) *Popper*. Glasgow: Fontana/Collins.

Massey, A. J. (1977) *Restricted Response Tests*. Occasional Publication 5. Cambridge: Test Development and Research Unit.

McPherson, A., Raffe, D. and Robertson, C. (1990) *Highers and Higher Education*. Edinburgh: Association of University Teachers (Scotland).

Mayston, D. (1992) *School Performance Indicators and Performance Related Pay*. London: Association of Teachers and Lecturers.

Mitchell, R. (1990) 'Site visits in the accreditation process of the Western Association of Schools and Colleges (WASC)', *Evaluation and Research in Education*, **4**(2), 75–9.

Mortimore, P., Sammons, P., Stoll, L., Lewis D. and Ecob, R. (1988) *School Matters*. Wells, Somerset: Open Books.

Murlis, H. (1992) 'Performance-related pay in the context of performance management', in H. Tomlinson (ed.) (1992) *Performance-Related Pay in Education*, pp.55–72. London and New York: Routledge.

Murnane, R. and Cohen, D. (1985) *Merit Pay and the Evaluation Problem*. Palo Alto, CA: Stanford University Press.

Murnane, R. J. (1987) 'Improving education indicators and economic indicators: the same problems?' *Educational Evaluation and Policy Analysis*, **9**(2), 101–16.

Murphy, R. J. L. and Torrance, H. (1988) *The Changing Face of Educational Assessment*. Milton Keynes: Open University Press.

National Commission on Education (1993) *Learning to Succeed: A Radical Look at Education Today and a Strategy for the Future*. London, Heinemann.

Neave, H. (1990) *The Deming Dimension*. Knoxville, Tenn.: SPC Press, Inc.

Nuttall, D. L., Goldstein, M., Prosser, R. and Rasbash, J. (1989) 'Differential school effectiveness international', *Journal of Educational Research*, **13**(7), 769–76.

OFSTED/Coopers & Lybrand (1994) *A Focus on Quality*. A review of the inspection system based on the first 100 inspections of secondary schools under Section 9 of the Education (Schools) Act 1992. London: OFSTED.

Ottobre, F. M. and Turnbull, W. W. (1987) *The International Test of Developed Abilities: A Report on the Feasibility Study*. Princeton, New Jersey: International Association for Educational Assessment.

Parsons, H. M. (1974) 'What happened at Hawthorne?' *Science*, **183**, 922–32.

Pearce, J. (1972) *School Examinations*. London: Collier-MacMillan Publisher.

Perkins, D. N. and Salomon, G. (1989) 'Are cognitive skills context bound?' *Educational Researcher*, **18**(1), 16–25.

Perutz, M. (1989) 'The new Marxism', *New Scientist*, 15 July.

Popper, K. (1959) *The Logic of Scientific Discovery*. London: Hutchison & Co.; New York: Basic Books Inc.

Popper, K. (1974) *Unended Quest: An Intellectual Autobiography*. Glasgow: William Collins and Sons & Fontana Paperbacks.

Porter, A. C. (1991) 'Creating a system of school process indicators', *Educational Evaluation and Policy Analysis*, **13**(1), 13–29.

Preece, P. F. W. (1983) 'The quantitative principle of teaching', *Science Education*, **67**(1), 69–73.

Raudenbush, S. (1984) 'Magnitude of teacher expectancy effects of pupil IQ as a function of credibility of expectation induction. A synthesis of findings from 19 experiments', *Journal of Educational Psychology*, **76**(1), 85–97.

Raven, J. C. (1958) *Standard Progressive Matrices*. London: H. K. Lewis and Co. Ltd.

Raven, J. C. (1962) *Advanced Progressive Matrices. Sets I and II*. London: H. K. Lewis and Co. Ltd.

Reder, L. R. and Anderson, J. R. (1980) 'A comparison of texts and their summaries: memorial consequences', *Journal of Verbal Learning and Verbal Behaviour*, **19**, 121–34.

Reynolds, D. (1976) 'The delinquent school', in P. Woods (ed.) *The Process of Schooling*. London: Routledge and Kegan Paul.

Richards, C. E. (1988) 'A typology of Educational monitoring systems', *Educational Evaluation and Policy Analysis*, **10**(2), 106–16.

Rowan, P. (1993) 'Nursery school provision'. Paper presented to the Annual Meeting of the British Association for the Advancement of Science.

Rutter, M., Maughan, B., Mortimer, P. and Ousten J. (1979) *Fifteen Thousand Homes. Secondary Schools and Their Effects on Children*. London: Open Books.

Sapsed, G. (1993) 'Performance-related pay in IBM', in H. Tomlinson (ed.) *Performance-Related Pay in Education*. London: Routledge, 73–87.

Scarth, J. and Hammersley, M. (1988) 'Examinations and teaching: an exploratory study', *British Educational Research Journal*, **14**(3), 231–49.

Scheerens, J. (1992) *Effective Schooling: Research, Theory and Practice*. London: Cassell.

Schon, D. A. (1983) *The Reflective Practioner: How Professionals Think in Action*. New York: Basic Books.

School Teachers Review Body (1994) *Consultative Document: Performance Related Pay*. School Teachers' Review Body. London: Office of Manpower Economics.

Schuller, D. (1991) *The Guardian*, 2 August.

Sen, A. (1993) 'Economics and ethics'. Paper given at the Annual Meeting of the British Association, Keele.

Shavelson, J. R. J., McDodonell, L. and Oakes, J. (1989) *Indicators for Monitoring Mathematics and Science Education: A Source Book*. New York: The Rand Corporation.

Shavelson, R. J. (1990) 'Can indicator systems improve the effectiveness of mathematics and science education? The case of the US', *Evaluation and Research in Education*, 51–60.

Simon, H. A. (1988) *The Sciences of the Artificial*, 2nd edn. Cambridge, Mass.: The MIT Press.

Slavin, R. E. (1979) 'School practices that improve race relations', *American Educational Research Journal*, **16**(2), 169–80.

Smith, D. I. and Kirkham, R. W. (1982) 'Relationship between intelligence and driving record', *Accident Analysis and Prevention*, **14**, 439–42.

Smith, D. I. and Tomlinson, S. (1989) *The School Effect: A Study of Multi-Racial Comprehensives*. London: Policy Studies Institute.

Smith, G. and James, T. (1975) 'The effects of preschool education: some American and British evidence', *Oxford Review of Education*, **1**(3), 223–40.

Smith, P. (1995) 'On the unintended consequences of publishing performance data in the public sector', *International Journal of Public Administration*, **18**(2/3), 277–310.

Smithers, A. (1994) *All Our Futures. Britain's Education Revolution*. London: Channel Four Television.

Smithers, A. and Robinson, P. (1988) *The Growth of Mixed A-level*. Manchester: Carmichael Press.

Smithers, A. and Robinson, P. (1991) *Beyond Compulsory Schooling: a Numerical Picture*. London: The Council for Industry and Higher Education.

Stephens, J. M. (1967) *The Process of Schooling: A Psychological Examination*. New York: Holt, Rhinehart and Winston.

Stewart, I. (1989) *Does God Play Dice? The Mathematics of Chaos*. Oxford: Basil Blackwell.

Straker, N. (1988) *Teacher Shortage in Mathematics and Physics: Some Possible Solutions*.

Sutherland, S. (1992) *Irrationality: the Enemy Within*. London: Constable and Company.

Sykes, G. (1990) 'Evaluation in the context of national policy and local organisation', in M. Granheim Kogan and V. Lundheim (eds) *Evaluation as Policy Making*. London: Jessica Kingsley.

Teddlie, C., Stringfield, S., Wimpelberg, R. and Kirby, P. (1989) 'School effectiveness and school improvement', in B. Creemers, T. Peters, and D. Reynolds (eds) *Second International Congress for School Improvement and School Effectiveness*. Rotterdam: Swets & Zeitlinger.

The Economist (1994) 22 January, p. 16.

Thomas, H. (1990) *Education Costs and Performance: A Cost Effectiveness Analysis*. London: Cassell Educational Limited.

Thomas, J. B. (1990) *British Universities and Teacher Education: A Century of Change*. London: The Falmer Press.

Tizard, B. and Hughes, H. (1984) *Young Children Learning: Talking and Thinking at Home and at School*. London: Fontana.

Tomlinson, H. (ed.) (1992) *Performance-Related Pay in Education*. London and New York: Routledge.

Turner, G. (1983) 'The hidden curriculum of examinations', in M. Hammersley and A. Hargreaves (eds) *Curriculum Practice: Some Sociological Case Studies*. Lewes: Falmer Press.

Tymms, P. B. (1990) 'Can indicator system improve the effectiveness of science and mathematics education? The case of the UK', *Evaluation and Research in Education*, **4**(2), 61–73.

Tymms, P. B. (1992) 'The relative effectiveness of post-16 institutions in England (including Assisted Places Scheme schools)', *British Educational Research Journal*, **18**(2), 175–92.

Tymms, P. B. (1993) 'Accountability – Can it be fair?' *Oxford Review of Education*, **19**(3), 291–9.

Tymms, P. B. (1995) Influencing educational practice through performance indicators, *School Effectiveness and School Improvement*, 6(2), 123–45.

Tymms, P. B. (in press) 'Theories, models and simulation: school effectiveness at an impasse', in J. Gray, D. Reynolds, C. T. Fitz-Gibbon and D. Jesson (eds) *Merging Traditions: The Future of Research on School Effectiveness and School Improvement*. London: Cassell.

Tymms, P. B. and Fitz-Gibbon, C. T. (1991) A comparison of examination boards: A levels', *Oxford Review of Education*. **17**(1), 17–32.

Tymms, P. B. and Fitz-Gibbon, C. T. (1992a) The relationship of homework to A-level results', *Educational Research*, **34**(1), 3–10.

Tymms, P. B. and Fitz-Gibbon, C. T. (1992b) 'The relationship of part-time work to A-level results', *Educational Research*, **34**(3), 193–9.

Tymms, P. B. and Fitz-Gibbon, C. T. (1995) 'Students at the Front: a successful teaching strategy?' *Educational Research*, **37**(2), 107–22.

Wainer, H. (1989) 'Eelworms, bulletholes, and Geraldine Ferraro: some problems with statistical adjustment and some solutions', *Journal of Educational*

Statistics, **14**(2), 121–40.

Waldrop, M. M. (1992) *Complexity: The Emerging Science on the Edge of Order and Chaos.* London: Viking.

Walker, D. F. and Schaffarzick, J. (1974) 'Comparing curricula', *Review of Educational Research,* 4 4(1), 83–112.

Wallen, N. E. and Travers, M. W. (1963) 'Analysis and investigation of teaching methods', in N. L. Gage, (ed.) *Handbook of Research on Teaching,* pp. 448–505. Chicago: Rand McNally.

Wang, M. C., Haertel, G. D. and Walberg, H. J. (1993) 'Toward a knowledge base for school learning', *Review of Educational Research,* **63**(3), 249–94.

Wiener, N. (1948) *Cybernetics: Or Control and Communication in the Animal and Machine.* New York: John Wiley.

Williamson, J. and Fitz-Gibbon, C. T. (1990) 'On the lack of impact of information', *Educational Management and Administration,* **18**(1), 37–45.

Williamson, J., Tymms, P. B. and Haddow, M. (1992) 'ALIS through the looking glass: changing perceptions of performance indicators', *Educational Management and Administration,* **20**(3), 179–88.

Willms, J. D. (1992) *Monitoring School Performance: A Guide for Educators.* Lewes: Falmer Press.

Wolf, A. (1991) 'Assessing core skills: wisdom or wild goose chase', *Cambridge Journal of Education,* **21**(2), 189–201.

Woodhouse, G. (1990) 'The need for pupil level data', in C. T. Fitz-Gibbon (ed.) *Performance Indicators: a BERA Dialogue.* Clevedon: Avon Multi-lingual Matters.

Woodhouse, G. and Goldstein, H. (1988) 'Educational performance indicators and LEA league tables', *Oxford Review of Education,* **14**(3), 301–20.

NAME INDEX

SUBJECT INDEX

ability   58, 60, 61, 69, 94, 95, 139,
    216
accountability   56, 74, 77, 154, 160,
    171, 197, 198, 208
ALIS (Advanced Level Information
    System)   5, 35, 51ff, 178, 203, 208,
    233ff
appraisal   240
APU (Assessment of Performance Unit)
    209
APVIC (Association of Principals of
    Sixth Form Colleges)   64, 159, 234
assessment
    authentic   76
    internal   74, 75, 77, 90
    modes of   88
    of achievement   71ff, 83ff
    transcript   69, 83ff
    separate modes   89
ATL (Association of Teachers and
    Lecturers)   190
attitudes   99
    measuring   100 ff

backwash effect of examinations   76,
    79
bias   75
blind   89, 116
BTEC (Business and Technical
    Education Council)   93, 98, 108,
    111, 156, 238

causal relationships   95, 104, 105ff,
    155, 160, 195
Centre for Evidence Based Medicine
    221
citations   viii, 78
cognitive error   46

COMBSE (Confidential, Measurement-
    Based, Self Evaluation)   56, 61
communal peace   116
complexity   7, 19, 25, 33, 38ff, 43ff,
    46, 92, 186, 192, 205, 215
confidentiality   25, 50, 54, 56, 58, 61,
    101, 164, 223
contextualization   141, 161
Coopers & Lybrand 1988 report   153,
    198
    1994 report   205
costs   17, 18, 26, 44, 60, 62, 74, 86,
    87, 89, 94, 96, 102, 113, 163, 164
    of inspection   102, 177, 202, 205,
    209
    of PRP   191
criticisms   viii
CRT (Criterion Referenced Testing)
    79, 94
cultural capital (see also SES)   143,
    144, 149, 176

data
    aggregate   142ff
    collection, checking   171, 173
    comparisons, Type II   12, 30
    fair comparisons, residuals, Type III
        11
    four kinds   11ff
    live   214
    raw, Type I   11ff
    really fair comparisons, Type IV
        11ff
delinquency   160, 173
delivery standards   82, 86
Department of Scientific and Industrial
    Research   183
department(s)   28, 30, 32, 40, 54, 58,